Winning Elections and Influencing Politicians
for Library Funding

WINNING ELECTIONS
AND **INFLUENCING**
POLITICIANS

FOR **LIBRARY FUNDING**

PATRICK "PC" SWEENEY *and* JOHN CHRASTKA

Foreword by Rebekkah Smith Aldrich

Neal-Schuman

An imprint of the American Library Association

An imprint of the American Library Association
Chicago   2017

Extensive effort has gone into ensuring the reliability of the information in this book; however, the publisher makes no warranty, express or implied, with respect to the material contained herein.

ISBNs
978-0-8389-1556-1 (paper)
978-0-8389-1576-9 (PDF)
978-0-8389-1577-6 (ePub)
978-0-8389-1578-3 (Kindle)

Library of Congress Cataloging-in-Publication Data
Names: Sweeney, Patrick "PC", author. | Chrastka, John, author.
Title: Winning elections and influencing politicians for library funding / Patrick "PC" Sweeney, John Chrastka ; foreword by Rebekkah Smith Aldrich.
Description: Chicago : Neal-Schuman, an imprint of the American Library Association, 2017. | Includes bibliographical references and index.
Identifiers: LCCN 2016059387| ISBN 9780838915561 (pbk. : alk. paper) | ISBN 9780838915776 (ePub) | ISBN 9780838915769 (PDF) | ISBN 9780838915783 (Kindle)
Subjects: LCSH: Library finance—Political aspects—United States. | Library fund raising—Political aspects—United States. | Libraries and community—Political aspects—United States. | Political campaigns—United States. | Communication in politics—United States.
Classification: LCC Z683.2.U6 S94 2017 | DDC 021.8/30973—dc23 LC record available at https://lccn .loc.gov/2016059387

Book design by Alejandra Diaz in the Adobe Garamond Pro and Gotham typefaces.

⊚ This paper meets the requirements of ANSI/NISO Z39.48–1992 (Permanence of Paper).

Printed in the United States of America
21 20 19 18 17   5 4 3 2 1

CONTENTS

FOREWORD

- Libraries are essential.
- Funding for libraries cannot be left to chance.
- It is not enough that people love us. We must be strategic. Focused. Savvy. Willing to play the game that others will play in opposition to an increase in taxes.
- We must play the game or be played.

At the Mid-Hudson Library System, a decade ago we began a project called "Getting to Yes," to ensure that libraries in New York could take full advantage of the opportunity to go directly to the voters to ask them, how much should your tax for library services be? That is a brave question, one that tests the limits of loyalty to the philosophy of a public library in the most concrete of ways. We learned very quickly that there is science behind winning, and methodical steps that need to be taken to ensure success at the polls.

We learned a new way of thinking as we created our Public Library Vote Toolbox (http://vote.midhudson.org), a resource focused on helping libraries to "get out the vote." After working on over one hundred campaigns I have learned to *never leave a vote to chance*, to focus on a deliberate strategy that moves from education of the community about the impact of a win or loss at the polls, to motivate people to come out and vote, and to the very deliberate and strategic identification and mobilization of actual "yes" voters.

This is a different skill set than most librarians, trustees, and Friends groups have. We are steeped in professional values that speak to the ideal that "libraries are for all": access, democracy, and social responsibility. We work hard to ensure egalitarian library service. We are not political strategists at heart; we are public servants. Our inherent skill set does not always translate to the hard-nosed tactics it will take to win at the polls, particularly in the face of an organized opposition to our efforts.

Make no mistake, in many communities across the country this will be a fight. *You are going into battle.*

EveryLibrary has stepped up to arm the national library community with proven, battle-tested tactics that work. They are doing the legwork to understand what actions translate into winning strategies not only from within the library community but beyond it. Will these actions ensure success every time? No. That is not the world we operate in. There are many variables and hyper-local issues that will come into play. However, using a campaign mentality that gives structure and direction to the work that needs to be done will *give libraries an advantage*. It will mean you can stand on the shoulders of those who have come before you, learning from their triumphs and failures. Why wouldn't you take all the help you could get to ensure your library can meet the needs of your community?

Thank you for picking up this book. The tactics you will find contained within it may be a wake-up call to you, revealing the true work it will take to win in your community. *Read the whole damn thing.* You need as many tools in your toolbox as possible, and think through all the angles—leave nothing to chance.

I always say to the libraries I consult with: "*No regrets.*" You want no regrets the day after the vote if your vote goes down. Many libraries have one chance, just one chance to change the course of history for their community through a library building referendum or major change in the foundational funding formula of their library. The morning after the vote, win or lose, you want to know that you left no stone unturned, that you missed no opportunity to influence, motivate, and mobilize. It can come down to a handful of votes in some close races and when that handful is not in your library's favor, that is not a loss. That is a failure on the part of your campaign. Harsh? Maybe, but it's the truth. A handful of votes is a few more phone calls, a few more one-on-one conversations, one more community meeting before the vote. Go all out. Make It Happen.

Every time a library wins at the polls it provides hope that our society is moving in the right direction. Every time a library wins at the polls it reinforces the importance, the deep-seated devotion that Americans feel towards an institution that ensures that all have access to information, literacy, and community. If that's not worth fighting for, I'm not sure what is.

As the EveryLibrary tagline states: "Any library initiative anywhere matters to every library everywhere."

I wish you luck on your journey. Remember, we are all counting on you.

—REBEKKAH SMITH ALDRICH
Coordinator for Library Sustainability
Mid-Hudson Library System, New York

ACKNOWLEDGMENTS

WE ARE GRATEFUL TO OUR EVERYLIBRARY TEAM FOR THEIR HELP, support, and encouragement in writing this book, especially to our EveryLibrary cofounder Erica Findley and our 2014 intern Rachel Korman. Erica's insights, ethics, and campaign work permeate this book, and Rachel provided invaluable early edits and insights for several sections. Our board colleagues Peter Bromberg, Mel Gooch, Brian Hart, and Lindsay Sarin are true partners in the work and have shaped our approach to campaigns and campaigning.

Special thanks to Rebekkah Smith Aldrich for providing the "Foreword." We admire her work on New York library campaigns and are inspired by her.

We have learned as much as we taught from the more than sixty library communities we have helped take to the ballot. We truly appreciate the partnerships that developed between us and campaign teams around the country. It has been a joy to help folks in small towns and big cities campaign for their libraries. We are most grateful to them all for their volunteer commitment and dedication to their libraries. They are democracy in action.

This book would not have been possible without the help and support of our EveryLibrary Advisory Committee members, and our vendor and individual donors and supporters. Their faith and their investment in our work is hopefully getting a good return for libraries.

John would like to give special thanks to his wife Deanna for her love and support on this book, and most importantly for her faith and encouragement that EveryLibrary was more than just a good idea and should be pursued.

Patrick would like to thank many of his colleagues online and in real life who helped and supported him in his early career. He also would like to give special thanks to Kate Tkacik, who supported him throughout his work with EveryLibrary.

Finally, we appreciate the hospitality of the folks in Seabeck, Washington, where a good portion of this and our next book was written. If you're ever on the Kitsap Peninsula, it's a lovely spot. You should grab a coffee and watch the seals.

INTRODUCTION

WE ARE ABOUT TO GIVE YOU A LOT OF ADVICE ON RUNNING ballot measures and tax referendums. The audience for this book is, in the main, library and community leaders who need to build a local library "vote yes" committee and win an election. We will discuss the right approach to setting up the committee structure, and identifying the core leadership team for the committee. We will take you through a deep dive into a technique called "power mapping" that will help set the committee up for success. New techniques and best practices for marketing and message development, fund-raising, and volunteer engagement are key topics. You'll see a big discussion of the best ways to do canvassing and direct voter contact. But many of these techniques for activating voters, donors, and supporters should also be read with an eye toward day-to-day advocacy or nonelection political goals like advancing a funding request through a town board, city council, or county commission. For most of this work, the techniques to accomplish those goals are exactly the same. For example, in a campaign, direct voter contact is used to meet voters in person, answer questions, and ask them for their vote. The exact same door-to-door or phone-bank techniques that we teach committees to use to identify voters and do "get out the vote" work should also be used to collect survey data for your strategic plans and meet your neighbors during library card sign-up month.

When we write about a campaign committee here, you can easily read our advice on organizing the volunteers and utilizing the campaign team as advice about how to organize and deploy the library's staff and board. The key takeaway from this book is not a series of templates and samples, though we have a few which will jump-start your ballot committee's work. Instead, we hope to provide a series of actionable units of advice about how political perceptions are formed, how political power works, and how you can use the right techniques to reach your funding or political goals.

Voters and pundits bemoan the fact that politicians have to run a "perpetual campaign," and that once elected, politicians' first order of business is getting reelected. The truth is that you have to do the same thing for your library. If you are reading this book because you have to renew your levy in three to five years, we are already worried about your next renewal too. If you are consulting this book because you are about to have a once-in-a-generation election, your normal way to fund the annual operations budget starts right up again after that Election Day ends. If you also have to motivate a board of trustees, a town board of selectmen, a few county commissioners or counselors, or a recalcitrant mayor to act on your library's budget, please read this book with that in mind. We've purposely written it to help you build a campaign to win an election. We want you to be able to influence funding outcomes in the future, too.

CAMPAIGN ANALOGIES

We use a lot of examples and analogies from well-funded, big political campaigns like running for president in this book. Presidential candidates, their behavior, and voter perceptions of them are convenient and well-known points of reference across the country. Using a presidential candidate analogy to frame a point doesn't require as much contextualization or back story because we have all heard of and seen both the winners and losers. Like all analogies, the examples break down at a certain point, and for local library elections that is around the scale of the campaign, the amount of money in the campaign, and the role that media and opinion-setters play in a national campaign. It is like when we attend a library conference session on customer service and hear about how the library should be like Disney or Nordstrom or Walmart and then mentally struggle through the session because those organizations have the money, infrastructure, and reach of Disney and Nordstrom and Walmart. But we want to highlight that two parts of the presidential campaign/library campaign analogy will always be applicable, and they are the biggest takeaways from this book: personal contact with your voters wins elections, and data about those voters drive the campaign.

POLITICAL PARTIES MATTER IN POLITICS

Political parties still matter in American politics because they organize and amplify political beliefs. Every election sees defections and divisions within a party. National elections are a process of continually remaking a coalition and resetting a perception of who the "we" is within a party. Parties serve a huge role in politics because they provide people with a quick and usually effective way to validate candidates and positions. Party membership or self-identification focuses voters onto a set of collective beliefs about America and about the role of government while vetting candidates who agree with that political worldview.[1] With the 2016 presidential campaign, we saw the Republican establishment struggle to integrate Donald Trump as their nominee and rally behind their candidate. To watch Trump or even Senator Bernie Sanders push the edges of what was considered mainstream in their respective parties was to watch a large bunch of voters trying to balance their own habits of voting for their party's nominee with the cognitive dissonance that comes when they recognized that neither person was truly "of" their party. Senator Sanders failed to make the transition. Trump is now president.

In a similar way, beliefs about libraries and librarians will matter in your election because voters who have a strong belief in the value of the institution and the impact that the people who work there have on the community are, essentially, coalesced together on Election Day as a pro-library party. There are already voters who live in your town that are pro-library and interested in funding libraries at the ballot box. That group of voters will form the base of your vote. You have to find them and activate them. They are not automatically activated in advance of an Election Day the way that Republicans or Democrats are about their candidates. We don't have a national library party in this country. While EveryLibrary is currently building the next best thing, which is a group of self-identified "special interest voters" who will turn out for library issues, it isn't in place yet. In the meantime, you will need to build what is essentially a local pro-library political party in the lead-up to your election. This book is designed to help you do that.

Elections are won by coalitions and not just the party's base. Party supporters need to be joined by a group of swing voters to win any election. Huge national voter surveys from organizations as diverse as Pew, Brookings Institution, Gannet, Harris Interactive, and Zogby regularly report that self-identified Democrats and Republicans count for about 35 percent of the electorate each. That is less than a majority. Without either party reaching out to build a coalition with independents and moderates, it is not enough to win an election. The "swing voter" exists, and it is the work of candidates and parties to attract them. The traditional Democratic coalition is often one between the "socially liberal/economically liberal" voters and the "socially liberal/economically moderate" voters. The traditional Republican coalition is "socially and economically conservative" voters plus "socially liberal/economically conservative" voters. These coalitions reshape with each election, but the coalition is what carries a candidate to the polls.

In a similar way, there are library-swing voters in your community. They don't vacillate back and forth about their use or their love for the library. They are "swingable" about how they feel about taxes. They have a personal value system and a worldview about the role that taxes play in society and in your community. It is a worldview that references national politics and trends but is informed by local politics and your town's history of good government when a library funding measure is on the ballot. No one has likely tried to map the work the library does to that worldview before. It is your campaign's job to do that. Library-swing voters may be activated for your measure because of the quality of the strategic plan, the impacts of the plan, or the leverage in the plan. But because they are not automatic pro-library voters, you have to work very hard to understand how to talk to them about a tax for the library and then do the hard work of reaching them where they live and vote. We want this book to give you an actionable pathway to do that.

Taxes make some humans crazy. Libraries and librarians are normally walled-off from the image of being the "tax man," but on Election Day you cannot avoid it. There are voters in your community who will not like that you are going to the ballot and asking for taxes. They do not believe in taxes. These are not the library-swing voters; those folks can talk about taxes. These are voters who already identify with a party that believes in shrinking government, that any tax is a bad tax, and that our institutions are only valid if they are supported charitably by individuals, nonprofits, and corporations. As you build your pro-library party and shape the coalition of voters you need to win, you will have opposition from this other party in town. This book spends a lot of time talking about how to anticipate that opposition. We want to teach you first how to neutralize it. We'd like to see you have a quiet and unengaged opposing party during your election. But if they do decide to run another "worldview" against you, we also want to prepare you and your "yes" committee to overcome the opposition and succeed.

Your local pro-library party already has a candidate: the librarians. It also has a platform: that the library exists to serve our community and should be properly funded to serve the people best. You will refine and expand on that platform for your own local library. The candidate in the race needs to be willing to run. If you can recognize that the techniques we share are not just about a tactical approach to building a ballot committee as an effective voter engagement organization, but they are also about building and focusing political power in your town, your campaign has the best chance of winning.

PERSON-TO-PERSON CONTACT IS STILL KING

Politics is a human endeavor. The role that people play in campaigns even outweighs the role that big-money advertising plays. Every single presidential election in the modern era has been won or lost based on the quality of their "ground game." Whether it was the Obama campaign deploying volunteers to walk neighborhoods in certain states in 2008 and 2012, or the Republican National Committee quietly but effectively going door-to-door with canvassers in swing precincts to support candidate Trump, person-to-person contact about a candidate or an issue is still the biggest determiner of voter behavior in elections. People *react* to TV, radio, online, and print ads. People *interact* with other people. When a volunteer shows up at an average voter's door or picks up the phone to call, their conviction or belief in a candidate, issue, or party carries a lot of weight with that average voter. We know this neighbor-to-neighbor contact is the best way for a small, underfunded campaign to reach voters because it can be done by volunteers and is, when data-driven, extremely effective. We know that this human-to-human contact is the best way to break through in town about the library or to update the image and brand of librarians. This book is intended to show you the right way to train, empower, and deploy your campaign volunteers to make voter-to-voter contacts.

A winning library campaign is always a proactive campaign. A ballot initiative is an amazing opportunity to share your library's brand in a unique and important setting. You, as a library leader, have to set the campaign theme, develop relevant messages for groups of voters, and build the campaign committee apparatus to get that message into the field. Whether it is carried door to door by volunteers, planted in a front lawn on a yard sign, shared across social media, written about in a letter to the editor, or broadcast on a drive-time radio ad, it needs to activate your pro-library base and convince the library-swing voters. We hope to help you set smart goals for your campaign, plan what campaign strategies are right in your community, and prepare you to operationalize smart tactics that activate voters for your library ballot measure.

A POLITICAL ACTION COMMITTEE FOR LIBRARY COMMUNITIES

It was with all this in mind that we set out to create EveryLibrary as the first national political action for libraries. We are not writing this book from the perspective of a nonprofit or a unit of government. We are writing it in the hope that your library community can become informed about the campaign process, focused on the success of your library ballot measure, and as activists after Election Day. Our goal from the start was to fill an underserved niche in the library advocacy ecosystem, one that is focused on Election Day and budget day. We did not set out to create another nonprofit or membership organization. We wanted to create the right type of organization to work within the law––and to the fullest extent of the law—to influence public policy and to lobby for pro-library outcomes on bonds, referendum, millages, mill levies, warrant articles, parcel taxes, or any other tax measure that goes before the voters, anywhere. EveryLibrary was set up as a 501(c)(4) "social welfare organization" to talk about politics and political action for libraries specifically. As a 501(c)(4) we can also be considered a Super PAC for libraries, in that we raise and expend money to influence policy and support other local political organizations that want to pass or defeat voter approved measures.

Since 2012, EveryLibrary has worked with more than sixty public library communities with voter-approved measures on the ballot to renew or expand operating funds, or building bonds to remodel, replace, or build new libraries. Our work has touched village, town, city, county, and multi-county library communities in red states and blue states alike. The advice we are giving to you here comes from more than forty-five wins and $200 million in stable tax funding that we have helped these libraries secure. It also comes from more than a dozen stinging losses where we have not been able to help shape an effective library coalition among the voters. Each of the teachings we are sharing here, and each of the learnings we're hoping you'll capture, have been tested in the real world in towns that are as big as New Orleans and as small as Darby, Montana. Each of our library communities is different from each other as can be. But for each of them, their voters want the same set of answers: Where is my money going, and who is spending my money? We hope to help you articulate your library's answers in a way that gets your community to "yes" on election day.

NOTE

1. John S. Jackson, *The American Political Party System: Continuity and Change over Ten Presidential Elections* (Washington, DC: Brookings Institution, 2015).

CHAPTER ONE

Getting Started

T DOESN'T MATTER IF YOU ARE A LIBRARIAN, STAFF MEMBER, leader of the "vote yes" committee, or even a concerned citizen. It is your call to service that drives your actions. Many of us in librarianship have a belief in public service or a personal belief that we can make the world a better place through the services offered in a library. Those of you reading this book might be a library volunteer, a library supporter, a library director, a trustee, or a library staffer. In each case, we want you to understand why it is that you felt the need to become involved and why you chose this profession, or to get involved in this campaign. This is because the first step towards inspiring others to get involved in your campaign for an improved library through political action, is understanding what inspired you to get involved.[1]

Understanding your call to service is not just important for inspiring others but also for inspiring yourself. We're not going to lie to you, and this is something that you should understand early in this book, *running a library campaign is very hard work.* You are going to give up most of your weekends and weeknights for at least three or four months to do mundane tasks like data entry or budgeting. Your house will become a meeting place filled with campaign materials. Your garage or front porch will be your campaign sign warehouse. Your friends and family might publicly disagree with you, or your partner will get angry about feeling neglected while you are deep in a campaign. Your friends will go camping or on fabulous vacations and have parties and you'll be working on winning an election by being stuck at some meeting that is going terribly. People will speak poorly about you at council meetings, write editorials about how you are the devil personified because you want to raise taxes, and they'll point to the car you drive as evidence that you are nothing more than an overpaid government employee. You will probably get e-mails and phone calls of the most ungrateful kind. Worst of all . . . you almost definitely volunteered to put yourself through this. All of this means that there will likely be times that you find it difficult to stay engaged, focused, and committed. You are going to need to inspire yourself throughout this process at least as much as you are going to need to inspire others, and remembering your call to service is a great way to remain energized and inspired.

So the question remains, why do this? Why is it that you choose to provide improved library services to your community? Why is it that you believe in libraries at all? These are questions that we can't answer for you. Actually, if we could answer those questions for you, we still wouldn't. It needs to come from you. It will benefit you to sit down and spend some time contemplating why it is that you are making this decision to invest so much of your time and energy for your community. This isn't a decision that is taken lightly, and there are many who do this work who fight through some bewilderment about why they even bothered to try to make a difference in the cause they care about. The first step in starting any campaign is answering these questions for yourself and having a gut check about your ability and willingness to make the investments and sacrifices necessary to win.

In the book *Campaign Boot Camp 2.0*, Christine Pelosi has a similar set of gut check questions that she calls the Public Service Fitness Test. This is an excellent exercise to take yourself through to make sure you understand why you feel you were called to take action to support libraries.

- What is your vision of an improved library or set of library services?
- What do you believe about a library's ability to improve a community?
- What is your bold stroke or big idea to improve library services with increased funding?
- How does that vision fit into the values of the community?
- What are the core values of the library that will guide your campaign?
- What traits of other libraries with increased funding do you find admirable?
- What has the library or librarians done for the community?

- Do you understand the demands of running a campaign?
- Are you willing to commit to the time requirements necessary to win a campaign?
- What political courage have you exhibited throughout your life?
- Name your biggest sacrifice or risk.
- Are you willing to ask friends, family, and neighbors for contributions to the campaign?
- Are you comfortable personally asking community members to vote for your campaign?
- How well do you handle crisis or personal criticism about your work or the library's work?
- Are your friends and family ready for you to commit to the work and dedication of a campaign?*   ✪

* Pelosi, *Campaign Boot Camp 2.0*, 46–47.

After you understand why you decided to stand up for your library and get involved in a campaign, it's time to understand why other people will join you in this work. In order to do that, we need to understand where we are now and what resources and knowledge we have that can guide us in our work. Unfortunately, we don't have a whole lot of good recent data to use for library campaigns. The most recent data that we have about voter attitudes about libraries came from a 2008 study by OCLC and the Gates Foundation.[2] Because the study was released in 2008, the data comes from polling and surveying done in 2007 and that means the data is pre-Great Recession, pre-Obama, pre-Tea Party, and pre-Trump. Voter attitudes can change quickly, and we need to know the most recent attitudes around voters' willingness to support or oppose library taxes. However, even with this lack of data, we have seen the trends from the OCLC study "From Awareness to Funding" to hold true within a reasonable variation (although it is slipping more each year).

The other issue with the data about voters for libraries is that it mainly showed that many of our preconceived notions about who supports libraries are incorrect, but this did not help us narrow down which sets of voters do support libraries. Our voter data on library issues is out of date. Many major issue- and cause-based organizations and political parties run new polling, surveys, and data sets each year. Those fresh data sets help the campaigns understand who is most likely to vote on an issue, and that insight about who the voters are and what they care about helps drastically reduce the cost of running the election or issue. But our data won't do that for us. In fact, if anything, it increased the cost of the election because it didn't narrow down who we had to contact and eliminate the preconceived notions about who our voters are. In the end, it wound up widening our scope of potential voters instead of narrowing it.

THE DATA

The great news for libraries is that they are undeniably well supported by the majority of the public. According to the latest Pew Libraries data, "76% of adults say libraries serve the learning and educational needs of their communities either 'very well' (37%) or 'pretty well' (39%).[3] Further, 71% say libraries serve their own personal needs and the needs of their families 'very well' or 'pretty well.'" They also found that "two-thirds (66%) say that if their local public libraries were closed it would have a major impact on their communities as a whole" and another 25 percent believed that closing libraries would have a minor impact. Pew even found that almost half of all Americans have visited a library in the last year. While these numbers are great, they are not politically motivated opinions.[4]

What is interesting is how this data varies when Americans are asked about voting. There is a significant shift in the data when Americans are asked if they are willing to vote for a higher tax rate in order to preserve libraries. The Pew studies show that people love libraries, but in "From Awareness to Funding" the OCLC found that only 37 percent of the population is definitely willing to increase funding for libraries through taxes, and there is another 26 percent of the population who will never vote yes for libraries. The interesting thing about these two groups is that they are steadfast in their commitment. The library could teach everyone to read and also cure cancer and the 26 percent who are no voters wouldn't vote for the library. Likewise, the library could ask for a tax rate of one dollar or one hundred million dollars and the 37 percent group wouldn't waver from voting yes.[5] Both of these groups have fundamental beliefs about libraries and taxes that guide their decision to vote yes or vote no. Moving people from one group to the other is difficult, if not impossible for any campaign with limited resources.

You might remember that in the 2012 campaign, Mitt Romney got in trouble for saying that he was only speaking to 47 percent of Americans.[6] While this comment is often cited as one of the reasons that he lost his campaign, he was absolutely correct when it comes to campaign strategy. We have no doubt that his campaign team told him that the correct strategy was to spend campaign resources on that 47 percent. The problem was that he just never should have said it out loud to anyone outside of his campaign. We have the same problem in library campaigns.

You probably did the math and understand that 26 plus 37 does not equal 100 percent of the voter population. There is a missing 37 percent somewhere in the middle. This is the group of voters that exist in between those who have absolutely decided how they will vote for the library. This is the target demographic for any library campaign and this is our version of Mitt's 47 percent. What this means is that there is a demographic of voters in the field who haven't made up their minds about how they will vote in an election for libraries. Since only 37 percent of the voters will definitely vote yes for the library, and that doesn't equal the needed 50 percent to win (for most campaigns), we have to figure out how to pull in the remaining percentages from that middle 37 percent. We also know that the 37 percent are yes voters and the 26 percent are no voters and that it would take massive resources to change their minds, so we then know that we don't want to spend our money there. Instead, we want to spend our resources convincing the middle 37 percent whose minds we can change. So what do we know about these voters?

Sadly, we know very little. In fact, the data that we have shows more about what we don't know about voters than what we do know about them. The "From Awareness to Funding" study tells us that libraries are typically a nonpartisan issue with large support from moderate Americans on both sides of the political spectrum.[7] It also tells us that there is no evidence that people who use the library are any more likely to vote for it than someone who does not use it. This means that library cardholder rates in a community don't indicate the likelihood of an issue passing or failing. While all of this might seem like it runs counter to common belief (because it does), you can see these trends play out in your library. For example, you probably know of people who are wealthy in your community who have nannies to do storytimes for their kids and can buy everything they need from Amazon but believe that libraries are good for society and will vote yes. You also know that guy who comes into the library every single day and is there all day on the computers, but while he's there, he's researching Obama's birth certificate, 9/11 being an inside job, and any other antigovernment conspiracy theory. Despite relying on the government services provided by the library, you know that he'll never vote to support the library.

There are only two beliefs that we have identified in our work that influence people's willingness to vote for libraries. These are people's belief about government's ability (or responsibility) to provide services to the public, and people's belief about their librarian. Voters who believe that the government can or should provide services to the public are typically people who will vote for the library. These people have beliefs about librarians as agents of good, have an understanding of the work that librarians perform, and possibly even have some nostalgia about the librarian of their youth. This is why we talk about librarians getting into communities and talking to the public about the work they do. Conversely, people who hold the belief that tax dollars should not go to government services or that government should be shrunk and privatized are less likely to vote for the library. In this second group there is usually another subset of the population who are voting against the library as a proxy for all government or because they feel cheated due to the behavior of other government agencies. For example, the mayor promised to fix the roads and there's still a pothole in front of their house after two years, so why should they believe that a library project will be any different from what they believe to be a failed roads project?

With these three distinct groups of voters, it becomes important to understand how we strategize to engage them in a way that wins. In order to do that, you need to understand that your campaign is going to have limited resources available to use. Overall, you are going to want to spend as little of your resources as possible on persuading the unpersuadable in either the top 37 percent or the bottom 26 percent. Your campaign also needs to know who is in each category of voters by smart voter identification (voter ID) work. Finally, your campaign wants to make sure that the right people show up to vote. That's why your resources need to be focused on tactics that support three significant activities:

- Voter identification work to find out who is voting yes, no, or maybe
- Persuasion work for the undecided voters
- Get-out-the-vote work for the committed yes voters

We'll talk more about strategies to complete this work throughout this book, as well as the messages you will need to target different kinds of voters in later chapters. Each group has their own characteristics and needs to be managed in different ways to embolden them as supporters or quiet them as opposition. But let's discuss why it costs so much to move people from staunch opposition to strong support.

LIBRARIANS AS CANDIDATES

When we use the word *librarians* throughout this book, of course we mean everyone who the public believes are librarians and not just those with a master's degree in library science. To the general public, everyone who works in and around libraries is a librarian. The public doesn't really understand that a librarian has an MLIS degree or that the person shelving the books or running the book sale is almost never a credentialed librarian. It would be a terrible waste of campaign resources to first spend money educating people about who exactly is a librarian, and it would ultimately be detrimental to the campaign since you can use the public's ignorance about master-degreed librarianship to your advantage.

Your library staff, your librarians, are the candidates of the campaign and they need to understand that role. That's because your staff is asking for money and support from the public through their votes just like a candidate would. The public is going to want to know how library staff have spent tax dollars in the past and they are going to have questions about how those dollars will be spent in the future. The public will want to hear a vision about the future from librarians, and they will want librarians to openly and honestly discuss the issues with the public. In order to facilitate this, staff should feel empowered and given permission to do what is legally permissible for them to do during a campaign.

A problem that we often hear about is library staff being afraid of getting involved in the campaign. Staff shouldn't be scared of the campaign, but they do need to be educated about what it is they can say and do throughout it. Essentially, on public time, and with public resources, they cannot tell people how to vote in any election, and that includes the library's election. That means they can never tell someone to vote yes (or no) for the library. But they can openly and honestly answer any other questions. They can discuss what will happen if the library measure passes, and they can talk about what happens if the library measure fails. Having these conversations with staff about their role and responsibility to openly and honestly answer the public's questions is a conversation to have early.

While staff can't send campaign e-mails from their work e-mail addresses or make calls about the campaign from their work phone numbers, they are citizens when they are not at the library or being paid by the library. This means that if staff want to volunteer for the campaign on their own time, they should be more than welcome to do so. In fact, to deny them that is a denial of their First Amendment rights as citizens. Staff should be given explicit permission (but not asked) to support the campaign if they choose to. When staff are off the clock and away from the library, they are allowed to use their personal e-mail addresses or phones to work on behalf of the campaign.

LADDER OF ENGAGEMENT

One of the best metaphors for understanding how an individual or groups of people move from a lack of awareness to an attitude where they vote, donate, or act is called the "ladder of engagement." A ladder of engagement is a process mapping tool used by political campaigns and nonprofits to understand what steps are needed to convince people to take action on behalf of their cause or organization.[8] The basic concept is that very few people will suddenly go from being unaware of an issue to immediately taking action on that issue after a single contact. It typically takes many contacts over extended periods of time to get someone to believe enough in a cause that they will spend their money or their time on that cause as an advocate. So a campaign has to take the time to make someone aware that an issue exists, educate them about why it's important to believe in that issue, have them take some small initial action on behalf of that issue, and finally give them opportunity to take really meaningful action. What is interesting here is that this is probably the same path that you took to becoming an advocate or activist for libraries.

A ladder of engagement looks like this:

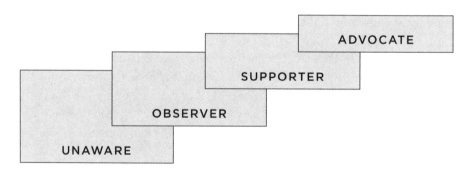

The squares get smaller as they get higher. This is because not everyone will be moved to the top of the ladder. There just isn't enough money or time to make that happen. And in any population, some people will care a lot and others will care only when asked. But if they are on the ladder, then they have the potential to move up. You will spend resources on making people aware of your library campaign: some of those will start to pay attention and observe what's happening, some of those will support your campaign, and then finally some of those supporters will donate time and money to your campaign or take some action to advocate for your library's campaign. You first need to find them and get them on the ladder.

There is a great example of the ladder of engagement that was used in Obama's campaign in 2012. Just like any library campaign, President Obama wanted people to take action for his campaign by donating time or money and committing to vote for him. In order to do this, Obama's campaign created a ladder of engagement that took people from unaware to evangelized.

The Obama campaign's ladder of engagement looked like this:

- First step, people were encouraged to take an easy action: to "like" Barack Obama's Facebook page.
- Second step, the campaign posted a link to Facebook asking people to "sign a birthday card" to Obama in the lead-up to his birthday. When people took this step they filled in their name and e-mail address. Now the campaign had the most valuable piece of information in their database: an e-mail address.
- Third step, the campaign sent an e-mail to supporters asking them to fill out a survey, or share a personal story. This is a new step: it encourages people to become more committed to the campaign and builds a profile for the supporter so the campaign can better target them in the future.
- Notice at this point that the Obama campaign has made only easy asks of people. They haven't asked anyone to give up any money or time. But they have built a relationship with people and gathered some useful data, like an e-mail address and location.
- Fourth step, people get a fund-raising e-mail. But instead of a direct request for money, they are asked to contribute to the campaign in return for a bumper sticker or T-shirt. Never underestimate the power of swag![9]

Your library campaign should have a similar starting point on the ladder of engagement. You should start with some kind of awareness or marketing campaign to talk about why the library is important and why there is a ballot issue in front of them. After they are aware of the campaign, allow them to take a first step in engaging with the campaign, something small and easy such as "liking" one of the campaign's images on Facebook and then liking your campaign's Facebook page. Once they have become an observer of your campaign through the Facebook page, then you can ask them to become a supporter through a pledge to vote yes. Finally, after they have pledged, you can use that list to get them to become an advocate for the campaign by attending a fund-raiser or event where you can then ask them for more money or to volunteer for the campaign. Take a few minutes and outline a few ladders of the engagement. It's okay to have more than one way to get your community to become advocates.

CAMPAIGN TIME LINE

Creating a strong campaign time line is what will keep you on track throughout the campaign. It's a working document that acts like a checklist to make sure that you hit every goal each week or month. While we haven't yet introduced many of the tactics or strategies that you will need to understand in order to create a strong campaign time line, we want to lay out the overall concepts of what would be considered an ideal one-year campaign time line. This will help you visualize your campaign as you read this book and understand when various tactics and strategies throughout this book will come into play. Most campaign time lines are built backwards from Election Day in order to help you prioritize where the bulk of your money and resources should be spent.[10]

Election Day

Throughout Election Day, you are going to keep an eye on election results. Some campaigns will spend time finalizing any get-out-the-vote work (or GOTV, as it is usually called) by continuously updating their voter files and reminding anyone who hasn't voted to go to the polls. It's also a great idea to host an election results watch party for campaign volunteers, donors, and supporters. This can be online with a mutual hashtag, or it can be in person at some venue. This is a good time to give your volunteers and your coalition partners an opportunity for closure to your campaign. It will allow those who took part in the campaign to come together to discuss next steps and plan for a future that is dependent on the outcome of Election Day.

Three Days before Election Day (GOTV)

Get out the vote (GOTV) is the time of your campaign when you should be expending any last resources to get voters to show up at the polls. This is when you are really pushing your GOTV strategies. At this point, it's far too late for voter ID. Most people will have made up their minds by now, so it's just time for your campaign to try to send as many people to the polls who have identified themselves as yes voters as possible. However, if you haven't yet reached your win number, then you should be doing the final big spend on persuasion.

One Week before Election Day (GOTV)

A week before the election, your campaign should be working to remind all of your yes voters to show up on Election Day. Early in the week you should mail any direct mail pieces that you are using to ensure that they get to your yes voters in time for the election. You can also conduct any final persuasion pieces during this time, but focus on yes voters and maybes. Don't send mail to the no voters because you don't want to remind them to go vote no for the library. This is also a great time to use up your extra money on big spends on social media ad buys. Your volunteer program should be winding down, but you should be finding a few volunteers to spend the day watching the polls. You can also e-mail your yes and maybe voters a few times throughout the week reminding them to vote and asking them to remind their friends and family to vote "yes" for the library. Hopefully, you have your win number by this time. If not, you will have to spend more on persuasion during this week than at any other time in your campaign.

One Month before Election Day (Persuasion and Voter ID)

You should have identified a large segment of yes voters prior to this month and voter ID should be winding down, but finish your lists before the last week of the campaign. Throughout this month you will want to focus your money and volunteers on persuading the undecided voters through social media, door-to-door work, phone banking, and outreach. You should schedule the largest part of your media during this time through editorials, radio ads, and television ads. At this point you should have found audiences for your messages and you are focusing your messages on those audiences in various traditional and digital media platforms. You should consider holding the bulk of your persuasive events like rallies and marches during this time. If there is anyone whom you haven't reached yet to identify as a yes voter, do it now and keep adding people to your lists of yes voters as they are persuaded to your side.

Two Months before Election Day (Voter ID)

You need to know who your voters are and who to spend money trying to reach. So during this month you want to spend your resources on identifying voters and ramping up the most effective campaign messages. This can mean that a large part of your door-to-door work and phone banking will happen at this time. You want your volunteers out in the community and finding as many people to vote yes as possible and you want to be focusing on using tactics that identify yes voters. Your campaign should be doing everything it can to build up its e-mail list and its social media presence. If you are planning on using direct mail in your campaign, this is one of the least effective times to use it. However, this is a great time to host house parties and fund-raisers and other events to raise awareness and attract attention to your campaign. This is also when you will give out yard signs (or find out who wants a yard sign if you aren't legally allowed to put them out this early) and give other identifying items to community members in order to solidify their yes votes. In all of your activities, start driving the messages of the campaign into the psyche of the community and ensure that all volunteers are well trained on what those messages are. Your activities around fund-raising will continue throughout this time, as well as finding more volunteers to help with the campaign.

Three Months before Election Day (Voter Education and Getting on the Ballot)

During this month the general voters and public will most likely just start taking an interest in anything on the ballot. The average voter won't care too much about ballot issues until this time. That's why this makes it the perfect time to start educating voters that there is a ballot issue for the library, what it means to the library, and what they can do to find out more information. This is also a good time to conduct testing messaging because any failed messaging is far enough away from Election Day that you have time to recover. You don't want to start testing new messages the week before the election since a bad message can damage a campaign with no time for recovery. Get your messages out into the public and see what works best with which audiences. This is when you really start dramatically and very publicly talking about the need for library funding. Let people know that there will be real consequences if the ballot measure fails and what those consequences will be. The library director and other "experts" should be out in the community talking about how important the funding is to the library and they should be attending as many community meetings and events as possible.

This is also when many jurisdictions have a deadline for getting on the ballot. Make sure that all your language is legal and enforceable. Get your endorsements for your ballot measure from the coalition partners you talked to in the previous month.

Four Months before Election Day (Coalition Building and Fund-Raising)

This is the month that you start collecting your resources and building the backbone of what you need for the campaign. You should create your campaign website, get the voter files, start collecting donations and holding fund-raisers, train your volunteers, make good on donation pledges, and so on. This is when you start solidifying your campaign activities, your budget, creating your media calendars, and identifying your strategies and writing them down into a full-fledged campaign plan. Start creating any graphics or other media that you might need for the campaign. You should also be calling on coalition partners like school districts, unions, and whoever else you met with and identified during the surfacing phase of your campaign. It's time to start cashing in on those relationships.

Five Months before Election Day (Polling and Data Collection and Donation Pledges)

At five months you are ready to take your first public opinion poll about the community. You have heard from influential people and organizations in your community and should have some general feeling about the level of support for a ballot measure. If you reach this point and it's become clear that there is no support, or you can't find people to commit to your ballot committee, and nobody you know will volunteer or even consider donating, you still have time to abort, fix the issues that people have identified, and start again. However, if you find that you feel like you have the support you need for your ballot issue, take the time and money to run a public opinion poll. It will help you make sure that your gut instinct is correct and it will bring to light any red flags before you have taken people's money or too much of their time. If your campaign polls more than five points below the threshold for winning a campaign, you might consider taking a step back and reconsidering your position. An unbelievably amazing campaign can bring up ten points, a really good campaign can bring up five, but any more is almost unheard of and you want a good five-point margin for a win. The further behind you are in the polls the more money, time, and people you're going to need to win. If you need to recover five points to guarantee a win, you might rethink your strategy.

Throughout this time, you can keep building your resources. It's not time to take money from people just yet. But it's a great time to start talking about pledges to give. Go to your big donors and ask them if they would pledge to give a contribution to the campaign based on the outcome of the poll. Go to your volunteers and start getting commitments from them that are also based on the outcomes of the poll.

Six Months before Election Day and Earlier (Listening Tours and Donor Relationships)

Six months away from Election Day you should be more clearly defining the kinds of resources you will need to win your election and you should start pulling them together. You should start with people that you have spoken to and built relationships with during your surfacing phase. Revisit them and get a firm commitment to take part in the campaign. Start your committee meetings and solidify your campaign committee members and organize their roles and responsibilities. Start thinking about what kinds of funding you will need and how much money you will need to raise and from whom. As part of this process, start brainstorming who can be asked for donations and ask your campaign committee to start making lists of people they know who can volunteer and ask to donate. Take the time to make big lists with as much information about the potential donors and volunteers as possible. Have the committee members start power mapping the community and scheduling meetings with influential people while asking these community members about their support of both the library and a library campaign, and listen to the responses of these kinds of influential people and early adopters. It's important to take the time to ask questions and listen at this stage and not ask too many questions or make demands of the people on your lists just yet. Simply start building the relationships.

One Year before Election Day (Surfacing)

This is the surfacing phase of your campaign. Spend time in the community and establish the library as the expert. Get librarians out into the community and spend money on marketing and advertising the library services in as many media markets as possible. Discuss the way the library benefits children, teens, parents, students, seniors, and business owners. The director should be meeting with as many people as possible and speaking as much as possible throughout the community. Take the time to meet with as many organizations as you can and get to know them well. This is a good time to start talking about how important the library is and to start talking about a vision of the future of the library. Remember, there is no opposition to the library yet because there is no discussion of tax increases or ballot issues here. Take advantage of that vacuum.

CAMPAIGN ACTIVITIES

With this rough time line in place, it becomes easier to start filling in the specific tactics that fit within each area. There are hundreds of different tactics that a campaign can use, and we have discussed some of the larger and more common tactics throughout this book, but no two campaigns are the same. Each campaign should spend time thinking about the tactics that will work best for it. In some cases it will be in the best interest of the campaign to have a loud and largely visible campaign, and in other cases it might be a better strategy to run a quieter and more strategic campaign. In some areas, the campaign will want to spend more time and energy on face-to-face work and in others, the campaign may focus on more targeted messaging through highly specific social media audiences. Factors like budget, terrain, number of volunteers, demographics of the community, connectivity, and so on influence the tactics that you use, and your campaign should spend some time thinking about what will be more strategic for your campaign. To that end, figure 1.1 is a rough guide of a wide range of tactics that can be used. You can find an editable blank campaign time line at action.everylibrary.org/campaignresources.

FIGURE 1.1

Campaign Activities Plan

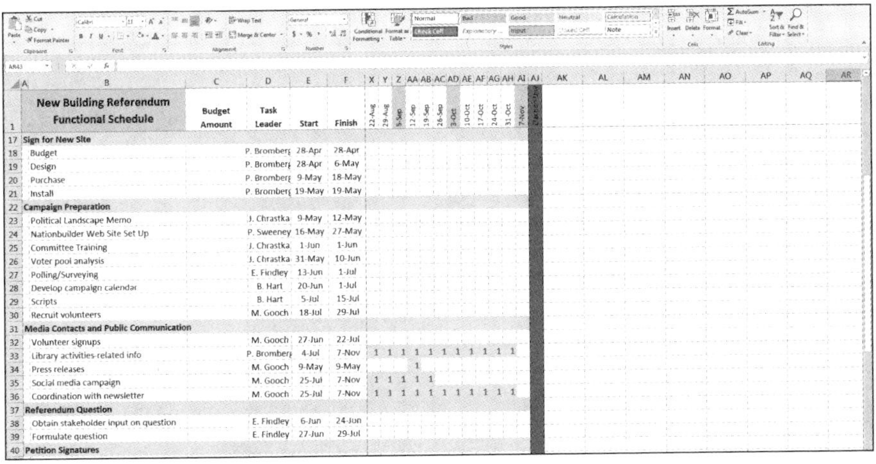

	New Building Referendum Functional Schedule	Budget Amount	Task Leader	Start	Finish	22-Aug	29-Aug	5-Sep	12-Sep	19-Sep	26-Sep	3-Oct	10-Oct	17-Oct	24-Oct	31-Oct	7-Nov
17	**Sign for New Site**																
18	Budget		P. Bromberg	28-Apr	28-Apr												
19	Design		P. Bromberg	28-Apr	6-May												
20	Purchase		P. Bromberg	9-May	18-May												
21	Install		P. Bromberg	19-May	19-May												
22	**Campaign Preparation**																
23	Political Landscape Memo		J. Chrastka	9-May	12-May												
24	Nationbuilder Web Site Set Up		P. Sweeney	16-May	27-May												
25	Committee Training		J. Chrastka	1-Jun	1-Jun												
26	Voter pool analysis		J. Chrastka	31-May	10-Jun												
27	Polling/Surveying		E. Findley	13-Jun	1-Jul												
28	Develop campaign calendar		B. Hart	20-Jun	1-Jul												
29	Scripts		B. Hart	5-Jul	15-Jul												
30	Recruit volunteers		M. Gooch	18-Jul	29-Jul												
31	**Media Contacts and Public Communication**																
32	Volunteer signups		M. Gooch	27-Jun	22-Jul												
33	Library activities-related info		P. Bromberg	4-Jul	7-Nov	1	1	1	1	1	1	1	1	1	1	1	
34	Press releases		M. Gooch	9-May	9-May				1								
35	Social media campaign		M. Gooch	25-Jul	7-Nov	1	1	1	1	1							
36	Coordination with newsletter		M. Gooch	25-Jul	7-Nov	1	1	1	1	1	1	1	1	1	1	1	
37	**Referendum Question**																
38	Obtain stakeholder input on question		E. Findley	6-Jun	24-Jun												
39	Formulate question		E. Findley	27-Jun	29-Jul												
40	**Petition Signatures**																

Everything you have read here comes together in the campaign plan. This is the document that guides the entirety of your campaign. If you followed along and built your campaign as you read through this book, it will be very easy to assemble your plan from what you have already completed. It's just time to bring it all together into one document. In this document you are going to lay out your political landscape memo, messaging strategy, committee member roles and responsibilities, your budget, fund-raising strategies, your volunteer strategy, voter contact tactics, and your media calendar and campaign time line in order to give a full picture of what your campaign will look like. Without this document it can be very hard to stay on track throughout your campaign but with it, you can check each week of your campaign to make sure that you are reaching your goals in order to make adjustments in other parts of your campaign if necessary. As many consultants say, if you don't have a written campaign plan, you don't have a campaign.

NOTES

1. Christine Pelosi, *Campaign Boot Camp 2.0: Basic Training for Candidates, Staffers, Volunteers, and Nonprofits* (San Francisco: Berrett-Koehler, 2012), 11–13.
2. Cathy De Rosa and Jenny Johnson, "From Awareness to Funding," OCLC report, 2008, https://www.oclc.org/content/dam/oclc/reports/funding/fullreport.pdf.
3. Lee Rainie, "Libraries and Learning," Pew Research Center: Internet, Science & Tech., 2016, www.pewinternet.org/2016/04/07/libraries-and-learning/.
4. John B. Horrigan, "2. Library Usage and Engagement," Pew Research Center: Internet, Science & Tech., 2016, www.pewinternet.org/2016/09/09/library-usage-and-engagement/.
5. De Rosa and Johnson, "From Awareness to Funding," https://www.oclc.org/content/dam/oclc/reports/funding/fullreport.pdf.
6. "Mitt Romney's '47 Percent' Comments," YouTube, 2012, www.youtube.com/watch?v=M2gvY2wqI7M.
7. De Rosa and Johnson, "From Awareness to Funding," https://www.oclc.org/content/dam/oclc/reports/funding/fullreport.pdf.
8. "Using the Ladder of Engagement," Using the Ladder of Engagement—New Media Campaigns, www.newmediacampaigns.com/blog/using-the-ladder-of-engagement.
9. Jack Milroy, "Digital Organizing 101: What Is a Ladder of Engagement and Why Do I Need One?" Medium.com, May 11, 2016, https://medium.com/@jack_milroy/digital-organizing-101-what-is-a-ladder-of-engagement-and-why-do-i-need-one-c523b5874e16#.5n1rru7i9.
10. Joe Garecht, "Tips for Local Candidates Preparing for the Next Election Cycle," Local Victory—How to Win Your Next Election, www.localvictory.com/strategy/next-election-cycle.html.

CHAPTER TWO

Surfacing

POLITICAL CONSULTANTS TAKE THEIR CANDIDATES THROUGH a pre-campaign process that is designed to build awareness about their candidates among voters and build affinity for their candidate among funders. This process is called "surfacing." We have all seen it at work for national and statewide candidates, but we may not have noticed it. The approach of surfacing a candidate is so effective that it is now pervasive. It is deeply ingrained in the media landscape and political process. It ends with Election Day, but it often starts with the candidate writing a book and doing a listening tour. This "surfacing" can take a person from a complete unknown to become a viable candidate in quick order. If you have ever scratched your head and wondered "Who is that and how is he or she running for office?" there is a public-facing surfacing project going on.

Surfacing is generally understood to be the first phase of a campaign. It begins even before public "campaigning" officially starts or paperwork is filed to form a committee. You can see examples of surfacing in the presidential election cycles. As this book goes to press, we have just wrapped up the 2016 presidential race. You may not recall all the names and faces from the original candidate pool in the fall of 2015. With an open race for president, it was quite large on both sides of the aisle. Five candidates from the Democratic side and seventeen from the Republican side attempted to be seen as viable, attractive candidates for primary voters and for their party's nomination. The process of winnowing them down to the eventual nominee started long before the first caucus in Iowa or vote cast in New Hampshire.

The earliest recognized preelection phase of a campaign occurred in 1976 when fourteen candidates began to appear in the earliest primary states at least two years before the primaries.[1] During this time the candidates began appearing at local churches, school board meetings, and various other community gatherings to introduce themselves to the local voting public and to help people become familiar with their beliefs and ideas. The candidates also wanted to establish themselves in the minds of the people on their own terms before their adversaries could take aim at them during the campaign. They understood that a well-established and unopposed story about themselves would carry them far in the primaries.

Since that time we have seen surfacing occur using a multitude of different tactics. The most visible to librarians would probably be the candidates' biographies that appear on our library shelves years before presidential election cycles.[2] However, less visible surfacing tactics include things like appearances at political events that were never previously attended by the candidate. Or maybe the candidate makes a large public donation to a veterans group. Many times the candidate will simply suddenly appear to be everywhere at once, conducting media interviews and giving his or her political opinions on radio talk shows or on morning news channels, or grasping for any kind of media coverage he or she can get.

Of course, these surfacing tactics didn't occur without planning and foresight, and they were performed with specific goals in mind. The foremost goal was to tell the story of the candidates in a way that resonated with voters and was free from attacks by adversaries. Since potential candidates have no campaign and therefore no opposition during this time, these tactics give candidates an opportunity to tell their story on their own terms. They can talk about issues that are important while they are on the offense instead of the defense, and they can solidify their messages and establish their authority more freely because nobody is there to attack their positions yet. This lack of opposition makes this phase of their campaign one of the most powerful and effective ones.

Likewise for library campaigns, surfacing is a crucial step that brings the needs of the library in front of key supporters, volunteers, and donors. This is a time when there is not yet any ballot language set before the voters. It comes before there is any public acknowledgment that the library will be appealing to the voters. There is no voter ID or persuasion, and there is typically no ballot committee during this time period. Even though the campaign hasn't yet begun, we would argue that this is the most important phase of a library campaign. Surfacing should not be overlooked by library leaders on their path to the ballot.

USERS OR SUPPORTERS

During the surfacing phase of your campaign, your library is not trying build a bigger base of library users, but is instead trying to build more support for the library in the community. As we have pointed out elsewhere, even people who don't use your library will vote for it if they have a good reason to. The people with enough money to send their kids to private schools, order books online, and have nannies read books to their children might still believe that libraries are important, but you may have to activate or instill that belief in them. We see many libraries that pay for Facebook ads or send out e-mails that only talk about what the library is doing or that tell people about the times of the next storytime. While a library can do that, it's much more effective to tell people why storytime is important.

For example, instead of saying that storytime is at 10 a.m. on Mondays, there is a much more significant long-range impact by saying that storytimes are key for the development of young minds in the community. Think of it this way: people are unlikely to vote to spend more of their tax dollars on a 10 a.m storytime, but they are much more likely to vote for the development of young minds in the community. Use your surfacing phase to tell people why library funding is important, not what is on your events calendar today.

LISTENING

One of the most important aspects of the surfacing phase is the candidate's willingness to listen. In fact, there is a term for this aspect of the surfacing phase: the listening tour. Good candidates want to be seen as being engaged and responsive to their community. Smart candidates also want to use the listening tour as a way to gauge voter interest in their campaigns. Everyone wants a media cycle "bump" as they go state to state or town to town on their tour. Likewise, a library, when not campaigning, should be spending significant amounts of time and money listening to its constituents. It's important to understand how the public perceives the library and what the public wants from the library. Because the library doesn't yet have a campaign and the public generally isn't focused on taxes at this time, they likely won't have a lot of questions or require a lot of answers from the library about taxes, so the library can make a better case for itself without that kind of opposition. That makes this time period one of the best opportunities for the library to ask questions and listen to the answers from the public. No matter how you meet with them the first time, just remember that this initial meeting is not about giving a library services 101 talk, it's about building a relationship so that you can mobilize them into action later.

SHOWING UP

To start your surfacing phase and listening tour, the first thing you need to do is simply know where to go and when to show up. By taking a careful inventory of the organizations or opportunities to engage in your community, you can start to build your community listening tour. Take some time and think about all of the organizations that you know of in your library's community. Is there a Rotary Club, Chamber of Commerce, Elks Club, and so on? If so, write them all down and then do some research about who you can contact in that organization to see if you can attend their meeting to introduce the library and get their feedback about the library. In most cases, these organizations love to have guest speakers and have people attend their meetings.

If you haven't built these connections before and are nervous about cold-calling strangers, it can be a daunting task. But there are a couple of tactics that you can use to introduce yourself to these organizations, and after the first three or four introductions it will become second nature. Typically, the larger organizations have websites with some kind of contact information, and by simply sending them an e-mail or calling them on the phone you can start the conversation. If the organization doesn't have a website with contact information, sending a letter of introduction via snail mail has worked for some people. In any case, you can't wait for them to contact you; you have to reach out and build those connections yourself.

Fund-raisers and networking events like those put together by organizations like Network After Work are great places to meet other professionals and listen to what they have to say. Networking events typically happen in large cities with younger professionals who are trying to build their new careers. These young professionals are looking for connections to advance their careers, but they are trying to find resources that can help them like those offered by the library.

The Sunnyvale Library is located in the midst of Silicon Valley in California. The library has done a lot of work with local startups and some of the well-established tech companies in the area. However, it hasn't done much to connect to young or new professionals, and there were a number of networking events happening in the area put together by Network After Work. When librarians began attending these events, the young professionals often asked why librarians were attending since this was an event for "professionals." However, after the librarians engaged them, discussed the things the library had to offer them, and asked them questions about how the library could support their profession, the conversation often changed dramatically. The librarians built connections with these attendees that led to programming ideas and partnerships, discussions about the library as an incubator for small business, and a number of new library cardholders. These are all discussions and outcomes that wouldn't have happened if the librarians hadn't shown up. ✪

If your community doesn't have a networking event, consider creating and hosting some at the library. There are many young professionals in every community who are looking for opportunities to grow their networks and get ahead. The library can insert itself in the middle of the young professional demographic in a community by becoming the place where young professionals meet. These are often community members who are starting their own businesses and creating new products, and by lining up events where local luminaries in the business world come to speak, or by educating the population about the business services provided by the library, the library can demonstrate its economic value to the community.

JUST ASK QUESTIONS

While attending these meetings and events, ask as many questions as you can. Ask the Chamber of Commerce what they would like to see from the library to support small or local businesses, or ask the Parent Teacher Association (PTA) or school board about how the library can supplement the educational activities of the school. People will be astounded that they are being asked questions instead of being fed messages or advertised to. They will be surprised that you aren't there to ask for money or support, but are asking them what you can do for them. They will respect the library as an organization that is responsive to their needs simply because you chose to show up and listen to their concerns. The truth is that there are very few other organizations in the community knocking on their doors asking them what can be done to support them.

Of course, you might not get answers that you like. That's okay for now. You are listening as well as talking, and the goal is to be seen as engaged as well as responsive. If you are getting answers that are inflammatory or in opposition to the library, take extra care to not retaliate or correct them. You are just there to listen to their concerns and start the dialogue, not offer solutions. Thank them for their honest opinions and let them know that you are willing to work with them to address their concerns throughout the next year, but make sure that you follow up with them to continue the dialogues about how you are addressing their concerns.

Make sure that you write everything down, and keep a journal of these kinds of oppositional statements because they are the same things you will hear during a campaign. Nothing is in front of the voters yet, so the oppositional statements or objections you hear are not about the difference between $5 a month and $10 a month in new taxes. At this phase, the feelings you hear are real and significant attitudes and perceptions about the library. If you get push-back in the absence of a discussion about new taxes, that push-back will be ten times worse during a campaign. The listening tour should allow you to evaluate your plans and also test out different ways to frame the problem(s) your plan is trying to resolve. We will be talking about how to address active campaign opposition in chapter 13. Your listening tour journal will come in handy when the ballot campaign needs to develop responses to the opposition.

USING THE MEDIA

The surfacing phase of a campaign is a great time to start engaging the local media and building relationships with reporters, local social media mavens, and local bloggers. When a potential presidential candidate is surfacing his campaign, you might start to notice that he is doing interviews on local media channels or speaking as an expert during a crisis on things like foreign affairs, unemployment, or national finance. For example, before Rick Perry officially began running for president, he began showing up on Fox News and its affiliates to talk about his track record of finding solutions for the financial crisis. He talked about his record of success, established himself as an expert, and discussed the hypothetical strategies that he would initiate if he were in the position of president.

Library leaders often have the same opportunities in their communities. By reaching out to the local media to talk about the library, or about the resources that the library offers to help solve local issues, the library can establish itself as an unopposed expert in the solution of those issues. For example, if there is a rise in crime rates, the librarian can reach out to local media to talk about the dramatic effect of increased literacy, education, and employment on crime rates. She can talk about how the library works to help adults gain the new skills they need for employment, or she can speak about the resources that the library offers small businesses. By starting these discussions in the community early, the library establishes its relevancy before it comes into question during a campaign. The community will already know and understand the value of the library before the library has to make that case while asking for an increase in taxes.

LOOKING THE PART

Appearances can make or break a campaign. The overall look and feel of a candidate can make a huge difference in the outcome of the campaign. There is a lot of data on people's perception of a candidate based solely on his or her public or visual appearance. Most famously, John F. Kennedy and Richard Nixon appeared side by side on the very first televised presidential debate.[3] Kennedy appeared as handsome, poised, and articulate and his appearance changed the public's perception and eliminated concerns that he would be too immature for the presidency. Meanwhile, Nixon's appearance reinforced the image of a menacing mug, clammy-faced, awkward candidate who was plagued by his gloomy five-o'clock shadow. There is some discussion about how many votes were swayed entirely by the appearances of the two candidates and whether it was enough to change the election, but it was enough for Americans to take notice of the contrast between the two candidates and be influenced in their subliminal decision-making process.

In any case, when appearing at events, speaking to the media, establishing expertise in subject areas, and generally being seen by the public, there is a level of psychological illusion used by politicians. For example, it was no accident when Rick Perry chose to wear glasses in his interviews and when he didn't.[4] He put on his glasses when he wanted to be taken seriously as an expert during his surfacing phase and throughout his campaign. While this is logically meaningless, it is a psychologically relevant maneuver. He was establishing himself as an intellectual in front of the crowds that wanted someone intellectual as president. It's also no accident that George W. Bush had photo opportunities in blue jeans on his ranch in Texas. He relied heavily on dressing for the demographics that would respond to that imagery to win his campaign.[5]

In his book *Rules for Radicals*, Saul Alinsky talks about the need for community organizers to look as though they fit into the community they are trying to help while at the same time not appearing too different than the community they are trying to affect for change. There is even an example in the movie *Homeland* when Matt Damon's character talks about wearing his father's old work boots and driving an old truck when talking to the working-class community members that he is trying to persuade to allow him to purchase the rights to their land. Finally, many of us remember President George W. Bush appearing on an aircraft carrier in a flight suit when he declared victory in Iraq. Each of these examples is contrived and meaningless when thought about logically, and yet they have a great impact on the psyche of the public.

Of course, there are examples of this tactic backfiring due to inauthenticity. When Paul Ryan showed up at a soup kitchen and washed dishes, it turned out that the kitchen was actually closed and the dishes were already done, and he was called out as a phony.[6] When Michael Dukakis drove an army tank to appear tough and capable, the George H. W. Bush campaign lambasted him in the media for being phony and it was one of the defining moments in his failed run for president. The ultimate reason that these tactics failed was really because they were inauthentic representations of the candidates. Don't make these mistakes and represent the library during a campaign as something that it has never been in the past. The public will see through these meaningless gestures.

There are many more examples of political figures staging events and using symbolism, but in each case the intended outcome is the same. They are simply trying to "look the part." If librarians are going to appear as candidates or leaders of causes and want to "look the part," they need to ensure that they are doing it in the most authentic way. This means that the candidates need to authentically fit the demographic that they are trying to reach. For example, it might not be in the campaign's best interest to send the children's librarian to a Chamber of Commerce meeting when there is a business librarian on staff. Librarians can utilize these same kinds of tactics in day-to-day outreach to various communities. For example, if a librarian is visiting the Chamber of Commerce or another business-related organization, then wearing business attire would be most appropriate. If the librarian is talking about issues in the community and wants to appear to the public as an expert, then she might consider wearing glasses or carrying a notebook. If a librarian is meeting with a highly conservative group of individuals, then wearing long sleeves over arm tattoos might not be a bad idea.

We say all of this with a lot of regret and hesitation. We would rather that librarians and all other humans could simply come as they are. Unfortunately, that's not the world we live in. But the reality is that if we want better funding, more resources, or more political support so that we can provide services that are desperately needed by community members, then we need to make some compromises to communicate effectively in order to achieve that goal. We think that Saul Alinsky made this point best in his book *Rules for Radicals:*

> If the real radical finds that having long hair sets up psychological barriers to communication and organization, he cuts his hair. If I were organizing in an orthodox Jewish community I would not walk in there eating a ham sandwich, unless I wanted to be rejected so I could have an excuse to cop out. My "thing," if I want to organize, is solid communication with the people in the community. Lacking communication I am in reality silent; throughout history silence has been regarded as assent—in this case assent to the system. As an organizer I start from where the world is, as it is, not as I would like it to be. That we accept the world as it is does not in any sense weaken our desire to change it into what we believe it should be—it is necessary to begin where the world is if we are going to change it to what we think it should be. That means working in the system.[7]

If you're nervous about how to go about cold-calling influential people in your community and introducing yourself to them, you can put together a sample "rap." For community organizers and political figures, a rap is a 5–7-minute introduction of you, your cause, and your call to action. It typically includes your elevator speech about yourself or your cause and then engages them in some kind of guided dialogue where you can educate them about the issue, agitate them in order to get them ready to take action, and finally commit them to a call to action. This is a highly structured device that helps you create a template for your introduction. But in practice, a real dialogue is fluid and is responsive to their input. In any case, a good discussion should go through a basic set of principles. In order to help you develop your rap, let's look at the example template that we adapted from the book *Tools for Radical Democracy.*[8]

Introduction	Hi, my name is _____ and I'm from the library ballot committee. I'm talking to people today about the library bond issue that we want to put before the voters on November 8th.
Self-Interest	Do you think that it's okay that our community has one of the smallest libraries in the district and that our children and community members aren't getting the library services they deserve?

(continued on next page)

(continued from previous page)

Accomplishments	Members of our committee, who are citizens just like you, are exceptionally proud of what the library has provided to the community. Things like literacy classes for children, help for small businesses, and education for adults who need new skills in the information age.
Education	I just heard from someone who started their own small business and they told me all about how they used the resources from the library to help them take their idea to market and now their business is thriving and contributing back to the community!
Agitation	What do you think about the fact that there are many days a week that our small library is too full to help more people in this community get the services they need to get ahead?
Call to Action	That's why I'm asking you to sign our petition to help us put this issue before voters on November 8th. Won't you please sign our petition?
Commitment	We are also having a meeting in two weeks to talk more about this issue. I hope you can come.
Data Collection	I'd love to write down your contact information if I could. Could I have your contact information to keep you updated?

WRITING THE BOOK

The best candidates know that sharing their own vision and telling their own story in their book are critically important. Donald Trump, a relative outsider to the political process in 2016, started running for president in 2012 with the publication of *Time to Get Tough; Making America #1 Again*. While then a state senator, Barack Obama did more to establish himself as a new generation of political leader by publishing *Dreams from My Father*. Hillary Clinton's perpetual campaign was established with *It Takes a Village* and was reintroduced most recently through *Hard Choices*. If you remember back to Ross Perot, in the lead-up to his 1992 run he published several books that activated his base of supporters by sharing his economic and political vision. He won 19 percent of the popular vote as a third-party candidate.

A candidate's book is a gateway to speaking engagements, to meeting friendly donors, to finding coalition partners and allies, and to gaining endorsements. A candidate's book establishes his expertise on a set of issues or policies. But most importantly, it lets him talk about his hopes for his state or nation; about why he is running for office. If it's Mitt Romney's *No Apologies* it may have charts, facts, and figures. If it's Carly Fiorina's *Rising to the Challenge*, you may be able to establish a correlation between poor sales and poor performance at the polls. It is worth wondering if 2000 would have been different for Al Gore if he had published *An Inconvenient Truth* then instead of six years later.

We think that your library already has its book, and it can help take you all the way to a successful Election Day. It isn't in the collection. It may be gathering dust on a shelf in your office right now. It's your library's strategic plan or facilities master plan. We'd like you to take it out, dust it off, and retitle it "Dreams of My Hometown Library" or "Make Our Library Great Again."

At EveryLibrary, we believe very strongly that your library's strategic or facilities plan should be used like the candidate's book to help you "surface" your library ballot measure. It is supposed to contain some facts and figures in order to shape a management approach, but your strategic plan is also supposed to be about the vision you hope to realize in the community through the library. For a building plan, if "form is supposed to follow function," what function do you hope to achieve by eventually breaking ground on that plan? Even a well-written annual report should be engaging to the public and tell the library's story with an honest and transparent dialogue about the library's mission and purpose.

GETTING SOMETHING BACK

The two most important resources in any campaign are people and money. But with a long and intentional surfacing phase, you can leverage the added benefit of time as a resource as well. Without time, you will need more money to campaign. You should use this pre-campaign surfacing period to continuously build your people and your money for your campaign at a later date. There are a wide range of opportunities for resource building during a surfacing phase, and you should think about every point of contact with the public as an opportunity to build one of those resources. Start thinking about ways that you can add more people to you e-mail list, get more likes on Facebook, and create relationships that will lead to campaign or Friends donations.

It's your job during the surfacing phase to ensure that you don't miss a single opportunity to build your resources. The primary resource that your library can build is a large network of people. There are many great tactics to use to build that network of people:

1. Pass around a clipboard during every storytime, event, or program that asks for people's e-mail address.
2. Place e-mail sign-up forms at the front desk or at the self-checkout stations.
3. Integrate e-mail sign-up forms into your social media plan and continuously import e-mail lists to your social media platforms.
4. All of your marketing should encourage people to sign up to receive e-mails or follow on social media.
5. Incentivize e-mail sign-up and give awards for signing up. For example, one library had a secret storytime at local parks that attendees could only find out about if they were on the e-mail list.
6. Always show up at meetings and community events with an intention to collect business cards or carry a clipboard for sign-ups.
7. Conduct a door-to-door library card campaign.
8. Meet with local politicians, local influencers, and potential donors on a regular basis to build relationships.
9. If you do any media ads, always ask for people to sign up for a library card (with e-mail address) or take some further action to get their contact information.

The single biggest impediment to effective communications by libraries is their lack of "opt-in" e-mail lists. Being disciplined during this time will mean that your library will have a broad reach during and throughout the campaign. Set yourself up for success early by building your campaign and its resources early.

NOTES

1. Robert E. Denton, *Studies of Communication in the 2012 Presidential Campaign* (Lanham, MD: Lexington Books, 2014), 4–6.
2. Ibid, 30.
3. "Kennedy and Nixon Square Off in a Televised Presidential Debate," History.com, www.history.com/this-day-in-history/kennedy-and-nixon-square-off-in-a-televised -presidential-debate.
4. "What's the Deal with Rick Perry's $500 Hipster Glasses?" *Christian Science Monitor,* 2014, www.csmonitor.com/USA/Politics/Latest-News-Wires/2014/0827/What-s-the-deal-with -Rick-Perry-s-500-hipster-glasses.
5. "The Many Faces of George W. Bush," TexasMonthly, 2015, www.texasmonthly.com/ politics/the-many-faces-of-george-w-bush/.

6. "How Paul Ryan Pretended to Volunteer at a Soup Kitchen," How Paul Ryan Pretended to Volunteer at a Soup Kitchen | Care2 Causes, October 16, 2012, www.care2.com/causes/how-paul-ryan-pretended-to-volunteer-at-a-soup-kitchen.html.

7. Saul David Alinsky, *Rules for Radicals: A Practical Primer for Realistic Radicals* (New York: Vintage Books, 1989).

8. Joan Minieri and Paul Getsos, *Tools for Radical Democracy: How to Organize for Power in Your Community* (San Francisco: Jossey-Bass, 2007), 47.

CHAPTER THREE

Schmoozing and Networking

THE FOUNDATIONAL SOCIAL SKILLS THAT ARE REQUIRED
to successfully build a network of supporters and allies are, unfortunately,
not taught in library school. In fact, your coauthor, Patrick Sweeney, and
many of the librarians that we have worked with are introverts. Before
learning these skills and practicing them, Patrick held the belief that people are just
plain born with networking skills or they're not. But that just isn't true, and networking skills can be taught. Schmoozing is a key aspect of successfully surfacing
your library by meeting with the public and building relationships through outreach
and networking. That's why we are going to take a deeper dive into the skills needed
to successfully schmooze.

As we said, your coauthor Patrick is a self-identified introvert who realized that
in order to get the things that he needed for his library or to accomplish some of
the bigger projects, he had to learn skills to build community relationships through
schmoozing and networking. So he spent a lot of time and effort building the skills
of an extrovert. Essentially, he needed to learn how to pretend being an extrovert in
order to make the connections he needed for his professional career and for the good
of his own organization. All of this came from observing extroverts and practicing
the skills that he learned from watching other schmoozers, attending webinars, and
reading articles about the "art of the schmooze." Because we believe that it is such an
important skill for a community organizer, we are going to explain what he learned
that worked for him so that you can use it to build your own networks, coalitions,

and groups of supporters. What follows are his tips and tricks for faking being an extrovert when you need to.

ATTITUDE

First and foremost, you should go into any networking opportunity or event with an upbeat attitude. You don't want to show up and complain or you will quickly get the reputation of a complainer and not a doer. It's important that you are not seen as a negative person. Many networking events are intended to be fun for extroverts. So come in with positivity and excitement about sharing with the people that you want to get to know. This is especially important because people tend to gravitate toward folks who make them feel good and are fun to be around.

TAKE A BREATH

Sometimes it helps to take a minute before you enter the venue. Pause, take a deep breath, and put on a smile. We all have bad days and that's okay, but you can't let those bad days ruin an opportunity to do something great. It's important that you leave all your problems at the door before you walk into a venue. Stopping to take a breath and center yourself just before you walk in is a great way to do that.

HANDSHAKES

It's funny that we were never taught handshakes in library school. A firm handshake is a great introduction and end to a conversation. People place a lot of value, both consciously and subconsciously, on the way that you shake their hand. This means that a handshake is usually the first opportunity for someone to judge you. When shaking hands with someone, don't just give them your fingertips; instead, give them a whole-hand handshake. A good confident handshake starts with a nice firm but not painful grip. It isn't weak or dainty. When shaking, your hands should always meet first at the webbing between your thumb and forefinger and then grasp firmly. Remember not to linger in their hand, and do make good eye contact while you shake their hand. Don't be afraid of practicing your handshakes with a buddy. We recommend holding things in your left hand when you're at a meeting or networking event. This ensures that your right hand is always free to shake hands. You'd be surprised how far a good handshake can take you. Another tip is to wear your name tag on your right-hand lapel or above a right pocket. This will put your name tag in an easy-to-read spot when leaning in to shake hands. The person you are meeting will feel slightly more at ease with you when they don't have to search for your first name. Unfortunately, they will probably not return the name tag favor.

EYE CONTACT

You should always be mindful of the need for comfortable eye contact. It's important to remember to keep your eyes on them and not be looking over their shoulder or at your feet or looking for other people. Of course, this doesn't mean you should stare unblinkingly into their eyes with an intense focus. It's okay to look around a little bit so that you're not staring them down, but people want enough of a gaze to let them know that you're interested in what they're saying. While talking to people, don't start fidgeting or scanning the crowd or looking for other places to be. Be present with the person you are talking to. If you have a hard time with fidgeting, hold something in your left hand such as a cup of coffee or water or some other drink.

BODY LANGUAGE

It's important to understand the way your own body impacts other people's response to you. If you are slouching, crossing your arms, or putting up physical barriers between you and another person, these are subconscious cues that they will pick up on. Doing things like checking your watch or your phone are great ways to make a person feel like you don't want to talk to them. Always keep your hands and arms open and accepting. Don't turn away from them or put yourself in a position that looks like you want to leave (unless you do).

One of the best examples of bad body language came from President George H. W. Bush during his 1992 debates with Bill Clinton when an audience member asked about the national debt.[1] In fact, no matter what political party you belong to, if you attend a campaign or candidate training, they will almost definitely show this video. In the video you can plainly see that Bush seems to be bored by the debate, isn't taking the question seriously, and his body language seems to show that he wants to escape the situation. Whereas Clinton is warm and welcoming, and his body language alone shows that he deeply cares about the questioner.

This is all great, but you should also be aware of differences in the way that different cultures and sexes engage each other in conversation. You should realize that some cultures speak while standing very close to each other, whereas Americans tend to stand farther apart. Studies also show that American men typically stand more side by side or offset while women tend to face each other directly while speaking. Be aware of these differences and try to respect them.

BUSINESS CARDS

It's very classy to always keep your business cards handy so you can quickly and easily pull them out. It's always awkward to stand around with someone while they are fumbling for their business cards, so don't make someone do that with you. We always recommend that men keep them in their right front pants pocket, or in their left breast pocket so that they can be quickly accessed. For women, it's a little more difficult because of the lack of pockets on so many women's styles of clothing, but keeping a purse or handbag on the right side where you can quickly reach in and grab it can help. When you get their business card, it is also a great idea to write something that you learned about them personally or a recommendation that you gave or received from them to help you remember them and personalize a follow-up later on. If you meet someone and you want to ensure that you follow up with them, you can turn the corner of their card to better keep track of it.

OTHER SUPPLIES

There are a couple of other things that you should bring with you when networking. First, you always need to keep a pen handy. Take notes on people's business cards that will remind you of who they are later, or to make changes or edits on their cards because the ones they have aren't always accurate. You can even let other people borrow your pen, and that can be a great icebreaker. Of course, make sure that your phone is charged and that you have your wallet and money, and so on. Even if you don't smoke, it can be very handy to keep a lighter with you or even an entire pack of cigarettes. There's just something about giving someone a light or a cigarette that makes them feel like they need to spend time talking to you. It's a great tool to break the ice in areas of the country where smoking is more prevalent.

INTRODUCTIONS

When you introduce yourself or someone else, it's always a great idea to build some kind of connection into the introduction. Just giving two people a name doesn't give those two people something to talk about. Instead, try to give some interesting piece of information about those people to each of them along with their name. If they are good networkers they'll be able to ask follow-up questions and have an easier time getting to know each other.

Your Pitch

Your pitch or personal elevator speech is typically 12–20 seconds about who you are and what you're about. At the end of this speech, you can have some prepared questions such as "And what about you?" This is a quick way to get your information out, engage them, or give them an opportunity to ask you something about yourself. Hopefully, they will either ask you more about yourself or share something about themselves that you can then use to engage them in your follow-up questions. Later on in the book we are going to talk about building a 27–9–3 campaign message. These messages are perfect to adapt to an elevator pitch about yourself.

Do Your Homework

Before you attend the event, it often helps to research who will be there. From this research you can plan whom you want to meet and set some goals about what you want them to learn about you or your organization, or what you want to know about them. For example, if you are at a fund-raiser and you find out that the mayor will be there, set a goal to talk to her and ask her three questions. Take a look at attendees' online profiles and ask them about things you noticed that they put on social media or on their website.

Small Steps

If you're an introvert, that's okay. The key to successful networking is to start small. For example: if you're usually a wallflower at social events, then it can be a daunting task to suddenly jump into the middle of a room full of people and talk to all of them. The key to a small start is simply showing up. If you attend your first event and all you do is stand against the wall and observe, that's okay. At the next event, take a step away from the wall. Then at the next event, introduce yourself to someone. Later, have a goal of meeting ten people and getting their business cards. It takes time to build up the courage and skills to really engage with strangers. That is okay.

First Contact

Often your entrance into a networking event sets the tone for the rest of the night. If you start the event by not talking to people, most likely you will end that way. But if you start the night by talking to someone, it typically flows throughout the event. We suggest you take the first couple of minutes of the event and introduce yourself to the host, or honoree or guest of honor. The easiest cold introduction or first contact is the most honest one: "I am new here and don't know anyone, so I thought I'd come by and introduce myself." Many times, they are excited to talk to someone and they can connect you to more people that you should know at the event.

Food and the Bar

Anywhere that people gather is a great opportunity to get to know the attendees, and people tend to gather around food and drinks. The great thing about this is that food and drinks usually offer some great introductory topics for conversations that can lead to more important topics. For example, start by talking about what someone is drinking, make recommendations for other drinks to gain some familiarity with the person, and then you can start asking deeper questions about what they're excited about at the event and then ask questions about what they are working on, and finally talk about how what you're working on can complement their work or vice versa.

Of course, once you get food or drinks, don't eat or drink alone. Sitting alone at a table sets a precedent that you aren't interested in being there and people will notice that. Instead, politely ask if you can join a table of people or ask other people to join you. Remember that they are probably as anxious and nervous as you and are just dying to find someone to engage with. Besides, nobody likes eating or drinking alone. This is your opportunity to be the hero and join them.

Short Sprints

There's no need to spend hours with someone or just a few people. You're at the event to meet and connect with as many people as you can and build the basis for a deeper relationship later. That's why you should try to spend 5–10 minutes with individuals at the most. The problem that you're going to run into here is that this behavior feels awkward and contrived. But that's because it is. However, you should remember that not only is your time valuable, but their time is as well. You should be strategic with your time and allow them to be strategic with theirs, and that means that you don't want to wear out your welcome. In fact, it's often best to leave someone wanting more time with you instead of wishing that you'd move on already.

Take a Break

If you're an introvert, you shouldn't be afraid to stop and regroup. When you do need that break, you can excuse yourself to some place like the restroom or a hallway. But you should never revert back to one of your safe spaces (like in a corner or against the wall) where you can get caught up feeling safe and never rejoin the group. Instead, take a quiet moment to collect your thoughts, add your notes to a business card, or just take a breath for a moment.

Connectors

At almost all networking events there are people who love to connect individuals or groups of people together. It's usually easy to find these people because they are surrounded by people having a great time. Always try to join these groups and introduce yourself to the connector. Many times, this person will do all your introductions for you and you can just be an engaging participant!

Be Genuine

Of course, you should always be in this work for the quality and meaningful conversations. You are not just here to use people for their connections or what they can do for you. You must genuinely engage them. This means that that you're not simply looking for people to get things from, but people that you are excited to share and work with or even be friends with. Genuinely try to connect with people on both a personal and professional level.

Rule of Threes

It's a great idea to try to get yourself engaged in groups of three or more. It is also a good idea to try to avoid couples, since they are generally talking about something that you don't want to interrupt. The dynamic between pairs of two and groups of three is different and the conversation is typically more free-flowing in groups of three or more. What is also great about groups of three or more is that they are more welcoming to outsiders coming into the group and you join by simply saying something like, "I don't know anyone here, can I talk to you for a while?" People love feeling like they are important, and giving them the power to introduce you can make them feel good.

Group Dynamics

When you become part of a group, watch the body language of the group. Make sure that there is always room for someone to join your group. Make the group shape look more like a C and not an O. This allows a space for people to join and leave the group. By continuously making sure there is that space somewhere in the group, you can create an opportunity for the group to change more rapidly. This is a good tactic because you won't spend as much time trying to find other groups, and having people come and go from your group means that you won't have to come and go from other groups. Of course, try to maintain groups of three or more for that more free-flowing and comfortable discussion. If you see the group dwindling, try to either invite more people over or excuse yourself.

Open-Ended Questions

Remember that people love to talk about themselves, so always ask open-ended questions. For example, "What did you find fascinating at the conference today?" or "How'd you hear about this event?" It can help to have a set of questions written down beforehand just so that they're fresh in your mind and ready to go when you need them. But you should always try to avoid questions that are complicated or could lead to an awkward conversation. For example, remember that it's a down economy, so don't assume people have jobs with questions like "Where do you work?" There are a few other types of questions that you should avoid asking. Don't ask off-putting questions that point out flaws or personal features or personal differences. As a general rule, asking about things that people choose to talk about is most likely okay, but things like skin color, gender, sexual orientation, and so on that people don't choose are generally not okay.

Make Recommendations

A great way to get more people to enjoy being around you is to try to make good recommendations. This can be as simple as a food recommendation or a recommendation of a potential major donor. The best part about recommendations is that they are something you can use to follow up with them about. If you make a recommendation, make a notation about it on their business card. Then in a week or two, you can send them an e-mail to ask how your recommendation turned out. When they know that you are a librarian, they may even ask about books!

Moving On

It is very important to move on from an interaction that isn't going well. You have many people to meet, and you don't need to fight through some interaction that just isn't working. You can often tell when an interaction isn't working because you're distracted or not focused on what's happening, or if they are giving those signals. So don't be afraid to just wrap the conversation up. You can excuse yourself by saying something like "I have to make a phone call," "I have to go to the restroom," or simply excuse yourself and politely walk away. If it's them giving the signs of boredom or inattentiveness, they'll probably be thankful for you moving on! Otherwise, one of the best ways to excuse yourself when you need to talk to someone else is to simply excuse yourself honestly and let them know that someone arrived that you wanted to talk to. If you use the restroom as an excuse, we recommend actually going there, even if it is just to wash your hands.

The Follow-Up

None of these connections will lead to anything unless you spend some time following up with the people you meet. Make sure you set aside an hour or two after the event and reconnect over e-mail. If you are working to follow up with a lot of people, it's okay to have some prepared statements or paragraphs to fill out the e-mail, but be sure to include something specific to that person. Ask about the recommendation you made, something from the conversation, and try to make some personal connection with them about your previous interaction to show that you care and were paying attention. Try to follow up between 48 hours to 4 days but no later than a week. Of course, don't be afraid to reach out by phone and give them a call.

Now that you have these schmoozing skills, you can use them to build your network. Well before your campaign starts, go out into the community and build the connections that you are going to need to win. There are plenty of opportunities to practice these skills and get those connections through many of the community meetings, city council sessions, and networking events that often occur in communities. No matter what, you are going to need these skills to build the network you will need for you to win your campaign.

NOTE

1. Smotus, "Clinton vs. Bush in 1992 Debate," YouTube, 2007, www.youtube.com/watch?v=7ffbFvKlWqE.

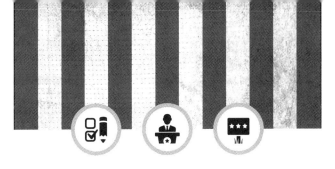

CHAPTER FOUR

Early Work and Political Landscape Memo

THE MOST IMPORTANT THING YOU CAN SAY IN A CAMPAIGN is "I don't know."

Before you even begin your library campaign, there is a large swath of work that needs to be completed. You must ensure that this kind of early work is done thoroughly and in great detail in order to ensure that the rest of your campaign will be the strongest and best it can be. This early work includes researching and polling your community, creating your political landscape memo or your campaign plan, and developing your budget. Without these primary documents in place, your campaign doesn't have a map to winning the election. The more of this work you do early in the campaign, the more you are going to know, and the fewer problems you are going to encounter later.

Let's start with some basic vocabulary. First, there is a significant difference between a goal, a strategy, and tactics. Each of these components is important, but they are rather different. Some campaigns make the mistake of confusing them. This understanding will help you think about how you are organizing and campaigning and make you a more effective campaign leader.

Goal. The goal of your campaign must be quantified, explicit, and specific. If your goal is to win the library campaign, then winning the campaign means you are trying to get a specified number of yes votes by a specific date. You need to quantify that in a specific and measurable number. For example, you know you need 1,000 yes voters to win by Election Day.

Strategy. In order to get to your win number, what will you need to do to get to your goal? You might decide that you are going to use a strategy of direct contact to persuadable voters. Making connections with 10,000 likely voters, with the expectation that 10 percent will turn out and are persuadable, means that you will persuade 1,000 voters by the end of the campaign.

Tactics. The tactics are the tools you will use throughout the campaign to achieve your goal. You can use a variety of tactics to carry out your strategies in order to achieve your goals. In our example of direct voter contact, you could choose either phone banking or canvassing as a tactic. Your campaign tactic might be to use door-to-door canvassing to reach 5,000 voters and to use phone banking to reach another 5,000 voters.

Example Campaign Plan Statement:

> Our campaign needs to convince 1,000 voters to vote yes for our library campaign by November. We will do this through persuading 10 percent of 10,000 likely voters to vote yes through direct voter contact. We will contact 5,000 voters through canvassing and another 5,000 voters through phone banking.

You should understand that this is a very simplified version of a campaign plan statement. A full campaign plan is far more complex and will use a wide range of strategies and tactics to fulfill its goals. But it is as fundamental as identifying your vote goal, developing a strategy to reach the goal, and having the discipline to use tactics that are productive in reaching that goal by Election Day.

KNOW YOUR RESOURCES

Every vote "yes" campaign, whether it is for the president or for a library, has only three resources: money, time, and people. The bulk of your campaign work will be finding enough of each to support your campaign strategy. Each one of these resources will need to be spent in the most effective and efficient way so that you can make sure you maximize the outputs from these resources. Unlike a fund-raising campaign, an advocacy campaign, or a normal marketing campaign, a vote yes campaign will end on Election Day, win or lose. We recommend planning to spend 100 percent of your financial resources by Election Day and to maximize your people resources to achieve your Election Day goal. There's nothing worse than losing a campaign with money in the bank that could have been spent and people ready to volunteer who weren't given a role.

Money

Everything in your campaign costs money—even "free" resources like volunteers. Campaign money comes from donations, and it will almost always be limited. You will need to work to maximize this resource through continuous fund-raising and by managing your budgets well. You should plan to spend all of your campaign money by Election Day. You should not use the campaign as a fund-raising opportunity for a foundation or a Friends group. Donor lists from a library ballot committee can be given to the library fund-raising organizations after Election Day, but the campaign should be broke when the campaign is done.

Time

There will never be enough time in the day to get everything done that you would like. There will always be one more thing to do. For most library campaigns, the time you are looking to put to work will be volunteer time. Time resources will only be maximized with effective planning because you will never be able to raise more time. The more planning and campaign days you have before Election Day, the better off you will be. It is never too early to start working on your library campaign.

People

Your people resources can be either volunteers or paid campaign staff. The library's staff cannot work on the yes campaign during their regular work hours. We occasionally work with library communities that can afford a paid campaign manager or coordinator (that is, paid campaign staff and not library employees). You have to continuously recruit new volunteers and manage the ones you have. This is the resource that will help you manage the rest of your campaign.

POLITICAL LANDSCAPE MEMO

A smart campaign begins with a thorough *political landscape memo*. This document is the structure for your campaign and includes the goals, strategies, and tactics your campaign will use to win. It will include a detailed analysis of the district, a description of the ballot measure, a frank assessment of its opposition, and an estimate of the anticipated time, money, and people that are available or needed to win the campaign. It's immensely important to have a strong political landscape memo as your campaign's first product. It will help form the rest of the campaign and shows the supporting community that you are serious about winning. It will help recruit partner organizations, donors, staff, and early volunteers.

Writing the Memo

The political landscape memo is the preliminary document that you will use to build your campaign. The document doesn't need to be much more than a review of what the current landscape is for the campaign. You don't need to talk about specific tactics here, and you don't need your budget details or time line laid out here, but some rough estimates of what you think your campaign can raise are helpful. This document should be only a page or two and written in an informal style that is easily read by anyone involved in the campaign to get a good overview of the campaign. This is not your campaign plan, though. It is just a rough overview to ensure that you understand your community, your voters, and your campaign.

Your District

The first step in building your political landscape memo starts by studying and understanding your district or voting area. You need to know your area inside and out. In fact, there are details that may feel irrelevant to your campaign until they become a problem. For example, if you live in the district, you already know the climate and the weather. But because your Election Day is in November and it might be snowy in November, you will want to think about how that will affect your voter turnout. Likewise, if Election Day is in June or August and "everyone" is usually on vacation or out of town, that will not only affect voter turnout but also the likelihood that volunteers will be in town during the last critical campaign days. There are also issues around local terrain and your volunteers' ability to go door to door. If the houses are too far apart, or they are mostly condos and apartments, or if the terrain is too hilly for volunteers, you might need to reconsider doing door-to-door work. Don't let these details go; they'll come back to haunt you later.

Your district information will help you determine your initial strategy, messaging, and targeting. If you are serious about winning your campaign, you will have these details committed to memory. Some other vital details you should know include:

Nonpolitical

- Physical boundaries (highways, trains, walls, etc.)
- Terrain (hills, rivers, mountains, etc.)
- Population demographics (age, sex, religion, race, education level, housing, etc.)
- Public transportation
- Major employers and industries
- Employment rates
- Current tax rates
- Media outlets
- Popular locations like bars, grocery stores, coffee shops, or restaurants
- Income levels, home prices, and trends

Political

- Type of election and offices on the ballot
- Typical voter turnout in similar elections (more about this later)
- Number of total voters (more about this later)
- Voter party affiliations breakdown
- Politician/political support
- Other local initiatives on the ballot
- National issues in the voters' minds
- Public opinion polling results
- Tax impact on the average resident or homeowner
- Perceptions of other tax measures for school, parks, and public safety

Library-Specific

- Number of library cardholders and as a percentage of the population
- Library visits per year
- Annual circulation
- Special programs and programming or services
- Strength of the Friends or foundation
- Library supporters, sponsors, and allies
- Outcome of previous library ballot initiatives

Where to Get This Information

Knowing you need to get this information is useless if you don't know where to get it. While this book is directed at librarians who can find all of this information fairly easily, let's take some of the work out of it by laying these resources out for you.

Nonpolitical

There are a number of resources where you can get this information quickly and easily. You can use www.city-data.com to find information from the most recent census and the American Community Survey compiled in an easy-to-understand format. There are also apps and websites that you can access on your smartphone that can help you find information on local hotspots and gathering spaces like Meetup .com, Facebook, Eventbrite, or Yelp.

Political

Typically all of this information is available from a local political party, previous campaigns, the board of elections, or from various vendors that sell voter files or voter rolls. The most critical pieces of information are typically voter turnout in similar elections and the number of registered voters. These numbers can be found on your state elections website or by calling your local board of elections. Websites like Ballotpedia.org can also be a great resource for the history of previous ballot initiatives and language and voter turnout.

Most Common Tools

- **www.census.gov:** demographic information such as age, race, sex, income, and housing
- **http://factfinder2.census.gov/:** the U.S. census online tool
- **https://nationalmap.gov/small_scale/printable/congress.html:** district maps (more detailed maps are available at your county elections office)
- **Voter rolls:** public documents that are made available at your county elections office or town clerk's office
- **Voter file and enhanced voter file:** sometimes this is available from your local party, previous campaigns, from various online vendors, or from many of the digital political platforms that you might use during your campaign like NationBuilder or EveryAction
- **Ballotpedia.org:** an online encyclopedia of American politics

Library

Hopefully, information about the library has been captured in the annual reports that are released to the public or sent to the state library. In California, for example, the state librarian makes these statistics available through their website. It may be different in your state, so be sure to ask.

THE INITIATIVE

In order to run an effective campaign, you need to know your initiative inside and out. Is it a bond, a levy, a referendum, or something else? Is it a sales or use tax, a property or parcel tax, or another type of measure entirely? What is the language of the initiative? Who filed it, when did they file it, and why? What is the background on the creation of this initiative? Is your library looking to increase funding, start a construction project, or increase services? Maybe it's an expiring tax structure that you need to renew, or it is an expansion of taxes that are already in place. Are you trying to create a separate tax entity? These are just a couple of the questions that you need to have an answer for. After you have a legal or technical answer, it helps to have an answer to "why" as well. Voters want to know why the library is on the ballot much more than what is on the ballot. This is just the surface of the questions that you are going to get on your campaign. Be prepared to answer them.

The Opposition

In our experience, it is often difficult to discuss opposition to the library before a campaign begins. It may feel at first like everyone supports the library. However, this is almost never true. You will always have some kind of local opposition, even if the opposition come around quickly to become supporters. You need to know who they are or who they might be before you begin. This will help you neutralize them or create a strategy to circumvent their claims against the library. The following questions may help you identify your opposition and help you frame your messaging in the future planning of your campaign:

- Is there a strong antitax group in the area?
- Is there already a vocal opposition to the library measure?
- Is there a group against the library staff or government employees?
- Does the community look unfavorably on the library leadership?

- Does the local political body support the initiative?
- Were there previous initiatives that failed?
- Are there comments on online media or blogs in opposition?

Your Supporters

Hopefully, you find it easier to find supporters for your campaign than it is to find opposition. After all, *you* are the first campaign supporter, and hopefully you know some like-minded individuals. Identifying potential supporters before the campaign begins will help you earn endorsements and quiet the opposition early. The following questions may help you find the support you need:

- Is there a strong Friends of the Library group or foundation community?
- Are people already vocal about their support?
- Are groups like the Rotary Club or Chamber of Commerce supporting the measure?
- Are local politicians supportive?
- Have previous measures passed, and who supported them?

These supporters need to be outlined in your political landscape memo in order to show that your campaign has the potential for early donors, volunteers, and endorsements. The ability to identify supporters early in your campaign planning is a signal that your campaign is viable and serious about winning.

Fund-Raising

When you begin thinking about fund-raising for your campaign, you should start with some fund-raising goals and keys strategies. There are many ways to raise money in a campaign, and briefly narrowing down your options early will help you plan. This means taking a few minutes and thinking about who in your community might be in a position to support your campaign. Do you have the money and social clout to create successful fund-raisers, a community of large corporations or wealthy individuals from which to solicit large donations, or the manpower to organize weekends of phoning for dollars? You might not have all the answers at this point and we'll discuss more fund-raising tactics in a later chapter, but an honest survey of your fund-raising resources should be discussed in your landscape memo.

Vote Goal

The most important part of your political landscape memo is determining your vote goal. A vote goal is not a theoretical number you need in order to win your election. It is the specific number for your entire campaign and everything you do throughout your campaign is aimed at achieving this number. Many of the budget items that we are going to look at later will depend on this vote goal to determine your costs because everything you do in the campaign will focus entirely on likely voters and you are going to ignore everyone else in the community.

To win an election in most states, the measure needs at least 50 percent plus one votes. Unlike candidates, though, there are a few states where a ballot measure needs to win a supermajority of votes to pass. This can range from 55 to 66 percent of the vote. Don't assume that the library ballot measure follows the same rules as candidates or schools, public safety, or other voter-approved measures. Know your specific winning-vote threshold and share it with your volunteers, donors, and supporters.

In any case, determining your vote goal is a simple mathematical equation. Simply multiply the total number of registered voters by the percentage of expected voter turnout. Then divide that number by two. If you need a supermajority, you can multiply the percentage needed (i.e., 60 percent or 66 percent) instead of dividing by two.

$$\text{(Total Registered Voters} \times \text{\% of Expected Voter Turnout)} + 1 =$$
$$\text{Minimum \# votes needed to win. / 2}$$

Or, for a supermajority:

$$\text{(Total Registered Voters} \times \text{\% of Expected Voter Turnout)} \times \text{[percentage needed}$$
$$\text{to win]} + 1 = \text{Minimum \# votes needed to win.}$$

SAMPLE POLITICAL LANDSCAPE MEMO

In the city of Springfield, there is a $3,000,000 library bond measure to raise funds for an expansion of an existing Carnegie building on the next general election ballot. The building was constructed in 1909 and is in need of not only a renovation to fit the twenty-first-century model of librarianship, but also a retrofit for earthquake support and an expansion to serve the community's children more effectively with a reading room and computer lab. The total cost of this project will be $3,750,000, and while the Friends of the Library have raised $500,000 and the city has secured a $250,000 grant, they still desperately need to raise the remaining $3,000,000 through this bond measure.

The city of Springfield is a small coastal community of 9,486 residents. These residents are mostly Asian, white, and Hispanic, with a significant active-living retiree community. The city did well throughout the Great Recession, with few layoffs and job losses, but home values did fall significantly due to a building boom just before the recession and many homes are under water. The climate throughout the election cycle is favorable to canvassing and outdoor meetings, and there are a few gathering areas where younger 25–35-year-old residents, who make up the bulk of the population, congregate. There are also a town recreation center and a few membership clubs in the retiree community.

The announcement of the construction project has led to the formation of a small antitax group in the area. This is a small group of citizens who are not well organized or well funded but are very vocal in the community. They began to form their opposition directly after the city council meeting where the bond measure was approved. They consist of a mother involved in the PTA and three retirees. They currently have a poor unfunded website but comment vigorously on online venues about their opposition to the project.

The library began its informational communications campaign immediately following the announcement of the bond measure. Staff have been educated about the regulations involving an information-only campaign. Brochures, flyers, and other informational materials are available at the library and on the city website.

There are a number of community members and organizations who have shown support for the bond measure. Three of the five city council members, including the mayor, support the measure while two are undecided. Members of the Kiwanis Club, thanks to the membership of the library director, and the local public workers' union have given donations and offered volunteer time for canvassing and phone banking.

The city of Springfield has 9,486 residents and 7,375 registered voters. Party registration is 36 percent Republican, 33 percent independent, and 31 percent Democratic. In the last general election the turnout was 2,803 registered voters, or only 38 percent. Given the contentious nature of this year's election due to a high-interest vote on an amendment to the state constitution, turnout may increase by a few percentage points to around 41 percent. We estimate that it will take 1,513 votes to win the election in favor of the library bond measure.

It is possible that the campaign committee can rely on large donations. There are four large corporations within the community that have ties to the library and a history of financial support. There are also six wealthy individuals who currently work with the library on a number of projects and can be asked for donations. The Friends of the Library have also committed to making two one-time donations in each of the fiscal years that this campaign will span.

Preliminary data and polling show that the library bond measure is well supported in the community and has a 63 percent approval rating, meaning that there is a high likelihood of passing. In order to ensure this, we are going to contact habitual voters, mobilize library activists (particularly Friends of the Library members), work within the retiree community, and move every identified yes supporter to the polls on Election Day through an active campaign of direct voter contact.

We estimate the cost of the election to be close to $10,000 due to the heavy reliance on campaign volunteers. These costs will be incurred through the purchase of yard signs, mailers, and other printed campaign materials. Other costs will be found in support for the lead campaign volunteers, canvassers, and phone bankers. ✪

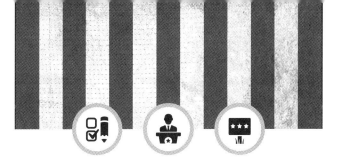

CHAPTER FIVE

Power Mapping

THE GOAL OF POWER MAPPING IS TO VISUALIZE HOW THE library and the campaign are connected to other parts of the community, to groups and organizations, and to specific leaders. It is vital for any "yes" campaign to learn and understand the landscape of these relationships.[1] Power mapping is a way to set up pathways for tapping into community power structures. Most importantly, it's a way to empower your group by showing your early campaign team members that they already know people in places of influence and thereby already have access to power and influence as an organization. A demonstration of these connections can help motivate and empower your campaign team during the earlier fragile weeks of advocacy campaign building.

During the early stages of building your campaign, you need to start by getting people from the community who are in positions of power on board. These people will be some of the strongest influencers throughout your campaign, and your campaign will benefit from their connections to the business, political, or community organization worlds. You will want to access their connections as soon as you can because these will be the first agents of change, your first connections to volunteers, and to some of your best fund-raising prospects. You can plan for doing this early work by conducting a power-mapping exercise with the library's staff and board members, library volunteers, your campaign volunteers, your friends and family, and anyone else who is willing to get involved in your campaign.

Power mapping is based on the idea that there are very few degrees of separation between any two people in your community. If you've ever played the game "6 Degrees of Kevin Bacon," you'll understand this activity immediately. That game is based on a similar assumption that any individual involved in the Hollywood film industry can be linked through his or her film roles to Kevin Bacon within six connections. By understanding the connections between people in your community in the same way that the Kevin Bacon game works, you'll identify your community connections to both your potential supporters and your opposition.

When we say "power" here, we are not only talking about folks with money or noticeable influence. We are also talking about formal organizations and informal groups that have a certain moral authority and validity in the community that comes from service. These groups and organizations do have their own networks (members or clients) who should hear about the library's ballot measure. For the library, "power mapping" is a process of identifying and communicating with organizations, agencies, and stakeholder groups that would benefit—through the library's increased capacity to partner—if the ballot measure passes. For your ballot committee and campaign, power mapping is focused on the leadership of partner organizations, agencies, and stakeholder groups and also extends to key individuals like potential donors, local politicians, community thought leaders, and the media.

Power Mapping

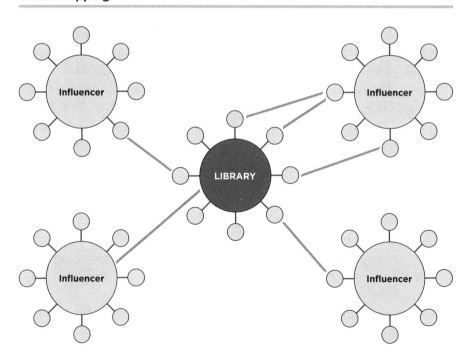

Sometimes it helps to start by knowing who you are targeting by identifying a specific person or an organization that you want to engage or influence. The target for your campaign is the person or organization in power who can address the issue that you are working on. For example, if you were looking to convince the mayor to keep from cutting library funding, then your target would be the mayor, or if you were looking to get a big donation from an organization, then the influential members of the organization would be your targets.

However, sometimes you might have a hard time knowing who in the community you need to influence, or you might simply want to explore how your organization is connected to the community or even what connections there are in the community. We often work on power mapping with a group from the campaign, and through this exercise they realize that there are people in the community who are invaluable to the campaign that they otherwise would not have known about. If that is the case and you want to find out who your campaign is connected to, or how it is connected to the community, you can start by taking a few minutes with your group and writing down the relationships that your group has connections to. This is a simple brainstorming exercise where everyone independently writes down names of people that they know of and then they spend some time sharing those names with their group. After that, the group chooses a few people to work on and takes a few minutes to think about how they are connected to them. There are many occasions when you will find that your ballot committee is connected to some organizations or people that you wouldn't have previously thought to connect to, or that you didn't know about. We have seen campaigns discover that someone is friends with the parents of a famous musician or other personality and with those connections, you can talk to those people or organizations about getting an endorsement or donation.

If you know who your target is, then members of your organization will work backwards from your target and identify anyone who can exert influence on them. It's important that your group thinks broadly about community connections and brainstorms as many connections as possible. These connections will be made up of anyone who can exert influence on a person, including people in the target's family, church, neighborhood groups, donors, and business relationships. Don't be shy about who you add to this map (like family members) because while you may not decide to use them, the connections they have to the target can lead to other connections with influence. This means that you need to be thorough and conduct your research on major players like donors, family members, and business ties as well as connections in small community or recreational groups. Don't leave anything untouched in this step. Once you have found the direct influencers of the target, zoom out a bit further on your map until you have identified 3–4 degrees of separation from your target, such as friends of family members of the person you want to influence.

Visually connecting all these individuals will sometimes show you some of the most important relationships between people. Once you have mapped the people who are connected to the people who have influence over your target, you need to draw lines connecting them while being careful to note what it is that connects them. You're going to find that people are connected across your map in interesting ways and create "nodes" of influence when they are grouped together. For example, when you step back and look at your map, you might find that the target's business partner is part of a community garden group with the target's wife and another major donor, but the target is not currently a member. This community garden group as a whole could be a major source of opposition or support, and with their ties to the mayor they have more direct influence.

No matter how you get to your target, once you have identified the connections you need to get to them, you are going to need to know very specifically what action you are going to ask them to take. Since they might have other ideas about how or why you should achieve your goal, you want to make it clear what you're asking for up-front. It's also embarrassing to find someone who is willing to help, but not have a plan for getting them engaged. This is why it's so important that the action that you would like them to take is specific and actionable. This means that you are going to ask them to go beyond just saying that they like or support libraries. Instead, you are going to ask the mayor to vote to put your library on the ballot at the May 2 council meeting, or you are going to ask the head of the Chamber of Commerce to write an editorial in support of the library bond measure to be published before the November election, or you are going to ask a large donor to pledge to contribute $5,000 to the campaign by October 1. Think about this as an opportunity to ask only one question of a person of influence in your community. You don't want to waste it by asking for something that they don't have to commit to or that won't lead to an action.

CAN'T FIND CONNECTIONS?

Sometimes there is someone in your community who is just not connected in any way that you can identify. That's okay. Just because you can't power map your way to someone of power or influence, you can always rely on an old-fashioned cold call. You can always contact someone in your community on behalf of the campaign or the library. Your library's campaign is a great excuse to reach out for an introductory meeting. In that case, you should contact them via e-mail or phone and simply ask them to join you for a coffee so you can introduce yourself and what you are working on. Your introductory meeting just needs to be an opportunity to explore each other's goals and find ways that the library can support their work, or ways that the library can support their work if the initiative passes. Take the time at the first meeting to primarily listen to what they have to say about their concerns, their fears, and their interests. After listening, you will have a better idea about how your library can work to help them. In a follow-up contact, you can review what they said, discuss the ways that the library can help address their goals, and then ask them to get involved in some way that makes the most sense for them. That can be through their money, their endorsements, their time or resources, or their connections. There are many people in big companies or organizations who love libraries and would love to get involved but will only get involved if someone asks them. Don't make the mistake of not giving them the opportunity.

One of the most important things you can do with anyone you contact who is on board with your campaign is to ask them who else they might know or who they might be able to introduce you to. Don't let opportunities to grow your campaign pass by just because you didn't ask.

FROM POWER MAPPING TO COALITION BUILDING

Building a coalition early in your campaign from these organizations and individuals that you've identified is extremely important to winning a campaign. Through your power-mapping exercise, you should have been able to identify a number of groups in your community that your library can work with as well as how to get your foot in the door with them. One of the best things you can do is ask for partnerships, endorsements, or assistance from groups that you've identified in order to lend your campaign more power through the development of a coalition.

Building these coalitions for libraries is a way to ensure that the library has the ability to develop and maintain power within the community. These coalitions are what will allow the library to shift power through its connections in a way that assures that it is able to advance its interests. If there are groups within the community that have similar goals and values, they should be asked to join your coalition. If all of these groups work together to advance the state of literacy or education in the community, they have a much better chance of making an impact through their alliances than if they worked independently.

A good coalition starts with relationships. These relationships are built on the idea that the goals of the organizations are compatible.[2] If you are trying to develop some priorities in the community around early literacy, it might not be beneficial to work with the Chamber of Commerce. Instead, you will typically find that the PTA or other local parents or education groups would be more likely to join you. No matter who you find in the community to partner with you, that partnership is most likely based on three key points. These are

1. that your goals are similar and compatible,
2. that working together will enhance both groups' abilities to reach their goals, and
3. that the benefits of coalescing will be greater than the costs.

For example, if the mayor of your city is big on public safety, you might want to find a way to get public safety on your side. Building your relationships with the police in your community can be the first step in accomplishing this. As a primary step, you can power map your way to someone within the police department who has a preexisting relationship with the library. Then you can reach out to that person or get introduced through those connections that you identified. In order to build your relationship, your library can extend some kind of introductory program or token such as helping the police promote their image in the community by conducting police storytimes. Take time at these events to talk to the police about what the library can do to support their public-safety agenda. Offer the library's resources as a way to incorporate a holistic approach to crime prevention through the opportunities offered at the library. By working as a coalition with the police on a holistic approach to crime prevention, your library has been lent the power of the police department and the police have improved their image in the community by working with the library.

JUMP-START YOUR POWER MAP

One way to quickly kick off an effective power-mapping session is to ask your people to write down answers to a few leading questions:

Q1 What community groups do you belong to?
Q2 Where do you live and where do you spend your time?
Q3 Who do you know who knows everybody?
Q4 Who do you think we are missing?

When you have exhausted your own networks and those of your colleagues, it is time to break out the yellow, blue, and white pages and start looking around town for who you missed. Even the most exhaustive research project will have holes. Forgive that failure and move on. Likewise, there could be arguments about what grouping to put an organization in. If they are important enough to the project to make the list, our advice is to just put them on the list, because the next step is to send your committee leadership out to talk to them. The strongest piece of advice we can give is to centralize the list on some type of shared document environment. If you can't track and record your meetings, the power map is just an exercise. ✪

Example Organizations to Build a Coalition With

The organizations that you partner with and build coalitions with don't necessarily need to be political in nature. Sometimes these organizations simply have similar goals and values. What is great about working with a library organization is that a library can support a wide array of the goals and values of other community organizations. By understanding the goals and values of these other organizations, it becomes easier to build bridges between them and the library.

Rotary Club

Rotary International is an international service organization whose stated human rights purpose is to bring together business and professional leaders in order to provide humanitarian services, encourage high ethical standards in all vocations, and advance goodwill and peace around the world. Rotary members are highly likely to volunteer in their communities and take part in many of the civic programs in the community. This is a good organization in which to find volunteers and by which to connect to many of the other organizations that are doing work for the social good of the community. Rotary Clubs also often invite guest speakers to their breakfast, lunch, or dinner meetings.

Chamber of Commerce

A Chamber of Commerce (or board of trade) is a form of business network; for example, a local organization of businesses whose goal is to further the interests of businesses. Business owners in towns and cities form these local societies to advocate on behalf of the business community. Local businesses are members, and they elect a board of directors or executive council to set policy for the chamber. The board or council then hires a president, CEO, or executive director, plus staffing appropriate to size, to run the organization. A Chamber of Commerce is primarily concerned about the economic health and the prosperity of businesses and entrepreneurs in the community. The library and the ballot committee should spend time talking about the economic benefits of a library, the return on investment, services to entrepreneurs, the library as a business anchor, and themes around economic freedom to this group to make the biggest impact.

Garden Groups

If there is a master gardeners group or a local community garden, the library can easily build some strong bridges here. I have seen campaigns collapse because a strong garden group was upset because the new library might cast a shadow on the garden. But building a relationship with these groups through things like a seed library, gardening classes at the library, and so on can ensure that you have the connections to this group when you need them.

Unions

Labor unions are organizations of workers who have come together to achieve common goals such as protecting the integrity of their trade, improving safety standards, achieving higher pay and benefits such as health care and retirement, increasing the number of employees an employer assigns to complete the work, and better working conditions. The trade union, through its leadership, bargains with the employer on behalf of union members (rank and file members) and negotiates labor contracts (collective bargaining) with employers. The most common purpose of these associations or unions is "maintaining or improving the conditions of their employment." The union has a vested interest in helping the campaign win an election because there are often many library staff members who are a part of the union and pay dues. The union can often provide financial support to the campaign as well as encourage its members to actively take a role in the campaign through volunteerism. Many times, a union will also offer "in kind" contributions to the campaign like office space, Wi-Fi, phones, or printing services.

League of Women Voters

The League of Women Voters can be one of the strongest political groups in a community. Even though they are nonpartisan, the members of this group often have strong political connections. The league can also help connect you to resources in the community or connect you to leaders in the local chapters of the political parties. This group is also often looking for places to host (nonpartisan) political events, and that can be a great opportunity for the library.

Parent Teacher Association/Organization

The PTA/PTO is made up of the parents of children who attend the local school district. This group is primarily concerned with the educational opportunities in the community. Reaching out to this group to talk about how the library benefits the schools or how the library supports the curriculum is a great thing to do during your surfacing phase. Many of the parents in this group also take part in other activities in the community or are community leaders, so there are great people to connect with who are a part of this group.

Food Pantries

Food pantries and other social services organizations in a community can help reinforce the notion that the library is a part of a broader solution. There are libraries in California that do Food for Fines programs or work with the local pantry to support lunches to children during summer reading. These social service groups are great to get involved with, but too much of a focus on them can harm the library campaign if it begins to look as if the library is only a social service organization. There are almost always vocal members of the community who will rally against tax dollars that provide social services. However, having a healthy network that includes both wealthy entrepreneurs as well as struggling families and access to the activists who support those families can help place the library in a strong position.

Local Political Party Chapters

It doesn't matter if it's a local chapter of the Democratic Party or the Tea Party, the library should build a relationship with these groups. While it might seem that some political parties' agendas are at odds with the values of the library, we would argue that's not the case. As the saying goes, "There's something in the library to offend everyone," but it's also possible that anyone who uses the library can find something that they support. Because the library accomplishes such a wide array of goals in a community, there is almost always a way into each of these groups. In fact, while antitax- and antigovernment-themed political parties have agendas that might oppose a library tax, they often simply want to be included in the process and if they are included, they turn from a vocal opposition to a silent one. This means that while the members might vote against the library, they will do it quietly without telling others to vote no, which is just fine.

Who Talks to Who? And When?

Now that you have a solid list of what organizations, agencies, and stakeholder groups to talk with, it's time to decide—and assign—who should go to talk one on one with the leadership of those groups. Our advice is to send the campaign team member "closest" to the organization first. If you don't have anyone close, then send the person who is most conversant in the issues that they are concerned with. The campaign manager does not have to make every meeting; the whole campaign leadership team staff should be involved in this project. Our other advice is to not send people without training, and to not send anyone out who self-identifies as unwilling. Sometimes hesitancy looks like unwillingness, and training provides the confidence to go out and do a new project like this. But when there is true reticence on the part of committee leadership or volunteers, it is a best practice to let them opt out.

This worksheet in figure 5.1 will help you work through this process. You can download an editable power-mapping worksheet at action.everylibrary.org/campaignresources.

FIGURE 5.1

Power-Mapping Worksheet

(Name of organization) _____
Brainstorm your connections to this group. Who do you know?

_____

_____

_____

Write a few short sentences about what you know that they believe in. Why are they organized? What makes them take action for a cause? Feel free to use your phone or Google!

_____

_____

_____

What is your goal for interacting with this organization? What would you like to take away from your relationship with them?

_____

_____

_____

Write a few short sentences about how the library can intersect with the beliefs of this organization or individual. Can your library provide them with a service? Can you collaborate on a project? What is it?

_____

_____

_____

Who will you contact to help you connect with this group? When will you do it?

_____

_____

_____

NOTES

1. "Grassroots Campaign Training," PDF (Washington: Democracy for America, June 10, 2016).
2. Ken Thomson, *From Neighborhood to Nation: The Democratic Foundations of Civil Society* (Tufts University, 2009).

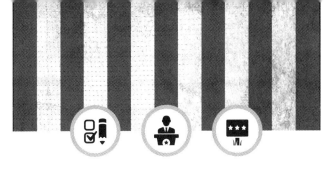

CHAPTER SIX

Building Your Vote Yes Committee

THE CORE MEMBERS OF YOUR BALLOT COMMITTEE—THE initial group of people who are dedicated to fighting for your library election—are critical to the success of your initiative. Every other aspect of the campaign is built from this core team. The committee leadership team can be people who are seasoned political operatives or are just good-hearted folks who want to become organized and active for the library measure. It doesn't hurt you or help you either way because the principles of running a library committee are based on organization, planning, and execution, and not in the everyday politics of running for elected office. This book is intended to fill in the gaps for the uninitiated as much as to correct the conventional wisdom that seasoned political players bring from nonlibrary campaigns.

These individuals who come together as the committee leadership team will be the basis for your fund-raising, outreach, and local support. You need to assemble them with care and an understanding of their roles and responsibilities.

LEGAL DISCLAIMER

Each state has relevant laws concerning the formation, conduct, and dissolution of ballot measure or issue committees. We'll talk more about those issues generally in the next chapter. This section is not intended to offer legal advice about the legal structure or financial decisions or reporting requirements of your committee.

Rather, we are interested in providing a general description of the roles and responsibilities that a committee leadership team needs to have considered and filled by either volunteer or paid campaign staff. In some states you might need to have a leadership team in place—or at least a treasurer—before formally filing the committee paperwork. In other states this might not be required. That's why we always tell campaigns to talk to their local board of elections and state elections or ethics office to find out how to legally form a ballot committee. However, even if you don't need a full leadership team or even a treasurer, you will need a dedicated cohort of volunteers to support your campaign and ensure that tasks are done in a timely and organized manner.

A good "yes committee" has three key areas of responsibility. These are

- Strategic planning
- Support development
- Fund-raising

STRATEGIC PLANNING

The first area of committee leadership responsibility includes developing the mission and the vision for the library campaign. This will be the group of individuals responsible for creating the political landscape memo and setting the strategy to win the campaign. They are going to need leadership and project management skills to make sure that they can accomplish this, as well as a strong attention to detail. Their leadership in carrying out the strategy that they develop will have a significant impact on the success or failure of the campaign. They should have the ability to monitor the ongoing activities of the campaign and find positive solutions to any challenges.

This doesn't mean they need to agree on everything. In fact, it is better if they have some differences of opinion, but they should be able to resolve those differences in a professional and positive manner. An early and important discussion for the committee is to talk about their "ground rules" for decision-making. If they want to operate on consensus or take votes about decisions, we are agnostic about how they want to organize. What is most important is that they all realize that the campaign has an Election Day coming up, and the committee has one goal—to pass the library measure.

SUPPORT DEVELOPMENT

The second area is about broadening the campaign's base of support in the community. Your committee needs individuals who are able to interact and conduct outreach to the community in order to bring in more opportunities for the campaign. They should be just as comfortable speaking in public and meeting with local officials and organization leaders as they are comfortable with meeting community members. Cultivating this support means that they need to have the ability to track support and train and develop new leaders and activists from these supporters throughout the campaign.

FUND-RAISING

Fund-raising is a crucial aspect of any campaign. Your committee leaders should be able to draft and stick to a budget, as well as be willing to use their connections and positions of power in the community to raise money for the campaign. If they are not willing to ask friends, family, and colleagues to financially support the campaign, they can't be expected to ask anyone to support the campaign in an authentic way. These individuals also need to have the ability to create fund-raising events and a fund-raising structure within the campaign.

FINDING COMMITTEE LEADERS

Your potential committee leaders may feel intimidated at the start, but once you begin sharing with them the hope you have for the community if the measure passes, folks who agree with that hope start to self-identify quickly. They may come from your existing pool of volunteers, your board of trustees, or other organizations in the community. You can also ask for nominations to the committee from this base of individuals. The kinds of people that you are looking for are typically people who have already expressed some kind of support for the library and are passionate about the services that the library provides to the community. However, not all passionate people should serve on the committee, and there are a few key things to consider when adding people to it.

Primarily, it's important to choose people who are well connected to other related areas within your community. Your library committee is an excellent tool to reach out and build relationships with other organizations that will be useful throughout the campaign. For example, you want to look at individuals who serve on the Chamber of Commerce, in local government like the mayor or city council members, the local PTA, or an especially powerful neighborhood organization. In some libraries, the Friends group or foundation members can be relied on to be strong members of the core committee. Sometimes it can be people from your corps of volunteers or even people who have donated to the library in the past. In any case, it's important to recognize that the committee leaders can be major influencers and a huge asset to your campaign while laying the strong foundational support that your campaign will rely on.

BREAKING THE ICE

We like to help new library ballot committees gel quickly around the goals, strategies, and tactics of the campaign. But before we get into helping them write their political landscape memo or start their power mapping, it's nice to find out why they care enough to volunteer for such a big project. If folks already know each other from other library leadership roles, this is a good chance to refocus them on the ballot campaign. If people are new to each other, it's good to find a common ground that is mission-driven. Here are some suggestions for campaign core group icebreaker questions:

Q1 Why is the library important to you, personally?

Q2 Why did you volunteer to work with the committee?

Q3 Who does the library serve? Pick a specific group instead of "everyone."

Q4 Why is the library important to those people?

Q5 What will this (new funding/new building/renewal and so on) do to serve those people?

Q6 Why do you use the library, personally?

Q7 Who is going to be uncomfortable with the library ballot measure?

Q8 What groups do you belong to?

Q9 Where do you live and where do you spend your time?

Q10 Who do you know who knows everybody?

These icebreakers aren't designed to be light-hearted or simple "get to know you" questions. We want to start the committee leadership down a strategic path that includes an awareness of the political landscape, the power map of the community, and the plan for the library's future. We can guarantee that the type of people who sign up to work on a ballot committee will find the questions fun anyway.   ✪

There are a number of other ways to find committee leaders from outside of your library if you can't find any inside of it. One of the easiest ways is to post on volunteer job boards on sites like Craigslist or a volunteer recruitment website like VolunteerMatch. You might also take the time to reach out to other organizations in your community that might not be thinking about the library. It could be a great excuse to make connections that your library didn't have before. There are usually also local branches of the political parties or organizations like the League of Women Voters that are well connected to people who are already interested in politics. It is almost always the case that the people are out in the community and are just waiting to get asked to get involved in something they believe in. You just have to go out and ask them!

If you're having a hard time finding community members to be a part of your campaign team, then there should be some rethinking of your library strategies. If you can't identify 3–5 people in the community who would be willing to fight for the library, it's going to be extremely difficult to find a majority of voters to vote in your favor. You might want to consider putting off the election for a year or two while you and your staff conduct more outreach, invite more individuals to take an active role in your library, and build up stronger partnerships within your community. After all, it is always better to put off a campaign for a year for a sure win than run it this year for a probable loss.

No matter how you find your committee leadership team, they each need to be well vetted. Since these are such critical individuals for your campaign, we highly recommend that you interview and reference-check each of them. You don't want to find out later that someone who is vitally important to your campaign has a history of illegal or immoral activity. You also need to make sure that each individual is capable of the high level of activity that will be required of them throughout the campaign.

TRAINING YES COMMITTEE MEMBERS

Just like any other volunteer or staff member for your library, your committee leaders will need to be trained. Your committee leaders are going to come into your campaign with preconceived notions about libraries. They might be nostalgic about libraries as book repositories and they might not fully understand the needs or functions of a modern library. That's okay, and it's not a disqualifier. But it's extremely important that once these individuals are trained they can answer questions about the library's budget, staffing levels, funding history, and the building history. They will be asked to answer those questions while they are working on the campaign. Committee leadership and volunteers need training to make them feel confident about the measure they are publicly and visibly supporting. So take plenty of time to give them a full tour of the library, review the budget, and let them ask the hard questions. Invite them to attend a storytime or other program and interact with staff. You could even invite them to volunteer for various tasks within the library if they have questions. The more that they understand about the library and feel that they are a part of the library community, the stronger their beliefs will be about the library and the harder they will work for it to win.

BOARD MEMBERS' PERSONAL AGENDAS

It's also important to realize that your committee leaders have an agenda, and you need to understand their agenda. For example, if they believe in the library because they believe in its ability to foster economic development, it is almost never a bad idea to encourage that belief and to use them to speak to organizations where their view of the library would be beneficial to the campaign, like the Chamber of Commerce. If they have aspirations to be local politicians, give them the information they need to meet with the county council or town manager. Likewise, if they believe in education, teach them about the educational activities of the library. Encourage them to speak at the Parent Teacher Association or school board meetings. Your committee members' agendas can be a strong asset for your campaign, and fostering those agendas can make them even stronger allies.

Anyone you didn't choose for the core leadership of the committee can be given places within the campaign, and you can find out more about these other roles in chapters 11 (volunteers) and 7 (campaign structure).

FILING THE COMMITTEE

Each state will have its own name for the type of ballot support committee you need to file. It could be called a "Campaign Committee," a "Ballot Committee," "Issue Committee," or some other title. But each of these committees forms the legal and financial structure needed in a campaign to collect and expend funds. Occasionally there are local ordinances for activities such as when you can display yard signs, but the vast majority of laws about political campaigns are state laws that focus on financial issues. If your campaign wants to fund-raise or if it wants to expend funds (which nearly all campaigns should do), you will need to set up some kind of legal entity in your state to do so. The requirements for these legal entities vary from state to state. Many states have a monetary threshold requirement before you are legally obligated to create the legal ballot committee. Every once in a while we hear from a library community that they don't want to set up a campaign committee because it's not required for how much they plan to expend on the campaign. But we always advise our committees to file the paperwork even if they will be under the legal spending limits.

WHY SET ONE UP

There are many important reasons to set up a ballot committee as a legal entity even if it's not required. First and foremost, a ballot committee provides a level of protection to the people working on the campaign. A ballot committee also acts as a shield between the library and the campaign. For example, many ballot committees include library staff members who volunteer their services on their own time. If there is no ballot committee in town and the "yes" activities are conducted by an ad hoc group of citizens that includes a library staff member, there can be accusations about the staff member's involvement. Even if the campaign does not expect to exceed the threshold required for reporting, having a high level of financial transparency and reporting can protect everyone in the campaign. For example, if people believe that the campaign is being financed by the library director who is working on the campaign (and who will "benefit" from the outcome of the election) and there is no structure that provides transparency about campaign finance, your campaign will be opened up to legitimate and unanswerable questions from the general public. With an established ballot committee, you can answer these questions through the required reporting.

Another good reason to set up a ballot committee is that it allows you to take advantage of the ability to raise more money if you need it. It's easily conceivable that your campaign is forced to spend more money than you originally planned either due to unexpected opposition or a sudden loss of support from a damaging news article or other surprise late in the campaign. You don't want to have to do the work to set up a ballot committee while you are also trying to raise money and also trying to do damage control. It can also be embarrassing if someone comes to your campaign to donate a large sum of money and you can't take it because you aren't a legitimate organization that is legally allowed to accept or expend a larger amount of money. That scenario is a fast way to lose a high-level supporter because they don't believe that you are taking the campaign seriously enough to set up a campaign committee.

WHEN TO SET ONE UP

We believe that if you are reading this book, it is now time to set up your ballot committee. Whenever we work with a campaign that is planning to go to the voters at any time in the next 5–10 years for any reason, we recommend they set up a ballot committee as early as possible. In fact, wherever it is legally and logistically possible, library leaders should have a ballot committee set up in perpetuity. This is one of the biggest recommendations we can make for libraries that have to regularly go to the voters. If you have to ask voters to approve a bond for a new library or a renewal of a tax every 5–10 years, you should have a legal entity already organized in your community that is ready to raise and bank political funds for an eventual campaign. This is partly because your library's foundation or Friends group (as a 501(c)3) is legally allowed to make some contributions to these kinds of voter advocacy committees. These contributions have a maximum fiscal-year limit tied to the expenditures of the 501(c)3, but every year they can make some contribution to the campaign.

Besides collecting small yearly donations from your supporting nonprofits, your committee can take in a few small donations throughout the years as well. These donations can be larger one-time contributions, or they can be smaller monthly or quarterly contributions. By setting up some kind of digital donation platform that allows monthly donations, you can solicit a dozen or so people to donate just $10–25 a month and over the course of 3–5 years. For example, 12 people giving 25 dollars a month for 5 years is $18,000. That's a healthy budget for many small-to-midsize campaigns. For larger campaigns that usually take place in larger communities, you might be able to find 100 people to donate $25 a month for 5 years and that can add up to a budget of $150,000! By doing this, your committee will not have to spend as much time fund-raising during a campaign. It instead has the potential to have more than enough of a budget to use high-level campaign tactics.

WHO FUND-RAISES FIRST?

In some places you might find the goals of a ballot committee at odds with the library's existing nonprofit support organizations who may perceive that the committee will take donations away from them. We disagree. It's important to remember that the day of the vote is likely the largest fund-raising day for the library that year, or maybe for a generation. Securing new operating funds for the library through a tax is truly sustaining. And when a new library building can cost tens of millions of dollars in tax money from voters (and you're almost definitely going to need a new library eventually) but a campaign can cost only $100,000, that would mean that $100,000 in donated funding to a campaign committee could return $10,000,000 in library funding, or a return on investment of $100 for every dollar spent. That's a great investment for your library.

One type of fund-raising shouldn't be seen as cannibalizing from another fund-raising effort. For most library donors, they have never been asked to donate to political activity before, so they could become new donors for the cause. For those potential donors who have never responded to a literacy or summer reading ask, a political campaign for the library—and the leverage that comes from winning a tax measure—may be the first time they have ever donated to the library before. If there is an understanding between the ballot committee and the other nonprofit support groups before the campaign to share donor lists, that is smart, strategic, and additive to the success of the ballot measure. We'd like to see everyone who was activated for the library during the committee work stay on as Friends or foundation volunteers after the election. And win or lose, your library needs more donors with a recent history of giving to stand ready to give again.

In some states the name of the ballot committee will be determined by election law, but in others you have a little more freedom to choose. In any case, the name of the ballot committee should reflect the goals of the campaign.

Something like "Vote Yes on Measure L Committee," for example, is clear and concise and effective. Some campaign consultants even recommend naming the campaign committee in a way that might influence voters or remove opposition, such as "Taxpayers for a Better Library" or "Taxpayers for Measure L." Each of these is effective in its own way. In any case, no matter what name you use in your campaign, make sure you spend a few extra dollars and buy all possible similar URLs to your campaign. We have seen opposition groups purchase and camp on URLs that almost appear to be from the campaign itself.

It is also not a bad idea to purchase the URLs of potential opposition groups to slow their effectiveness. For example, you might also consider purchasing "TaxPayersAgainstMeasureL" as well as "TaxPayersForMeasureL." There was a great example of this tactic in the 2016 campaign when someone purchased "trump.tv" and "trumptv.com" before Donald Trump could purchase them and turned them into vehicles to educate voters that Donald Trump wasn't even organized enough to buy a URL before announcing plans about Trump TV. This shows that if you buy a good opposition URL, you can even turn it into a fun website that actually supports your library campaign. In any case, all of the URLs can always just redirect to the main campaign URL. ✪

HOW TO SET UP A BALLOT COMMITTEE

Setting up a library ballot committee is usually a relatively quick and easy process. Each state offers both online and phone support for questions, and questions should be directed there and not left up to hearsay or friendly advice. There are many differences between each state, so unless we discuss the process for each state (that would be its own book) we are going to speak in generalizations for most states.

In most states, you need to do three steps in order to establish the committee:

1. File for and receive an Employer Identification Number (EIN) from the Internal Revenue Service (IRS);
2. Open a bank account for the committee using that EIN and under the committee's legal name; and
3. File the requisite paperwork with your state election authority that shows one to three people as the "leadership" of the committee.

You may run into some bureaucratic hurdles. In one state where we frequently work on campaigns, committee leaders are faced with a catch-22 where they need to open a bank account before they file the registration paperwork with the state board, while at the same time needing to have the paperwork approved before they can get the bank account started. The committee leadership called their state board of elections helpline and were relieved to learn that there was another "provisional" piece of paperwork that could be used by the bank.

The IRS has set up a relatively easy online process where a committee chair or the treasurer can apply for and receive an Employer Identification Number online. Be aware that there are scam sites on the Internet that charge up to $150 for "expedited EIN approval." However, filing for an EIN with the IRS is both free and immediate. You receive the committee EIN at your e-mail address within a few minutes. Once you have signed and sent in your filing papers, you can generally start acting as if they were already accepted. Many states have "safe harbor" provisions that allow the committee to begin acting in an official capacity even before you receive confirmation back from the state election authority. You usually don't have to wait until you get the official approval from the state office before you can begin to act like a ballot committee and fund-raise or expend funds on the campaign. But as always, know and follow your own state laws.

In almost all states it is relatively easy to find the state-specific requirements for a ballot committee on the state election authority website, including which forms to sign. A simple Google search can return the results. Or you can find some information about your state's requirements on voter information sites like Ballotpedia. EveryLibrary maintains a list of filing requirements for each state at everylibrary .org/campaigncommittee. While our list was created by a team of research experts, we still recommend talking to legal counsel and confirming the requirements with your state agency. Campaign finance laws can and do change.

It should be noted that ballot committees are generally not subject to any federal reporting requirements. Neither the IRS, the Federal Election Commission, nor the Securities and Exchange Commission has reporting requirements for state ballot committees. Likewise, local ballot committees do not generally have to file state or federal taxes or submit a 1099 or state nonprofit report like a 501c3 or 501c4 would. A ballot committee is an organization that normally operates solely under the purview of state election laws. Ballot committees are intended by state law to provide financial and organizational support in a relatively short time frame. Some states only provide for the existence of a ballot committee when there is a reasonable likelihood that a ballot measure will come before the voters at some time in the near future. Other states provide for long-term, multiyear or semipermanent ballot support committees. These are akin to permanent campaign committees for candidates for office that only end when the committee is officially closed.

If you are considering a long-term ballot support committee to raise and retain funds for an eventual library levy, bond, measure, or referendum campaign, you should consult with an experienced election attorney before deciding on a legal structure for the committee. You may also consider forming a 501c4 social welfare organization if your state does not provide for a long-term committee structure. We don't recommend creating a 501c4 to support a single ballot measure in a single jurisdiction for a single election without first consulting an attorney. The reporting requirements of a 501c4 are similar to a 501c3 and include both state and federal requirements.

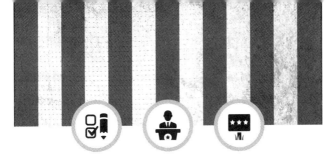

CHAPTER SEVEN

Committee Roles and Responsibilities

"VOTE YES" CAMPAIGN STRUCTURE

Any strong campaign for libraries varies significantly from the next. There are a wide range of variables that have drastic effects on the campaign such as access to resources, size and scope of the jurisdiction, type of ballot measure, and so on. However, the success of the campaign will depend greatly on the structure or backbone of the leadership team running the campaign. Typically, this structure won't vary too greatly between campaigns, although you might have changes in the number of volunteers or paid staff and their exact assignments. In just about every case, there is someone responsible for managing the field, fund-raising, communications, and staffing/volunteers. It's important to have this structure in place so that everyone involved knows their role.

For a library campaign, with the exception of the campaign manager, this structure is usually made up of volunteers and not paid staff, but it remains the same in either case. Each committee chair under the campaign manager has a significant number of tasks to complete throughout the campaign. While these chairs are responsible for ensuring that these tasks are completed and the chairs will be held responsible, they should work with their corps of volunteers to complete them and do not have to complete each task themselves. In fact, they should not. Those individuals under the campaign manager need to be strong delegators and leaders themselves.

The campaign structure could look like this example:

```
                    ┌─────────────────────┐
                    │  Campaign Manager   │
                    └─────────────────────┘
```

Communications Chair	Volunteer Chair	Fund-raising Chair	Field Chair	Treasurer and Compliance

CAMPAIGN MANAGER

The campaign manager has the most important role in the campaign and can be a paid professional, a consultant, or a volunteer with some significant campaign experience. This is the person who should be responsible for all aspects of the campaign. Specifically, this person is responsible for the time, money, and people. One of the most time-consuming roles of the campaign, and the one in which many managers struggle, is with people management. The campaign manager ensures that everyone knows their roles and the goals of the campaign and treats the campaign team with dignity and respect. In a lot of cases, and especially around library campaigns, the team is a corps of volunteers and they are going to be looking to a strong leader to show them how to win. At the same time, this person needs to be able to answer to the people below him and should have assembled a group of volunteers who will give him honest answers and will hold each other accountable in a respectful manner.

TREASURER OR COMPLIANCE OFFICER

The treasurer of a ballot committee is responsible for ensuring that all the money raised and spent for the campaign is accounted for and reported to the relevant state election or ethics authority. The treasurer is responsible for opening, maintaining, and eventually closing the committee's bank account. This person also ensures that the committee has filed all of the relevant tax and financial disclosure forms required by the state. In most cases, the filings for a ballot committee are only state filings and are not with the IRS or other federal regulatory agencies.

However, it is important for you to know and understand the laws and regulations concerning the type of ballot committee you plan to create. The treasurer often also works as the compliance coordinator to ensure that any other nonfinancial paperwork has been filed.

FUND-RAISING CHAIR

The fund-raising chair works to ensure that the campaign has the funds it needs to remain active. She needs to meet the fund-raising goals set by the campaign manager. This person needs to be highly organized, detail-oriented, and not afraid to get out into the community and ask for money (which can be paralyzing for some people). Preferably, this person has strong contacts with community members and businesses and is willing to use those contacts to raise money for the campaign.

COMMUNICATIONS CHAIR

This is the person responsible for ensuring that the campaign has a unified theme and voice, and that the campaign message is consistent and is repeated often. He keeps the campaign "on message." This person reviews the campaign materials like e-mails, social media posts, paid media, brochures, and so on to ensure that they are consistent with the message. Often, the communications chair is the point person with the media for background while the campaign chair or an honorary chair would sit for an interview. Your campaign committee leadership team should establish its own ground rules, but we generally recommend that only people designated by the campaign manager and the communications chair should be speaking on behalf of the campaign.

FIELD CHAIR

The field chair ensures that canvassers, phone bankers, tablers, and other person-to-person outreach staffers complete their tasks. In essence, the field chair is responsible for the voter contact plan and ensures that it is carried out. This person helps organize the canvass territories, makes sure that data is entered back in the campaign office, and ensures the campaign has the volunteers it needs to get its message to the people through the fieldwork. Since this part of the campaign needs the most volunteers, this person needs to work closely with the volunteer chair.

VOLUNTEER CHAIR

Having a large and well-trained corps of volunteers is a key aspect of a good campaign. The volunteer chair works to ensure that the campaign makes the best and most efficient use of the volunteers to meet its needs and that this volunteer corps is well utilized and well trained. Since volunteers are "raised resources" just like money, this person should also have strong connections to the community and businesses and not be afraid to ask key community members to volunteer on behalf of the campaign.

There are a few other people who are important to the campaign and should be utilized whenever possible. These roles aren't always a necessity, but having them involved will definitely make your campaign run much smoother and lead to a greater chance of success.

LAWYERS

You might be familiar with election law and campaign regulations, but you should still seek legal counsel if any doubt exists. Any action taken by the campaign that may be illegal can sink your entire campaign regardless of whether it was done by accident or on purpose. However, legal counsel is extremely expensive, and you can get many answers from the government elections bureau in your area. Remember, nothing in this guide is legal advice. Just because it's written here doesn't mean it's legal in your state.

CONSULTANTS

Occasionally there are tasks that need to get done by a paid expert. For example, an effective video ad that strongly conveys your library's message to the voters is a difficult and time-consuming thing to do right and do professionally. If you are going to spend the money to put it on the air, spend the money to do it right! However, consultants are experts in many other areas as well and are a great resource if you think you have a problem and need professional advice to move forward.

LIBRARY STAFF, FRIENDS OF THE LIBRARY, AND OTHER ORGANIZATIONS

While there are some laws around a 501c3's involvement in a campaign, the Friends of the Library and other advocacy organizations can do a lot of work that will help or hurt the campaign. Make sure that you get buy-in early from these potential supporters. Be sure to keep them educated and involved and use them as support whenever you can, and of course, be sure to support them as much as you can.

While we are not lawyers and we are hesitant to give legal advice in this book, there are quite a few resources that can be used in order to navigate many of the laws regarding a 501c3's involvement in a campaign. For example, the library or the local government entity often has legal council that can assist with answering questions. It is also possible to try to have a lawyer on the ballot committee or in the Friends Group. However, there are many organizations that help nonprofits navigate the local legal system, pro-bono. One such organization is called Bolder Advocacy, and EveryLibrary has worked with them on a number of occasions to help library Friends and Foundation groups get answers to their questions.

ASK "WHO ARE WE MISSING?"

As we begin to build a support relationship with our campaigns, we always work with them to evaluate where they are strong and weak on a variety of topics. We ask them to talk about their own personal understanding of and confidence in the library's ballot measure. We challenge them to talk about where the relationships between the library and other organizations or groups in town are either solid or weak. It is also important to do an honest assessment of "who you are missing" from the leadership team or campaign insiders. Sometimes the folks who form the core of the ballot committee don't reflect the demographics of the community. If there is a part of the community that is missing, we encourage our committee leadership team to have an honest and frank conversation about who they need to approach to join the core committee team.

One of our favorite stories was with the "yes" committee in Northvale, New Jersey, as they organized to restore library services to their town through a ballot referendum in 2014. When we asked the question "who are you missing," we had a wonderful moment that probably won the campaign in the end. They were able to identify a group of neighbors who they, as another group of neighbors themselves, had never met. They were emboldened to reach out and bring these neighbors in by the fact that if library funding was restored on Election Day, the whole community would benefit. Everyone we were missing also had a stake in the win.

Other times, the library is isolated from community groups and organizations that support public safety, the parks, the arts, or youth sports. One technique for bridging this divide is to invite leaders from those other organizations to be "honorary chairs" for the library committee. In Paulding County, Ohio, the library committee got a lot of new attention and support when it was announced that the sheriff signed on to be an honorary chair of the library campaign. We have worked with other committees to identify and ask four or five people from outside the traditional library community to lend their good name and pen their networks to the committee as honorary chairs. It's an ultimate kind of endorsement to not only be listed as a supporter but to be on the letterhead of the organization, as it were.

WHAT IF YOU CAN'T FIND A CHAIR?

Sometimes the hardest part of starting a library ballot support committee is finding someone to be campaign manager or chair the campaign. Talented people are often willing and interested but consider themselves unavailable for such an important role. We always respect the time limits that people put on themselves for this kind of leadership burden. Often, committees try to break up the campaign manager role into two comanagers in order to make the burden less severe on one reluctant but able volunteer. If this works for you, great. But we have also worked with committees that have been very successful campaigners and decided to not have an official manager or comanagers and instead use the campaign plan and to-do list as "the campaign manager."

Responsible adults who are willing to take on a role like fund-raising chair, volunteer chair, communications chair, or field chair are perfectly capable of jointly managing both their tasks and the campaign. Often, we lose valuable time trying to find the right overall campaign manager instead of filling valuable roles across the campaign organization and getting to work. As much as a well-built campaign committee team with clear roles and responsibilities creates a win, don't let an idealized campaign structure get in the way of success either.

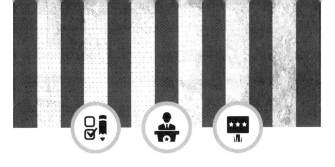

CHAPTER EIGHT

Getting on the Ballot

G ETTING ON THE BALLOT IS MISSION-CRITICAL. DETAILS
cannot be overlooked in this area. There are generally only two ways
to get a library measure on the ballot and that is by petition or by
placement by a unit of local government, including a library board. In
both cases, the library director and board or the leadership of the ballot committee
needs to pay significant time and attention to ensuring that all steps in the process
have been accomplished correctly and on deadline. We have seen campaigns end
before they even got started because they failed to realize that their ballot measure
was not completely legal, they did not receive the right number of petition signatures, or they missed an important statutory deadline. All of this can be avoided
by paying close attention to the details and using the resources that are available to
you to double-check your work.

If state law allows it, the most straightforward way to place a measure on the
ballot is by the local government body. This government body can be the library
board itself. Depending on the governance and financial structure, a government
body may be a school district board as in some jurisdictions in Pennsylvania and
New York. It can be a city, town, township, borough, parish, or county governing
authority. About two-thirds of our library campaigns originate with an independent
library board, though. In the other one-third, local politicians and administrative
offices need to approve a ballot measure and place it before the voters in the next
election. While it seems fairly straightforward, this pathway to the ballot is almost
entirely dependent on the relationships that the library has with local government

officials and their belief about the library. This is yet another reason why building strong relationships with the politicians and individuals of influence in your area is so important. (For more information about building these relationships, please see chapter 5, "Power Mapping.")

What is the legal basis for a library or municipal entity to go to the ballot? State law is sometimes confusing, and on a plain reading, statutes may seem contradictory. EveryLibrary and the Chief Officers of State Library Agencies (COSLA) have compiled an index of state statutes that concern how libraries can be legally constituted and governed, and what mechanisms within state tax codes are available to levy or enact. You can download and view it at http://openscholarship.wustl.edu/pollib/vol2/iss2/8/. ✪

PETITIONS

Another way to put a measure for the library in front of the voters is through a petition drive. While only twenty-four states allow citizens to put statewide measures before the public through this process, many local jurisdictions will allow the people to petition to put something on a local (city or county) ballot through a process often called a "citizen's initiative."[1] Typically, in order to put a citizen's initiative on the ballot, the people must circulate a petition and if it gathers enough valid signatures and is otherwise legal, the proposal will be placed on the ballot for a popular vote.

There are some benefits to running a petition for a library campaign. Most importantly, the data shows that these initiatives have a higher rate of success than ballot measures that were put before the voters by the local government.[2] This is probably because the people are more likely to support ballot measures that they believe have a high possibility of success. There is a kind of herd mentality when it comes to voting and people enjoy picking a winner and not upsetting the herd. So if something gathers enough signatures to get on the ballot then the public often believes that everyone supports the measure and will therefore be more likely to vote for it. It is also the case that circulating a petition is a great way to inform and educate the public about the initiative, and the public becomes persuaded through the petition process itself.

While these advantages of a petition are great, there are also some disadvantages. Most importantly, there is the chance that not enough signatures will be gathered to put it on the ballot. We have seen campaigns fail to get the right number of legal signatures and in so doing fail to get on the ballot. Petitions require a great amount of work and also cost valuable resources. There have been campaigns that have run out of volunteers for the GOTV campaign because they used them so heavily during the petition process. Because a petition-endorsed measure doesn't go through an approval process by the local government in the same way that a legislatively enacted measure does, it's sometimes possible to get enough signatures on ballot language that isn't legally acceptable. We always insist that petition campaigns have their language reviewed by legal counsel and the state board of elections or another relevant state agency before beginning to gather signatures.

GATHERING SIGNATURES FOR A PETITION

It is important that you know and understand your state's laws concerning who is eligible to circulate a petition. The law varies from state to state and is sometimes based on the type of measure listed on the petition. In one campaign the number of signatures required was very small, but the person who gathered and turned in the signatures needed to be a legal resident of the city where the library was located. In another, the petition campaign was able to hire out-of-state paid signature gatherers who then turned the completed forms over to a notary. In any event, your petition circulators should plan on doing both door-to-door and location-based signature-gathering in the lead-up to the deadline. Here's a sample script to help them get started.

Greeting: Hello, I'm _____. I'm a volunteer working with the Springfield Community Library Committee. Are you registered to vote here in Springfield? (If no, abandon)

I'm concerned about the future of the library. I'm part of a large group of neighbors that are putting together a petition for the library. This petition will allow us to vote on a measure on the November ballot to create permanent stable funding for our libraries. Will you please sign it and let residents vote on their own library?

If resident asks for more information: I'm asking you to sign the petition so we can vote on permanent funding for our libraries in November. This vote will be for a new library district, called the Springfield Community Library District. The funding will help sustain library services and provide more hours.

If resident says "YES": Thank you. If this measure gets on the ballot we will be looking for volunteers to help us with get-out-the-vote work. Are you willing to be contacted about this? May I also get your e-mail address so we can contact you?

If resident says "NO": I appreciate that. But without this library funding we will have a problem providing library services in Springfield. Can I ask you again to simply help us put this library measure on the ballot and let the voters decide?

Please note that in some states, asking petition signers to do anything else beyond their signature (like sign up for future volunteer opportunities or join a mailing list) may be prohibited activity. When it is allowed by the law, you should always do it and your petition circulators should carry a separate committee volunteer sign-up form and campaign literature to hand out. ❂

The number of signatures required for a petition is almost always determined by the number of voters in a previous election. That's why you often see, after a year of low voter turnout, a high number of measures on the next ballot. But one of the biggest hurdles and stumbling points of a petition is simply not getting enough signatures. This can happen for a wide variety of reasons, but it usually happens because the campaign simply underestimated how many people and hours it would take to gather signatures, or had no good plan to gather those signatures. It has also happened because the campaign got exactly the right number of people to sign the petition, but didn't get enough extra to account for an inevitable percentage of signatures that would be invalid. It's always a good idea for a campaign to get 20–30 percent more signatures than required in order to overcome the invalid ones. In rare cases, we have even seen a petition drive get the number of signatures they were told they needed but were simply misinformed by the local clerk about how many signatures were legally required, as happened in San Jose in 2012.[3] While the clerk is the authority on validating petitions, this kind of mistake is why we often recommend campaigns to ask more than one source about signature requirements.

There are a number of other ways that a petition drive can fail. Occasionally a detail is overlooked or missed in the requirements. For example, it's easy to miss requirements about the look and appearance of the petition, the length of time it can circulate, specific due dates, and the way the completed petition is submitted. Missing any of these statutory requirements can invalidate your petition and all your hard work gets thrown out with the signatures.

That's why we always recommend that any campaign that is choosing to go through the process of a petition thoroughly check and recheck their petition to ensure that it is valid and legal. Spending a few dollars up front on legal counsel can save a campaign thousands of dollars (or even the whole campaign itself) in the long run. Don't rely on just one source like the elections office, local government officials, or the city clerk for validation. Ask 2–3 local and state offices and ask for written guidance and instructions. Then get legal counsel to make sure everything is legally enforceable. A bad petition can ruin a campaign.

★ ★ ★

KILLING A BAD PETITION

In 2012 the library in Pulaski County, Kentucky, faced a "petition for dissolution" that was fielded by a group of Tea Party people who were upset by a one-dollar increase in property taxes.* The petition, which had a 6,500-signature threshold, started to circulate in the county and gain traction. If the petition was successful and gathered 6,500 valid signatures, under Kentucky law the independent library district would simply be dissolved. This fact mobilized many pro-library folks who began working against the petition drive in the county. They could not run a counter-petition and there was no way to sue to stop it had the petition succeeded. They had to work on killing it. They got organized very quickly and effectively to share information about the consequences of the petition to dissolve the library. The library itself hosted an adroitly written "Fact Sheet" about their financial and governance history while informing people that this petition might be "about" the library but it was not a petition "for the good of" the library.¹ This was bold of the library leadership team, and it helped.

After a lot of back and forth in local media, on social networks, and at community meetings the petition circulators backed down. The whole story about how the petition got killed has dozens of ins and outs, but the reason most cited was the November letter from the pro-library side that reminded neighbors across the county that petition signatures are a matter of public record and that the names of petitioners could be made public. They put a fine point on it in the letter by saying "If you own a business, you may lose customers. . . . If you plan to run for public office, it will become an issue for you. Your children and grandchildren will always know you had a part on closing the library. You may also lose friends."[‡]

If your library is facing a petition or other ballot action that could severely harm your budget or force the closure of your library, you have to act against it within the law and you have to organize pro-library folks to fight it. Each jurisdiction has different laws, rules, and regulations about how a petition is valid. Many of the cautions we provided here to petition circulators to safe-guard the integrity of the petition process can be used against a bad petition to bottle it up or invalidate it. Challenging signatures and questioning the language of a petition is a normal and necessary part of the democratic process. While these legal maneuvers about the bad petition were not available in Pulaski County, you can take inspiration from the boldness of the pro-library community in Pulaski County to organize and act. ✪

* John Celock, "Pulaski County Library: Conservative Group Tries to Disband District Over Tax Hike," *The Huffington Post*, November 20, 2012, www.huffingtonpost.com/2012/11/20/pulaski-county-library -conservative-group-district-tax_n_2165980.html.

† "About the Petition," About the Petition, 2012, www.pulaskipubliclibrary.org/petition/.

‡ Bill Estep, "Backers Drop Petition That Might Have Closed Pulaski Libraries," Kentucky.com, November 30, 2012, www.kentucky.com/news/state/kentucky/article44391552.html.

WHAT MAKES GOOD BALLOT LANGUAGE

The language on the ballot measure can have a profound effect on the outcome of the election. Of course, your ballot language needs to be legally enforceable, but language that is unclear or confusing can cause voters to accidentally vote against their intentions. Writing your ballot so that it is easily understood by laymen and not lawyers is always a good practice. The language of the ballot, the title, and the summary should be written in a way that is clear, concise, and accurate. The laws regarding how a ballot is written vary from state to state, even to the point that in some areas it can be written in a way that is also mildly persuasive. This was the case with the November 2014 Sonoma County (California) Library ballot measure in which the campaign stated the need for a yes vote in the ballot language. While this ballot measure didn't pass, this was a well-written ballot measure and was written as follows, with the persuasive statement on benefits to the community written into the language:

> Library Improvement Act: Shall the Sonoma County Library Improvement Act be implemented by imposing a one-eighth cent (0.125%) sales tax for ten years to restore and enhance library hours and services to benefit children, seniors and all residents of the County; with an annual audit to be conducted to ensure that funds are spent as mandated by the voters; and an increase in spending limit to allow use of the revenue?

This is in contrast to the June 2016 Kern County (California) Ballot Measure that was written with more strict guidance from the county lawyers and couldn't include more specific benefits to the community:

> Shall the Kern County Board of Supervisors enact a 0.125 percent (1/8 cent) transactions and use tax on all qualified retail sales within the County of Kern, for the benefit of the Kern County Public Library system, in accordance with California Revenue and Taxation Code §7286.59?

If there is an opportunity to write about the benefits of funding a library within the ballot language, we highly recommend that you do so. The voters almost always respond more positively when specific outcomes are written into the ballot language. If the clear benefits to the community are laid out within the text, the uninformed voter can make a decision based on clear language.

In November 2016 in Florida there was a proposed "Constitutional Amendment 1" on the ballot to enshrine the right of citizens of Florida to produce solar energy, which was already allowed for by state statute, as a fundamental right. The second part of the proposed amendment was to "[enact] constitutional protection for any state or local law ensuring that residents who do not produce solar energy can abstain from subsidizing its production."

The "for" language on the ballot read: "A vote 'for' Amendment 1 supported adding a section in the state constitution giving residents of Florida the right to own or lease solar energy equipment for personal use while also enacting constitutional protection for any state or local law ensuring that residents who do not produce solar energy can abstain from subsidizing its production."

The "against" language on the ballot read: "A vote 'against' Amendment 1 opposed constitutionalizing the right to own or lease solar equipment and the protection of laws preventing subsidization of solar energy, thereby leaving the personal use of solar power protected as a right by state statute and not by the constitution."

According to Ballotpedia.org, "Supporters argued that Amendment 1 would further protect the rights of Florida residents to own solar equipment, while also protecting electricity consumers from unfair prices and poor businesses practices. Opponents argued that Amendment 1 was put on the ballot by big utility companies to protect their control over the energy market and inhibit net metering. They claimed Amendment 1 was designed to prevent increased solar energy production by Florida residents and the sale of that solar energy back into the electric grid under the pretext of consumer protection."[4]

The amendment needed 60 percent of the vote to pass and got slightly more than 50 percent, which means a simple majority of Florida voters either wanted to enshrine a prohibition into selling surplus solar power back to the electrical grid into the state constitution, or they just read the language of the amendment for the first time on Election Day and thought it sounded good. Whoever controls the language on the ballot has the potential to control the frame of reference for voters who have not previously been exposed to campaign communications and messaging.

THE BATTLE FOR LAFOURCHE

Ballot wording and ballot titles matter a great deal. As we discussed in chapter 1, about 37 percent of voters are highly predisposed to vote "yes" for any library measure. In Lafourche Parish, Louisiana, Mr. Lindel Toups, chair of the Parish Council in Lafourche, knew that fact and tried to pull a fast one on the voters—and the library—during a special election in December 2013. The parish faced a federal consent decree to correct a real and significant problem with its jail. Mr. Toups wanted to take funding away from the library to build his new jail rather than raise taxes to be in compliance with the decree. But he needed to do it through an election. As a shrewd politician, he wrote the ballot title and language in such a way that a "yes" vote would defund the library. But the title and wording were very neutral and only mentioned the library. He knew that an uninformed voter would assume that anything with the word "library" would be *for* the library, and would be likely to attract that base of voters. The library staff were unable to do anything more than provide neutral information about the measure, and the special election was filed so fast that citizens didn't get organized.

Unfortunately for Chairman Toups, he is also a loudmouth and he made a series of inflammatory statements about the people who use the library in order to bring out anti-immigrant and antitax voters. It was more than an alt-right dog-whistle:

> *"They're teaching Mexicans how to speak English," the council chair-man said in reference to Biblioteca Hispana, a Hispanic-language segment of the Golden Meadow library branch. "Let that son of a bitch go back to Mexico. There's just so many things they're doing that I don't agree with. . . . Them junkies and hippies and food stamps [recipients] and all, they use the library to look at drugs and food stamps [on the Internet]. I see them do it."**

This caught our attention at EveryLibrary. Because the library staff was unable to advocate, and because there wasn't a local "vote no" campaign, we moved into action. With about five days before the election, EveryLibrary designed, fielded, and funded two concurrent online and social media ad campaigns targeting voters in Lafourche. One campaign carried a "Get the Facts" message to alert people that a "yes" vote would defund the library. The other was a "Books Not Crooks" theme designed to focus attention on Chairman Toups and his bait-and-switch between the library and a jail. In the end, the library and parish won by defeating the measure with a 53 percent "no" vote. We knew, like Toups did, that unless voters were educated about what the measure's language really said, they would vote with their gut or their heart. We have a recap of the campaign at https://www.youtube.com/watch?v=Fr70ftmVm_Q. ✪

---

* Eric Besson, "Election 2013: Voters Asked to Rededicate Library Funding toward Jail," *The Times of Houma-Thibodaux*, November 20, 2013, www.houmatimes.com/news/article_d1cd291e-4bd9-11e3-acb2 -001a4bcf887a.html.

BALLOT TITLES

Some political consultants argue that the ballot's title is one of the most important aspects of the campaign. This is because many voters will only read the title and not the language of the entire measure. If the title is unclear or confusing, they are more likely to vote against the measure. Or worse, they may make the mistake of voting against their intentions and vote no, when a yes vote would provide the outcome that they were expecting. Of course, the ballot title should not be misleading or deceptive and it should be a neutral summary that is accurate in its description of the ballot.

VOTER GUIDES

In states that publish a voter guide, there is an opportunity for the library campaign committee to write and submit a more persuasive text for voters who read the guides. In some states, there is a "plain text reading" or "impartial analysis" of the ballot language to ensure there is no confusing legalese used in the ballot measure. In other states, there are opportunities to list endorsers and opponents as well as the ability to write in arguments in favor and arguments in opposition to the ballot measure to be included in the guide.

When drafting a ballot argument, put yourself in the shoes of a voter who has no recent experience of the library and no context for "how we got here" to the ballot. A persuasive ballot argument should first simply frame the problem that a yes (or no) vote will address. It then goes on to endorse and validate the measure or referendum that is on the ballot. The argument should show what the good outcomes will be if it passes. It also needs to explicitly state Vote Yes (or No) in each paragraph. Your ballot arguments should be shorter than the legal word limit because most opposition-written arguments will be written like a manifesto. If there are two arguments to read, less engaged voters will read the shorter one.

Know and understand your committee's rights and the rights of individual voters to participate in the ballot argument process. You can find many examples of the latest library ballot measures on Ballotpedia.org to help guide the writing of your ballot measure title and language. Think of the library committee's statement in the voter guide as a final argument about the library measure.

★ ★ ★

SAMPLE BALLOT ARGUMENT

The current library in Springfield does not adequately meet the needs of our community. Its space is too limited and the arrangement with Springfield High School, while friendly, isn't flexible enough for a full-service library and isn't good on a high school campus. We are voting Yes for the library measure to fix this problem, and support a more livable Springfield with a usable library.

Our Yes vote is based on a recent citizen task force report that recommended a new Library for Springfield. They conducted wide-ranging community surveys to determine how a new, stand-alone, modern library could meet and anticipate the needs of our growing town. The site selection process was transparent and anticipates continued growth. We are excited by the opportunity for Springfield. We are voting Yes because a new library will improve pre-K literacy and school readiness, be a 21st century partner in K-12 education, create a new sense of community as a gathering place where all our neighbors can meet, and provide an anchor for business development in Springfield.

Studies show that libraries have a return on investment for the community of three to six times the investment. We are voting Yes for a new library that will be able to offer cultural programs such as art displays, book signings, performances, and community events that would make Springfield great. There will be adequate parking and easy access to downtown shopping, dining, and services. A new library will boost property values and make downtown Springfield more attractive for retail businesses.

We urge you to vote YES for the NEW SPRINGFIELD LIBRARY.   ✪

NOTES

1. "Ballot Initiative—Ballotpedia," Ballotpedia, https://ballotpedia.org/Ballot_initiative.

2. Sasha Issenberg, *The Victory Lab: The Secret Science of Winning Campaigns* (New York: Crown, 2012).

3. "Blunder Could Leave San Jose Library Measure Off the November Ballot," CBS San Francisco, June 8, 2012, http://sanfrancisco.cbslocal.com/2012/06/08/blunder-could-leave -san-jose-library-measure-off-the-november-ballot/.

4. "Editorial: Reject Deceptive Claims about Anti-Solar Amendment," *Tampa Bay Times*, October 27, 2016, www.tampabay.com/opinion/editorials/editorial-reject-deceptive-claims -about-anti-solar-amendment/2300324.

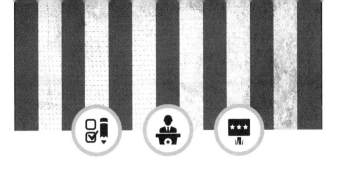

CHAPTER NINE

Campaign Budget

B UILDING A CAMPAIGN BUDGET PLAN IS ONE OF THE MOST unexciting yet most important things your library's campaign can do. While creating a campaign budget is terrifically easy, it does take time to build and it requires an ongoing attention to detail throughout your campaign. However, the nice thing about having a strong budget plan for your campaign is that it acts like a checklist so you know what you're accomplishing and you know that you're doing what you think is right. If you are ever having a panic attack about your campaign, you can take a look at the budget and see what activities you have accomplished and see what you need to be doing next. A budget also helps keep you from buying unhelpful things like branded pens and pads of paper when a spend on a persuasive mailer would be more effective.

We often get asked how many dollars a campaign should spend "per voter" in order to ensure a win. The truth is that if there was a magic number to ensure a win, we wouldn't have to write a whole book about political campaigns. The amount that a campaign spends is dependent on a wide range of factors, and no two campaigns are the same. In fact, we have seen libraries win by large margins with a low budget and we have seen libraries lose with a giant budget. But you can plan a budget for your campaign that will realistically give you a good chance of winning.

While you can make the argument that the candidate with the most money almost always wins, there are plenty of stories about candidates who lost even though they were well funded. When you do see an upset in an election, it's almost always

95

because the candidate with the smaller budget spent their money more wisely. The well-funded campaign can spend on everything, but the underdog has to spend on the right things. In the end this means that it's not how much you spend on your campaign, it's how you spend it.

There are two secrets to building a budget for a political campaign. The first is that you should start on Election Day and work your way backwards. This is because your largest expenditures for voter contact and get-out-the-vote work come in the last week of the campaign. The second is that you should plan to have zero dollars left in the campaign bank on Election Day. It's a terrible thing to lose an election when there is still money in the bank. That's why you need to use all of the resources available to you to ensure that you are going to win by as much as possible. Even if you are polling at 80 percent the week before the election, spend your last bit of money to make sure you keep that margin. The only exception to this rule is if you know you are going to run again very soon regardless of the outcome of the election. Or, of course, if you want to make a large contribution to EveryLibrary at the end of your campaign!

Make sure that your budget is a living document. This means that it gets updated with every dollar that gets spent in as close to real time as possible. It's almost impossible to do it all in your head, so take advantage of the wide range of budgeting tools out there that can help you out. Even if it is something as simple as an Excel spreadsheet, make sure your functions are correct and the running total is updated and accurate at all costs.

Figure 9.1 shows a sample budget. You can find an editable campaign budget sheet at action.everylibrary.org/campaignresources.

SO WHAT SHOULD YOU BE SPENDING YOUR MONEY ON?

Here are some general guidelines for a good campaign budget. Contacting and persuading voters are the primary goals of your budget and therefore it should be your largest expenditure. This part of your budget should amount to, at the very least, 60 percent of your total budget. For all-volunteer-run campaigns it can be as much as 80 percent or even 90 percent. For campaigns that need to hire staff, your budget will include salaries or honoraria and overhead costs for office space, supplies, and a website. Administrative costs should not exceed 10 percent of the budget, however. Unless you are paying for really good campaign managers or need supplemental paid services like canvassers or phone bankers, the salary and fees should not be your primary expense. Some other expenditures that come in at around 5–10 percent

FIGURE 9.1

Sample Budget

CAMPAIGN BUDGET

	Month 1	Month 2	Month 3	Month 4	Month 5	TOTAL
EXPENSES – INCOME OUT						
Office						
Office rent and utilities	500	500	500	500	500	2500
Phones/credit	400	300	400	800	1000	2900
Supplies (paper, pens, etc.)	100	100	100	200	300	800
Computer/Printer rental	150	150	150	150	150	750
Internet Access	50	50	50	50	50	250
Coffee/Tea	30	20	20	40	90	200
Printing/Photocopying						
Flyers/Leaflets	150		150	250	500	1050
Paraphernalia (buttons, stickers, signs, etc)				500		500
Fundraising						
Events	1500		800	200	1000	3500
Meetings		200	200		500	900
Voter Contact						
Voter List	400					400
Canvassing (Door to Door)		250	250	500	1000	2000
Community Meetings	200	200	200			600
Get Out the Vote				2000		2000
	Month	Month	Month	Month	Month	
Media & Communication						
Radio Ads					1000	1000
Billboards					1000	1000
Website	200	200	200	200	200	1000
Press Events	200			400	700	1300
REVENUE – INCOME IN						
Candidate contributions	1000		1000		1000	3000
Political Party contributions	5000			3000		8000
Donations	500	250	500	2000	5500	8750
Fundraising events income	2000		600	300		2900
TOTAL EXPENSES	3880	1970	3020	3790	9990	22650
TOTAL INCOME	8500	250	2100	5300	6500	22650

each include supporting your volunteer field operations, research and polling, and fund-raising. And sometimes there are unexpected costs.

Because voter contact is the most expensive part of your campaign, it is important to understand what voter contact includes. Voter contact is any expenditure used to identify voters, persuade them to vote for you, or to help them show up on Election Day. That includes things like social media spends, TV or radio ads, yard signs, mailers, and door hangers, and sometimes supplies for your volunteers, canvassers, and phone bankers are included here.

NUMBER OF VOTERS AND THE WIN NUMBER

The reason we talked earlier about the number of likely voters and getting to a "win number" in the chapter on creating the political landscape memo is because these numbers are the first places you start when you're building your budget. Essentially, you know that you have x number of voters who need to be contacted and identified, and then convinced to vote yes for your library. For example, if you know that you need to contact 5,000 people and one of the ways that you are going to do that is through direct mail, and each piece of mail costs $1.50, then you know that you will have to spend $7,500 on direct mail. The same formula applies to other tactics as you build out your budget.

POLLING NUMBERS

The number of times that you need to contact people in a campaign to convince them to vote for your library largely depends on how well you poll. For example, if your library campaign did really well and easily got the majority that it needed, you won't have to contact voters as many times. However, if you polled poorly, you're going to need to spend a larger part of your resources on identifying yes voters, persuading the maybes, and then contacting your likely yes voters as many times as possible to ensure that they show up to vote yes for your library.

TACTICS

This is where we start to really build your budget. Your campaign leadership team should sit down and have a discussion about what kinds of techniques to use to contact voters. You should ask yourselves if your voting district has a large area that is impossible to canvass due to rough terrain, or if there is a large population of unconnected voters in your area who won't be reached by social media, or if there is a larger younger population who don't have phones at home and will be hard to reach through phone banking. The answers to these kinds of questions are what is going to guide you in determining what tactics you will use for your campaign.

Each tactic has its own cost associated with it, and knowing how many people need to be contacted and how many times they need to be contacted by each tactic is what is going to guide a large part of your budget-building process.

Of course, as a library campaign, your funds are going to be limited. Unfortunately, almost nobody is going to fund a library campaign at the level of a Koch Brother campaign, and this means that decisions will need to be made about where to spend money. But that's okay because a campaign can be outspent and still win if it spends its money more intelligently than the opposition does. That's why figuring out how to spend your campaign funds is just as important as raising your campaign funds. Your campaign has to be focused on what it takes to win. That means that every dollar you spend has to be focused on returning real, measureable results to the campaign. So how do you make the decisions about what your campaign needs to win?

★ ★ ★

No matter what tactics your campaign uses, anything that is paid for by the campaign committee should be labeled as "Paid for by _____" in order to ensure that the public does not think that library or public funds are being used to fund the campaign. In some places, a campaign must legally say who paid for the campaign materials. We once worked with a campaign that didn't label their campaign materials and they handed out yard signs from within the library (don't do that), and someone alerted the press thinking that the library was spending public money on campaign resources. Luckily, they were able to quickly address the issue, but it could have blown up their entire campaign. You can avoid this by simply labeling your campaign materials as "Paid for by_____" whether it is required in your state or not.   ★

NEED VS. WANT

We've all seen campaigns with great "swag" like pens and notebooks and branded clipboards. But those kinds of things don't make a difference when you're trying to win. In a campaign, anything is classified as a "want" if it doesn't directly identify or persuade voters. Something is categorized as a "need" if it directly identifies or persuades voters to vote in your favor. For example, nobody is going to see a branded clipboard or a free pen and make a decision about how they are going to vote. Throughout your campaign you will have to make decisions about whether something is a need or a want. One of the first things you should ask yourself when your budget is tight in your campaign is, How will this activity convince someone to vote yes, or what will it tell me about the voter? If you can't answer that in a measurable way, it probably falls into the want category.

Want

If it doesn't ID or persuade voters, it is a want and not a need. The things you want in a campaign are things like branded office supplies, volunteer T-shirts, water bottles, tote bags, and so on. While volunteers might like to have matching T-shirts and those shirts might help build bonds between volunteers around your campaign, the T-shirts aren't going to convince very many people to vote yes. If your campaign has enough money that it doesn't need to make decisions between buying campaign-branded water bottles and buying social media ads, for example, then by all means, feel free to buy swag for your volunteers or for your office. But in almost all cases, that money can be more wisely spent.

A want can also be something that doesn't reach the right people in your community. There are many things a campaign can purchase that don't reach the right voters in the community or the ones who matter to winning the campaign. One of the things that fits in this category is a billboard. While a billboard can be great for name recognition, you are spending money to tell everyone in your community, when in reality, it is only the voters who need to be reached.

Need

A need is something that your campaign does to directly ID voters or persuade voters. For example, media ads, canvassing, phone banking, and sometimes direct mail are great ways to persuade voters to vote for your library's ballot issue. If you are spending money on something but there is no way to find out how someone is voting, or convince someone to vote yes for your issue, just don't do it.

However, sometimes you can use "wants" to ID voters if it's done strategically. That means that what you're giving out is something that the voters want and whenever you give one out, you get something back. For example, you can give out branded pens, yard signs, stickers, buttons, and so on to anyone who pledges to vote yes for the library. In this way, you are encouraging people to self-ID as yes voters for your campaign, so you don't have to spend other campaign resources on them. It's a great way to incentivize the voter ID process. But if your campaign is simply trying to put out as many of these materials as possible into the community and your campaign is not doing it in a strategic way, then it remains in the "want" category.

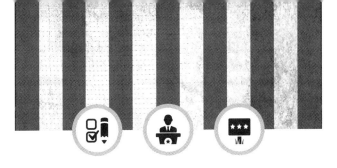

CHAPTER TEN

Fund-Raising

EVERY LIBRARY CAMPAIGN HAS TO RAISE AND SPEND money to maintain the needed level of activity. Political campaigns are becoming more and more expensive, and campaigns need to raise greater amounts of money to remain competitive. The fact is that in order to keep up, library campaigns need large funds to compete in the political arena. Without these funds there can be no staff, no office, no phones, no signs or advertising, and no media coverage. Basically, without money, there is no campaign.[1] Even if your campaign plans don't include an office or paid staff, every other component of a well-run and effective campaign needs funding support—either cash or in kind—to succeed. In order to ensure that your campaign has the money it needs, your committee members need to spend some time developing its finance plan.

30 PERCENT RULE

While it is often the least fun thing to do in a campaign, we want to make it clear early in this chapter that you will have to spend large amounts of time fund-raising for your ballot initiative whether you like it or not. This is true of any political campaign. In fact, a typical ten-hour day for freshman congressmen includes 3–5 hours of call-time and meetings with potential donors.[2] Likewise, you should expect to budget 30 percent of your campaign time and resources to fund-raising activities like phone calls and meetings. However, you can get this done early in your campaign. If you spend the first month of a four-month campaign on fund-raising activities, you can spend the next three months on activities to win your election with a much lower fund-raising workload. This kind of early planning and initiative is what will give you the tools to win your campaign before the opposition can even realize there is a campaign, so do it early and get it out of the way.

GOALS, TIME LINES, AND BENCHMARKS

So you know that the campaign for your library ballot initiative will cost money. How much money depends on many factors, namely the size of your district and the strength of the opposition. Your initial research as outlined in your political landscape memo should give you a starting point for determining how much you need to raise for your campaign to win the ballot measure. From this, your finance director can create some budget scenarios for lean, modest, and robust fund-raising scenarios. With these already in place, it will be easy for your campaign to adapt to any scenario that presents itself.[3]

STRATEGY AND TARGETING

Of course, if you know how much money you need, the next step is figuring out how to get that money. People will give money to your campaign for a lot of different reasons, and understanding these motivations will be the key to being successful at fund-raising for a library campaign. Any potential donor has a reason to give. You're simply identifying that motivation and giving the donor the reason to engage financially in the campaign. That's why your pitch should reflect their motivations. So whenever your library campaign asks for money or time or any other resource, listening will be one of your strongest tools when asking for money. If you listen to your potential giver, you will be able to find their reason for giving. Even better, start gathering information before the campaign that will help you get a better idea about donors' motivations for supporting the campaign even before giving them your pitch. In this way the donor should play a big part in the crafting of the campaign message and not the other way around.

According to Democracy for America, a national political action committee (PAC) for training progressive candidates, these motivations for donating will most generally fall under four general categories of stakeholder groups in order of proximity: relational, ideological, aversion, and access.[4]

STAKEHOLDER GROUPS

If you chart these groups in a series of circles, it would look like this:

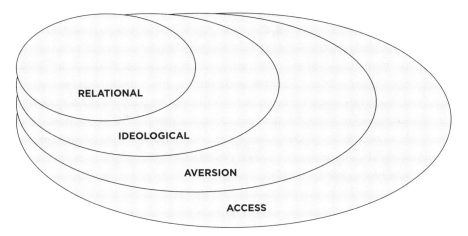

Your library's campaign is at the center of the circle, and each ring in the circle represents a different group of stakeholders in the library's campaign.

1. *Relational:* The closest to the center and the first circle of donors that you should tap into are those with whom your library has a strong connection and relationship. This could be your Friends group, library board members, library volunteers, patrons who regularly attend library programs, friends and family of your library staff, and contractors. These groups of people will generally give to the campaign because they have a relationship with the library. Often these relationships override the donor's political views. Starting your fund-raising here will jump-start your campaign, and this is how you can finance the start-up costs of the campaign. Most important, your success with this group demonstrates your viability to subsequent circles.

2. *Ideological:* Passionate people will give to passionate causes and organizations. The library that has a strong message for the community that the donor wants to see pushed forward will be able to effectively tap into this group. These are people who believe in the literacy benefits of libraries, libraries as economic

drivers, as community spaces, and so on. Their ideological considerations about social or economic issues will often trump whether or not they believe the campaign is viable or not.

3. *Aversion:* Aversion to the opposition is a powerful motivating force. You will find that there are people who give to the campaign because a victory for the library could be a win against whomever they perceive as the opposition. You can activate these donors by showing that a win for the library will be a win in the fight against the opposition.

4. *Access:* Many donors participate in the political process to advance their own institutional or economic interests or in order to gain access to individuals or institutions. For example, Betsy Devos contributed over 900 million dollars to gain access to the political system where she was then appointed as Secretary of Education. This desire for access can include businesses, trade and professional associations, labor groups, and special interest groups. The opposition is unlikely to receive support from this circle of donors. Major issue-based interest groups fall in this category. These donors often give later in the cycle to demonstrate their support for the clear winner.

By categorizing your donors in order of proximity, you will find those donors who are closest to the center to be the easiest group to fund-raise from. As you move away from the center circle, the donors in those categories will require more time and effort to solicit donations. Just like with your volunteer teams, you need to start fund-raising closest to the center of the circle and work your way out.

MOTIVATE YOUR DONORS

If you're talking to relational donors such as your friends and family, then you shouldn't be talking to them as if they're ideological donors. Your pitch to your donors needs to match the donor segment of which they are a part. This is because many people want to give to your library campaign, but they will only do so if you can understand what motivates them to participate. Each of the donor segments has different reasons to give, and you need to match your pitch to their motivations.

For Relational Donors

These donors care about you and they want to see you win and succeed. Their giving probably isn't as closely related to the library as it is to their relationship to you. They are giving to you and not necessarily the library campaign because they feel that you need them to give.

> **Sample ask:** "This is an important institution in my life. I need to do this, and I need your help."

For Ideological Donors

These are people who care about the library as a cause. They share an interest in what you or your library is passionate about. They are committed to the library and its issues and the value it provides and they want to see that continue.

> **Sample ask:** "I knew that if I let the library fail, that many children in the community wouldn't have access to books or a literacy environment."

For Aversion Donors

These are people who are interested in seeing the opposition to the library measure fail. This could be a personal reason, an agenda against the antitax movement, or directed at a particular person in the opposition. A win for the opposition would affect this donor in a negative way. This donor has something to lose if the opposition wins. He wants to know that the campaign is aware of his fear of losing and that the campaign knows that they are providing hope to him that he will make a difference.

> **Sample ask:** "Without libraries, you have an illiterate nation. We know Republicans like illiteracy, we can do better than that."
> —*Howard Dean, former head of the Democratic National Committee*

For Access Donors

These donors are difficult to capture in a library campaign. They are typically interested in backing a candidate that will give them some kind of visibility or access to the political arena or some aspect of society. However, these are also people who are interested in having a say in the day-to-day operations and decision-making process of the library, or building a relationship with the library that gives them something. They are going to want to know that the library supports their issues and not necessarily that they support the library's issues. This kind of donor could be an organization like a union or even library vendors who have something to gain.

> **Sample ask:** "I want the library to win so that they will have the resources to buy our databases."

SOME RULES OF THUMB IN FUND-RAISING

1. Typically, you'll find that while your top donors will be only 20 percent of your total donors, they will make up (or they should make up) at least 50 percent of your total donations. These are the people and organizations who have big money and will hold on to it tightly.
2. The donors who give a moderate amount to the campaign will most likely be around 30 percent of your total donors and 30 percent of your total funds.
3. The small donors will be somewhere around 50 percent of all your donors, but they will most likely make up only about 20 percent of your total donations.

If you're familiar with the 80-20 percent rule or the Pareto Principle, you will understand that there is a consistent rule of thumb that 80 percent of your outcome will come from 20 percent of your input. While this principle originated in Italy in 1906 to state that 20 percent of the population of Italy owned 80 percent of the land, it has since been shown that the 80-20 rule applies to business, politics, wealth, customer service, and many other aspects of life.

For our purposes, we can say that 80 percent of your campaign's fund-raising time will be spent on that top 20 percent of the donors who provide 50 percent of the funds. ✪

HOW MANY ASKS DO YOU NEED?

When you're making your plan to ask people for donations, you will need to plan on asking five times the number of donors needed. This is because you will most likely only talk to around 40 percent of the people you call, and only around half of those will give you a contribution. This means that if you call 100 people, then you will only talk to 40, and of those 40 only 20 will contribute to your library campaign. So if you need 20 people to contribute $50, then you need to plan on asking 100 people or five times the number of donors you need.

With this math in mind, you need to develop your fund-raising goals at each level. Let's use an easy example of $10,000. If your largest donor level is $500 and you have a large-giver goal of $5,000 (50 percent of your goal), then the total number of large donations needed is 20. In this case, you will need to ask 100 people (20 × 5).

If your medium-giver level is set for $100 and you have a medium-donation goal of $3,000 (30 percent of your goal), then you need to get donations from 30 people and that means you need to ask 150 people (30 × 5).

If your small-giver level is $25 and your small-donation goal is $2,000 (20 percent of your goal), then you will need 80 donations to reach that goal and that means that you need to ask 400 people (80 × 5).

While you might be thinking that your library's campaign will need much more money raised than our example and you are daunted by the number of small givers you will need, you don't need to worry. It's easy to ask large groups of small givers at the same time. For example, you could host a fund-raiser with cheap entry fees or plan a sale of baked goods or stickers or other swag. The small donors are also good targets for house parties or talks.

FUND-RAISING TOOLS

There are many tools that your library's campaign can use to ask donors for money. The following examples are the most common and the most effective ones.

In person: Personally asking donors for contributions will be your most persuasive and fruitful technique. It will also be your most time-consuming one. This is generally reserved for large personal donors whom you know personally or that someone in your library campaign knows personally. Make sure to prepare for the meeting to make it more personal. Meeting face to face is also a great chance to talk to your donor about people that they may know who would be interested in giving. Be sure to take notes.

Phone banks: This is one of your most effective tools for asking potential donors to contribute. Calling has a high response rate and takes up much less time than personal meetings, but the donor amount is typically lower. Your library campaign team should spend a good amount of time on the phones and keep good records of donors they have called, gotten contributions from, how much, and so on.

Canvassing: Taking the time to spend energy and resources walking door to door in your community and asking for money or support has the potential to return moderate gains. At-the-door donors are not big givers and smaller contributions should be solicited. Like face-to-face tactics, people who take the time to open the door and listen to your campaign message are going to be more likely to contribute. If people are not likely to give, they still receive the campaign message from a friendly and welcoming face and may find other ways to help the campaign. You can solicit these individuals to join as a volunteer, become fund-raisers or canvassers themselves, or otherwise get involved in the campaign. People are always more likely to get involved or contribute when asked directly and in person.

Events: Events are fun awareness tools for your campaign, but you should be cautious about doing too many because events can suck resources from a campaign. This is because events cost your campaign volunteers, time, and money. Small events, like house parties, are pretty safe but the larger your event, the larger your cost and your potential for losing money. If you're going to throw a large event, make sure you have your sponsors lined up before you plan the event. After the event, make sure you follow up with everyone who attended to ask again for another contribution. This follow-up is where you will get another round of donations and can really make that event pay off.

Direct mail: Even with e-mail, direct mail is still a pretty common tactic for library campaigns to use to solicit contributions. Your campaign can send mail to people who are potential donors in hopes that they will give. This kind of mail is called prospect mailing and while it typically won't generate a large return, it is a good way to reach people for their first donation and then use that donor list to re-solicit later.

E-mail fund-raising: This kind of solicitation doesn't always yield a high percentage of returns in the form of large or medium donors. But you can ask very large groups of people very inexpensively. If your campaign has a large and well-maintained e-mail list and web presence, you might see a significant overall return. For example, with a well-written e-mail you might see a return rate as high as 10 percent, but you can realistically only expect to see a 1–2 percent return rate. This means that if you ask 100 people, only 2–10 people will give and they will probably only give at the small-donor level. The big advantage to this technique is that it's a very cheap way to identify people who give to your cause and get the word out about it.

Social media: Many library campaigns make the mistake of believing that social media are a cheap and easy way to get potential donors to give or get involved in a campaign. This is typically not the case. As more social media sites like Facebook and Twitter move to a pay-to-play business model, campaigns are going to have to invest not only more time and energy into making them return significant yields, but also more money. This is not to say it can't be done, but it is typically not as easy or cheap as it might have been previously. However, a strong and fully developed social media campaign can generate large returns with the right investment.

WHO TO ASK

One of the first things your ballot committee and board should do is plan out who they are going to ask for money. The campaign adage is, if you don't believe enough in your campaign to ask your mom for money, how can you believe in it enough to ask your neighbor to vote? This means that you should not be scared to ask everyone you know for a few dollars to win the election. So, at your first ballot committee meeting, spend the first hour with the committee brainstorming the names and contact information for everyone they know. Don't leave anyone off the initial list. Once you have this long list, spend time discussing the people on it with the committee and create a master list that prioritizes everyone on it and ranks them in order of their likeliness to give. Use an Excel spreadsheet for this. Then add their contact information, note who will contact them and when, the amount of money they will be asked for (the "target ask"), and leave a column for their responses, pledges, and notes. It might look something like this:

NAME	CONTACT INFORMATION	TARGET DATE	TARGET ASK	WHO WILL CONTACT THEM	DONATE (YES/NO)	HOW MUCH DID THEY PLEDGE?
John Chrastka	867-5309	June 5	$350	Erica	Yes	$100
Peter Bromberg	555-8888	June 12	$100	Mel	No	0
Brian Hart	123-7654	June 8	$400	Erica	Yes	$400

If you get to your budget number without getting all the way through this list, that is great! You have some people in reserve that you can go to later if you need more money, or you can ask them now and plan a bigger campaign. However, if you don't get to your budget number, there are a few resources you can use to find more donors.

DONOR AND FUND-RAISER DATABASES

If you have access to your library's databases, there are a few that may help you develop your fund-raising plan. For example with AtoZ databases or Reference USA, you can download lists of known political donors in your community and spend time cold-calling them. You can also use those databases to get the contact information of the executives of the top companies in your area. Call them to ask them for a coffee or a meeting where you can make your pitch for larger donations. Some of the listings in those databases will also include the e-mail addresses of top executives, so you can follow up with an e-mail if you don't hear back from them. One of the other great databases to access is DonorSearch (www.donorsearch.net), where your committee members can look up the names of prominent individuals in your community to find out where they donated. If you don't subscribe to any of these data sets, you might also try OpenSecrets (www.opensecrets.org), where you can find out more information about corporate money in politics and help you identify more potential corporate or individual donors based on their donation history.

LOCAL NONPROFITS

You can try looking at some of the local nonprofit organizations to see who is donating to them. There are a couple of ways to find out who gives to local nonprofits, but the easiest way is to ask the nonprofits if they would be willing to share their donor lists with you. If the nonprofits have an interest in seeing the library succeed, if their purpose is supporting education in the community, for example, they are more likely to share those lists.

UNIONS

Your library may have a labor union of some kind. If it does, this can be a great group to tap into. They have a vested interest in making a contribution to the campaign since their members work for the library. These labor groups will often not give to a campaign unless they know the chances of winning the election. For example, in one campaign, the local union that represents library staff, did not want to support the library's campaign because the campaign didn't poll high enough. It took a lot of maneuvering to get them on board. It can also be hard to ask these groups for funding if nobody has a relationship with the local community organizing office, because the local chapters of unions can also be fairly personality-driven. There are times when the local labor representative is difficult to work with or hard to reach. We have had many experiences with unreturned e-mails and phone calls from labor unions, but through the persistence of the ballot committee they came on board and made contributions to the campaign.

POLITICIANS

If you have close ties with a local politician, they are often willing to share their donor lists with a campaign if those donors have maxed out their legal limit of contributions to the politician's campaign. This can be a great way to find some local donors that you don't know about or reach donors who don't know about the library campaign. Some politicians are even willing to fund-raise on behalf of a campaign or a cause they believe in. Having these politicians help fund-raise or make introductions on behalf of the campaign is a great way to generate legitimacy for your campaign in the minds of donors, and they'll be more likely to give. It is just another great reason to get to know the local politicians.

FRIENDS AND FOUNDATIONS

One of our best pieces of advice for a library committee is to set the committee up early and have the Friends of the Library or the foundation give their maximum allowable contributions throughout multiple years leading up to the campaign. In many states you can set up a general ballot committee years before something is on the ballot and then these groups can give donations multiple times, therefore saving you the trouble of spending large amounts of time fund-raising for the campaign. To find out if you can set up your ballot committee early, just ask your local elections office or your state secretary or state attorney's office about the paperwork.

HOW TO ASK FOR MONEY

Library campaigns are not free. While there have been campaigns that cost a couple of hundred bucks, there are also campaigns that cost hundreds of thousands of dollars. Your campaign will most definitely fall somewhere in between, and as a campaign committee leader you are going to be responsible for raising that money. This can be a difficult task and it makes some of the best campaigners nervous about what they have to achieve. Most likely, you are more nervous about asking the people closest to you for money.

It's pretty easy to ask strangers for money. In fact, there are hundreds of sites on the Internet dedicated to crowd-sourced funding which do just that. The most difficult part of fund-raising is asking those closest to you and those people with whom you have a relationship. But, as we talked about earlier, these are the people who are most likely to give, to give the largest amounts, and to connect you to other people who will want to give to your campaign. We need to get comfortable asking.

First, think about how you feel when you're asking for money. Do you feel pushy or like a spammer? Or do you feel bad trying to get people to separate themselves from their hard-earned money, time, or resources to support your cause?

Now think about how you feel when you give to some of your favorite organizations. Do you feel honored that you were asked to get involved? Do you feel connected and good that you gave? Do you feel engaged with the organization and its cause? Do you feel like you're taking action and fighting for what you believe in?

Almost undoubtedly, if you're giving your hard-earned money, you believe in the organization and what they're doing and you want to give to them. Your giving could be inspired by the leader of the organization, by fighting the opposition, or any of the above-discussed reasons for donor giving. But in any case, you are giving because you were asked, and because you want to. What we want to get you to understand is that people want to give, that they'll feel good about themselves for giving, and that they just need to be asked.

In order to better understand this relationship between giver and solicitor, we want to reiterate one of the fundamental rules and guiding principles of the campaign. *People don't do things for you because they like you, they do things for you because they believe that you like them.* This means that the fund-raising wing of your campaign should be significantly about making people feel good about themselves, that you like them, and that they are friends with your campaign.

THE FIVE TRUTHS TO FUND-RAISING

1. You need to put yourself in your donor's shoes.
2. Ask more people than you think you need to.
3. You have to be comfortable with people telling you no.
4. You don't need to ask everyone, but you will need to ask a lot of people. Don't focus on asking one person.
5. Your belief in your campaign has to be greater than what you're scared of. If you're afraid to ask for money, just get out of the way and let the cause talk for you.

COMMON FUND-RAISING MISTAKES

There are some common mistakes to asking for money from donors. While you'll probably make some of these mistakes, or you've already made them, don't let that stop you. Instead, learn from those mistakes and do a better job next time!

Be Sure to Ask Those Closest to You

Have you ever been picked last for a game? It doesn't feel good. Don't let your donors feel like that. Don't make them think about why you didn't ask them to get involved in the fight. Just as you felt good by giving your money and being a part of the team fighting for your cause, by asking people to get involved by giving, you're giving them a position to play on your team and for your cause.

Don't Beg

This means that you can't be embarrassed and apologetic to ask for money. Don't make the donor feel like you begged them for their money by telling them your sad story, because nobody likes to feel that they gave to a beggar. Instead, they want to feel that you empowered them by letting them give to you. The biggest mistake you can make is apologizing for asking for money because that makes you sound like a beggar. Instead, you want to make the donor understand how much you believe in your cause. They should learn why this campaign is important to get involved in and how much they are helping to fight for your library's cause. You are offering them an opportunity to feel good.

Don't Step on the Ask

When you're asking for money and working on the transaction, don't interrupt them or stop them or slow them down. One of the most uncomfortable parts of fund-raising are the few seconds just before someone gives and while they are writing a check. The best thing you can do is sit quietly and wait for the transaction to be completed. It's often easy enough to interrupt someone, talk them down because you're embarrassed or feel bad for taking their money, or even stop them during this time. Stay strong and remind yourself of why you're there and sit quietly while the transaction completes. If you need help staying quiet during this time, take a drink of water, write down a couple of notes, or distract yourself for a couple of seconds.

Using the Wrong Word

It's very easy to just make a simple mistake in your language. One example is the use of the word "can" vs. the word "will." At first glance these two words seem pretty similar but the connotation is very different. Let's look at two examples:

> I'm asking you to support us with a $100 donation. Can you do that?
> I'm asking you to support us with a $100 donation. Will you do that?

You might think these two sentences are too similar to make a difference until you realize that a yes answer is very different in each case. For example, a "yes, I can do that" response doesn't mean that they will. It means that they have the ability to do it. However, a "yes, I will give" answer means that they are agreeing to take action and that they will give to your campaign. Always use language that encourages action and not ability.

Only a No Means No

It's easy to mistake a maybe for a no. For example, a donor can say that they need to ask their committee, or their spouse, or that they need time to think about it. None of those things are a no. The only thing that means no is no. Until they flat out tell you no, they are still in the potential donor list. Don't be afraid to reconnect with them at a later date. In fact, ask them to give you the best date to get back to them. After the meeting, make sure you put a date to reconnect with them in your calendar or on the donor cards to remind you.

Not Asking a High Enough Specific Dollar Amount

It's not enough to ask for a donation, you need to ask for a specific amount. If you need $100, ask for that. If you know the donor can give $1,000, ask for that since it's easier to lower the dollar amount that you asked for than raise it. This is where donor research comes into play. You need to make sure you know how high a donor is willing to go. If you ask for a hundred, the donor will give you a hundred or they will give you less. They almost never will give more than you ask. If you do the donor research, you might learn that the donor has a track record of giving $1,000 and you shortchanged the campaign by only asking for $100.

Not Asking for a Match

EveryLibrary has been proud to be the first donor to several of our library "yes" campaigns. We want to put early or seed money into those campaigns because we know that our national support will help them get started as a campaign, but it can also be used as a "challenge match" in their local community. Many campaign committee leaders find that the trepidation they felt before starting to fund-raise disappears as they become more successful at it. If our challenge match provides them with a good reason to go out and make those first local asks, they can build momentum as a fund-raiser. If you are wondering where to get your first campaign dollars, ask your leadership team and closest circle of donors to pool their money into a challenge match. Then ask the next ring of donors to help your campaign "make that match" at a 2-to-1 or 3-to-1 or higher rate. It starts the fund-raising process off inside the campaign and it opens doors to donors who like to see their dollars go farther faster.

NOTES

1. "Finance and Fundraising," PDF (Washington: Democracy for America).
2. Ryan Grim, "Call Time for Congress Shows How Fundraising Dominates Bleak Work Life," *The Huffington Post*, January 8, 2013, www.huffingtonpost.com/2013/01/08/call-time-congressional-fundraising_n_2427291.html.
3. "Finance and Fundraising," PDF.
4. "Finance and Fundraising," PDF.

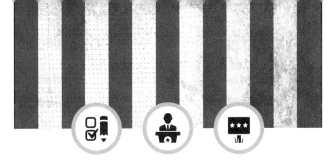

CHAPTER ELEVEN

Volunteers

VOLUNTEERS ARE NOT "FREE." BEFORE YOU BEGIN recruiting your volunteer team, you have to recognize that volunteers are not free. Every volunteer needs your dedicated time, energy, and to be fed (really, free food is a great motivator). It will (and it should) cost your campaign a large amount of resources to recruit, train, and manage volunteers.

Volunteers are not staff. You can't expect a volunteer to do a professional's job. That's what hired staff are for. If you need professional help, that's when you hire. Volunteers will take more time and make more mistakes and have a different set of costs than professional staff. Paid staff can be held accountable and have a stronger incentive to do well. Volunteers may have a high turnover or they can otherwise be unreliable. Even the most dedicated volunteer needs motivation and assignments.

If volunteers are not free or cheap, why would you want them? One of the most significant resources you have as a library campaign is your corps of dedicated volunteers. They can be your strongest advocates if they have good leadership. Understanding how best to utilize them, keep them motivated, and ensure they are involved in your campaign will separate a weak campaign from a strong one. The volunteers you have for your campaign will act as one of your strongest resources equivalent even to money and time and will ensure that your campaign has the capacity to continue throughout the election cycle.

WORK FOR YOUR VOLUNTEERS

A campaign begins to run into significant trouble when it lacks an understanding of the best ways to utilize volunteers as a resource. They are your campaign activists and should be invested in as significantly as your funding. There are three ways people donate to a campaign: some will give money, some will give their good name (endorsements), and some will give their free time. Their hard work should be treated with the same level of respect as your monetary donors and with all the thanks for a ringing endorsement. Always remember that volunteers will give as little or as much as you ask of them, and you only get what you ask for.

The first and most important step in developing your volunteers is to gain an understanding about why they are volunteering. In other words, what are their motivations?

There are typically four reasons why someone volunteers:

- They are passionate about libraries.
- They want to contribute or feel useful and be recognized.
- They are against the opposition to the library.
- They are seeking an opportunity for growth or advancement.

You should keep in mind that each of these reasons is important and none of them is better or worse than any of the others. You should make sure that you find out what your volunteers' reason is and understand that motivation to get the most out of them.

Your own level of enthusiasm and excitement will set the tone for your volunteers and that will affect the success of your campaign. Your volunteers need to be excited and engaged to be able to contribute to winning a campaign. Make sure that you demonstrate the level of enthusiasm you want from your volunteers. After all, it is your library; it is your campaign.

The first time the volunteer comes through the door, it is generally because of the campaign. The second time, and every time thereafter, it is because of *you*.[1]

WHERE DO YOU FIND VOLUNTEERS?

Interestingly enough, finding volunteers for your campaign is (or should be) similar to the way you find volunteers for your library or funding for your campaign. Simply put, start by asking those you know and then work out from there until you are casting a wide net.

Some Tactics for Finding Volunteers

Getting your first few volunteers is always the hardest. Just like you did with brainstorming who to call to ask for money, you can do the same thing for volunteers. Have your campaign committee sit down and spend an hour brainstorming everyone they know and then put them in order of those most likely to volunteer and start calling. If that doesn't work, here are some other ideas.

Utilizing Your Volunteers

Your volunteers are going to be your strongest source of finding new people for your campaign. This is because people typically associate with like-minded individuals. Ask them to ask their friends and family to volunteer or to bring them to the socials and appreciation nights.

Asking Other Organizations

There are many organizations that will help you with a library campaign. Many times the Chamber of Commerce, the local unions, the Kiwanis Club, or similar organizations will find ways to help. You can go to the universities and colleges to find organizations that require community service like fraternities or sororities or associations for young, politically active students. It's also great to ask organizations like the Girl or Boy Scouts for small projects like stuffing envelopes or other duties that they can do to earn merit badges or satisfy other requirements. Some schools require their students to do community service, and having children involved in a campaign is a great photo opp.

Outreach

While your volunteers are phone banking, tabling, or canvassing, be sure to train them to know what to do if they come across someone who is very enthusiastic about the library or the campaign. They should feel free to give out information about how those individuals can help or get involved.

Crowd Work

Every event you have for your library campaign should include some kind of data collection plan. Just a simple sign-in sheet with information about who showed up like the volunteer recruitment list will work, but the more detailed it is, the better. This is because every event is an opportunity to get more volunteers and contacts for your campaign. Every. Single. Event. No matter how small.

The Internet

There are many websites dedicated to finding volunteers for organizations. Websites like VolunteerMatch (www.volunteermatch.org) or VolunteerSpot (www.volunteer spot.com) allow your volunteers to sign up for trainings, help you track them, and assist you with scheduling workdays and times. While these are useful, don't forget about the standards like craigslist, your campaign website, blogs, and so on.

In the Library

The most obvious place to find your volunteers is inside your library. If you're like most libraries in the United States, you have any number of volunteers who already help you provide services to the public. You might have a board of trustees, a Friends of the Library group, a teen advisory group, or just a core group of dedicated volunteers. Be sure to ask them!

In the end . . . Always remember that you are your own most important recruitment tool.

HOW DO YOU GET THEM INVOLVED?

One of the most difficult aspects of getting your volunteers involved is *the ask*. Volunteers can be wishy-washy or noncommittal. Figuring out the best way to ask them to help you is key to establishing a successful volunteer corps. When asking for volunteers, be sure to use these six Cs from Democracy for America:[2]

- *Connect* **with them immediately.** This can be as easy as a handshake, commenting on their shoes, or referencing some trait or interest in common. It's even better if you have a history with the person and you have a story to relate.
- **Give them** *Context.* Let them in on the story of the campaign and the role they can play in that story. Let them know how they will fill a role and be useful to the library and the community at large.
- **Make them** *Commit.* Anything besides a "Yes" should be considered a no. Give them a solid ask. If you get an answer like "Probably," "Maybe," or "I'll try" that is not a "Yes."
- **Get their** *Contact information.* Every volunteer who commits should fill out some kind of form that gets their contact information. At the very least you need their name and phone number. But preferably you should also capture their e-mail, their Facebook/Twitter and any other social media address, and how the volunteer found out about volunteering.
- *Confirm* **them twice.** Once you have them committed, be sure to follow up and confirm their interest before the day they show up. Call them, e-mail them, or text them. No response from a volunteer is a no. A nonverbal yes is still a no. At least one of the confirmations should be a firm verbal yes.
- *Catapult* **them into the campaign.** Give them a role right away. Throw them into the campaign with a position, role, or task that they can do now.

ONCE THEY'RE IN THE DOOR

When a volunteer comes to the canvassing event, there is more information you should collect about them. First, be sure to greet them and make them each feel welcome and excited to be there. Then it's important to find out as much as you can about each volunteer or potential volunteer so you can ensure that they are engaged in the campaign and that you know the best way to utilize their skills. Be sure to collect data such as:

- Who came to the event
- Where they are from
- When they came
- What they did
- What they like to do
- What they do for a living
- Why they came to the event

Engage them one more time before they walk out the door. Try to shake their hand and thank them for coming. Please use their name. You should also ask them how they thought the event went and ask them to commit to the next one. Every event ends with a pitch to participate in the next event or, even better, attempts to establish them as a regularly scheduled volunteer.

EVENTS FOR VOLUNTEERS

Besides the regular events that your campaign runs to get the message out about your library's initiative, its services, and needs, you can also have volunteer-related events. These kinds of events are geared towards getting more volunteers and thanking the ones you have while also getting the word out about the campaign.

Social Events

Backyard barbecues, meet-ups, tweetups, bar crawls, and so on are great for recruitment and your campaign. These are opportunities for you to talk about your campaign with your volunteers and whomever they bring. If you do something in a more public space like a bar or restaurant or park, it's an opportunity for more people to see the campaign and gain visibility as well as attract more volunteers

Volunteer-Only Events

Hosting events and activities where volunteers are encouraged to bring a friend will boost your volunteer recruitment by encouraging volunteers to engage their networks. You can even use competitions to see who can bring the most volunteers with them.

Recruitment Events

Special meetings that are just about talking about the campaign, how to get engaged, and what can be done are also effective. These can double as a training event, and by the end you can have a new enlistment of engaged and trained volunteers.

VOLUNTEER TRAINING

Once you have your corps of individuals committed to volunteering for your campaign, you need to train them to do their jobs. Training is not a one-time thing; it should be ongoing and consistent. Many campaigns give the same training every day to their volunteers. In order to have a successful training, make sure you follow this formula:

- Review the campaign's message and the way in which the role of the volunteer fits into that message and the winning campaign.
- Demonstrate the tasks the volunteer needs to accomplish, with each of the steps clearly shown.
- Clearly explain your expectations for what a successful project or task looks like.
- Give them the opportunity to practice in front of you to show that they understand their job. Spend the bulk of your time on activities to practice so the volunteers are sure to have the skills they need.
- Give them the opportunity to ask questions and give them resources and tools to seek answers from or let them know who to ask if they have a question. Be sure to be clear that they are more than welcome to ask any question they need to. Nothing will derail your campaign like an eager volunteer with the wrong answers. Let them know that the two smartest things they can say on a campaign are "I don't know" or "I have a problem."

Once you have trained your volunteer, be sure to train them again and then continue to train them. If you have volunteers who have excellent skills, it is a great idea to give them the opportunity to lead the training. Giving volunteers the opportunity to teach or lead a training forces them to become better acquainted and skilled at the concepts that they are teaching. This will also give your volunteers a point of pride, a leadership opportunity, and a feeling that they are more useful and are adding even more value to the campaign. Of course, it will also free you up for other activities.

Create Leaders

It's always great to empower your most skilled volunteers to become leaders in the campaign. This will demonstrate to other volunteers that if they do a good job, they can get a better or more fulfilling position. It will also give your volunteers the opportunity to grow, take more responsibility and ownership of the campaign, and help you retain them longer. The best way to do this is to create a tiered model of volunteering.

For example, first-time volunteers can fold brochures, the next time they can help distribute them, the next time they can help decide where to distribute them, the next time they can lead the team of distributors, and so on. Be sure to have these tiers well thought out before you need to promote someone into a position. Don't just make them up as you go along because a volunteer will see your disorganization and lose faith in the campaign.

Throughout your leadership training of your volunteers, you should never stop training them. Remember that these leaders are not coming to you fully trained, but need to be constantly trained. For the leaders especially, they need to be taught to lead, they need to be evaluated, given guidance and feedback, to be held accountable, and they need opportunities to keep them interested. These volunteer leaders aren't being paid and they rely on your personal touch to keep them motivated. You are your campaign.

Keep Them Busy

Not having enough to do with your corps of volunteers will suck the momentum out of your campaign. Once that momentum is lost, it's very hard to recapture. Be sure to keep your volunteers busy with all of the tasks that a campaign has.

There is more than enough to do in a campaign to keep any number of volunteers busy, so be on the lookout for more opportunities for your growing number of volunteers. The best way to do this is to continuously assess what tasks need to be done. At least once a week, you should take some time to analyze how many volunteers you have, where you need volunteers, how many you need for each task, how long you need them, and when you need them for each of the week's goals. That analysis should be divided into each area of the campaign and by date and the time. It's easy to keep track with a form or calendar that is visible where volunteers can sign up and you can keep track of their work.

A calendar will help you plan your volunteers' time and energy and keep you and your campaign on task. This example calendar will help get you started thinking about weekly tasks even though it is incomplete. A better calendar will include times, the names of volunteers scheduled to complete the tasks, and many more tasks and goals. A sample calendar is shown below.

SUNDAY	MONDAY	TUESDAY	WEDNESDAY	THURSDAY	FRIDAY	SATURDAY
• Training • Canvassing • Phone banking • Enter canvass data	• Training • Editorial writing • Media outlook • Print 1,000 brochures • Mail lawn signs	• Training • Fold 250 brochures • Social media blitz • Plan weekend canvassing	• Training • Fold 250 brochures • Radio interviews • Order office supplies • Distribute posters	• Training • Fold 250 brochures • Fund-raiser • Social media blitz • Plan weekend phone banking	• Training • Fold 250 brochures • Volunteer party • Confirm volunteers for weekend outreach	• Training • Canvassing • Phone banking • Enter canvass data • Enter phone data
• Training • Canvassing • Phone banking • Enter canvass data	• Training • Editorial writing • Media outlook • Print 1,000 mailers • Mail lawn signs	• Training • Fund-raiser • Social media blitz • Stuff 250 mailers • Plan weekend canvassing	• Training • Order office supplies • Stuff 250 mailers • Television interview • Distribute posters	• Training • Social media blitz • Stuff 250 mailers • Plan weekend phone banking	• Training • Volunteer party • Stuff 250 mailers • Confirm volunteers for weekend outreach	• Training • Canvassing • Phone banking • Enter canvass data • Enter phone data

Beyond the scheduled tasks, it's also helpful to keep lists of simple odd jobs and ongoing tasks posted so volunteers can see them. If you have a surplus of volunteer time, or an unexpectedly eager volunteer, this list is available for any volunteer with little training to find something to make themselves feel useful to the campaign. If you don't have a campaign office, you can still do this with an online shared calendar or a shared document environment like Google Docs.

Keeping Them

There are many reasons why a volunteer leaves a campaign. Some of these reasons are your fault, some of them are their fault, and some are nobody's fault. In any case, it's important to do everything you can to keep them and keep them happy and engaged. An angry, disillusioned volunteer can end a whole campaign with their insider information and a will to use it. Here are some of the reasons why volunteers leave a campaign and some of the ways that you can avoid having them leave.

- *Not having fun:* A campaign is not a volunteer's paid work. They are there because they enjoy the work and believe in the goal. It's your responsibility to ensure that they continue to enjoy the work even when it gets hard. Having music playing in the office, colorful and upbeat wall decorations, and frequent social and community-building engagements can help ensure that they are enjoying themselves.
- *No recognition:* Everyone wants to feel like the work they do is important to the campaign, and sometimes they won't know this unless you tell them. This is the cheapest thing you can do in a campaign office, and it is often the most overlooked. Thank your volunteers as often as you possibly can.
- *No growth:* We already talked about building leaders in your campaign. Not only does this help your campaign become self-sufficient, but it helps volunteers have a greater objective and goal and it ensures that your hardest-working volunteers are rewarded for their time and effort.
- *Too much, too soon:* Many times volunteers are going to come to the campaign "hot and heavy" and ready to be engaged. They will put it all out in the beginning and then after a couple of weeks or months of grueling campaign work, they will feel overwhelmed. It's your job to talk to and listen to your volunteers about their amount of work and their feelings about their workloads. You can find ways to help them to ensure that they are delegating work, or asking for help, while still pushing them to do better work and asking them for more.

- *Cliques:* People in large groups tend to self-create smaller groups to get projects done. This is fine for the project, but when one group or another gets more attention or becomes an exclusive club, your team can run into problems. Make sure you work with both your paid staff and volunteer staff to ensure that they are engaging each other and not creating an unwelcoming environment for newbies. You can have volunteers with more time on the campaign take a newbie as a mentee and get the newbie engaged and feeling like part of the crowd early on.

- *Outside world:* Your volunteers have a life outside of your campaign. Be aware and welcoming of that. For example, when a volunteer is working on the campaign, they are away from their family. Some campaigns encourage volunteers to bring their families to the office and get the whole family involved.

- *Office politics:* While they're working in a political campaign, your volunteers don't want to be caught up in office politics. If your committee leadership team is caught up with internal drama or disagreement, be sure to keep the volunteers free and clear of that side of the office culture. Rumor mills and volunteer opinions on the culture of the management of the organization can destroy the whole campaign. Remember the old adage: loose lips sink ships.

- *Forgone conclusions:* You might already think you know if your campaign is going to win or lose. In either case, there is still some work to do to see it to the end. It is always possible that the opposition slips up at the last days and sinks their own campaign. Your team needs to fight to the end. Be sure you keep them positive and optimistic.

Allocating Your Volunteers

Every goal you have for your campaign is easily divided into a series of smaller tasks. In order to successfully manage your volunteers, you need to understand each of the steps necessary to complete each task and be able to assign those. For example, if you have a goal of mailing a hundred letters, you need volunteers to print them, to address them, to stamp them, to fold and stuff them, and to put them in the mailbox. Knowing each of the steps, how long each step will take, and how many volunteers you need to complete your goal will give you the ability to train and assign your volunteers accordingly. The basic steps are as follows:

1. Create a list of tasks needed to complete a goal.
2. Calculate the time it takes for each task to be finished.

3. Determine how many volunteers it will take to finish the required tasks in the time you have.
4. Assign and train volunteers.

Example: You want to send a direct mailer to every voter in your county. First determine your goal. Because you know that there are 5,000 voters from the information in your voter file, you know that you need to send 5,000 mailers.

Next, determine how much time it will take. If you know that each mailer takes a volunteer 45 seconds to complete (this is where knowing your campaign tasks comes in handy), then using simple math you now know that it will take 62.5 hours to complete the mailers.

45 seconds × 5,000 mailers = 22,500 seconds
Divided by 60 = 3,750 minutes
Again divided by 60 = 62.5 hours.

Next, determine when you need the mailer finished. If you decide you need them in 6 hours, then simply divide 62.5 by 6 and you see that you need 10.4 volunteers for six hours. Of course, there's no way to have .4 of a volunteer, so always round up. Volunteers will feel a great sense of accomplishment by completing a task early!

Of course, this is a very simplified version of a goal. Much more complex goals like rallies, media campaigns, or canvassing will take several small tasks and various steps to complete the larger goal.

While it's important for you to know how long a task should take, you should focus your volunteers on the completion of the task and not the time. This means, don't assign folding brochures to a volunteer for two hours, but instead assign a volunteer to fold 200 brochures. This helps volunteers focus on the completion of the task and it will help them feel that they have achieved a goal.

Volunteer Roles

While the campaign can have many tasks for volunteers for one-time projects, the campaign should include higher-level volunteers who are responsible for the necessary ongoing operations of the campaign. These are typically outreach and assistant roles. The following list is not a complete list of potential volunteer roles, but merely a suggestion of the most-utilized volunteer positions in most campaigns:

Canvassing trainee: The entry-level position for canvassing a precinct. After the initial training and role-playing for canvassing, there is still some experience that the volunteer lacks. During this time the canvasser should be partnered with a well-trained canvasser or a canvasser with more experience. This will help this volunteer gain confidence and some real-world practice of their skills while witnessing the canvasser work. This trainee should only remain in this level for 1–2 shifts, depending on the length of the canvassing day.

Canvasser: The fully trained canvasser who is responsible for being independently skilled to walk a precinct with little or no oversight from the lead canvasser.

Lead canvasser: The lead canvasser is responsible for ensuring that the materials for the day's canvassing are organized and ready. This person is typically responsible for a small group of canvassers and ensuring that the area in which they work is properly documented. The lead canvasser also acts as canvassing director in the director's absence.

Canvassing director: This person is responsible for planning the canvassing of precincts and overseeing the majority of the canvassing operations. The canvassing director is responsible for ensuring that new volunteers are trained and that all volunteers have the materials they need to complete their canvassing.

Phone bank trainee: This is the entry-level position for a volunteer to work the phones. During this time they should role-play phone calls, learn the script, and work with a well-trained phone banker to gain experience and confidence in real-world phone banking.

Phone banker: The fully trained phone banker who is responsible for being independently skilled to call constituents with little or no oversight from the lead phone banker.

Lead phone banker: The lead phone banker is responsible for ensuring that the materials for the day's phoning are organized and ready for the volunteer team. This person is typically responsible for a small group of volunteers and ensuring that the phone numbers that they call are properly documented. The lead phone banker also acts as phone banking director in the director's absence.

Phone banking director: This person is responsible for planning the calling of constituents and overseeing the majority of the phone banking operations. The phone banking director is responsible for ensuring that new volunteers are trained and that all lead phone bankers have the materials they need for their groups to complete their calls, including phones, scripts, and so on. The phone banking director is also responsible for ensuring that all calls are planned, carried out, and documented.

Media volunteer: Campaigns can generate a lot of press that is either written by the campaign, by the opposition, by the press, and especially online. It is a good idea to have someone responsible for keeping an eye on any local forums, news and media sites, and any influential bloggers or social media community members. This volunteer shouldn't be the one to respond, but simply reports to the campaign leadership team about any findings.

Scheduling assistant: This volunteer helps oversee the calendar for the campaign. She helps canvassers, phone bankers, mailers, potential donor events, and so on make sure that they don't plan conflicting events. If there is a project or a task that needs scheduling, it should go through one person. This helps everyone know how to schedule.

Print and design volunteer: This volunteer ensures that all materials that are needed for the campaign are designed and printed. This volunteer will be an individual with high-level skills in design. She can also design logos and digital flyers for social media campaigns. It is important that one designer work for the campaign, whether it's a volunteer or a paid position. This ensures that all materials have a familiar and similar look and feel.

Office assistant: This is one of the highest levels of volunteering for a campaign. This volunteer ensures that the office is well supplied, the calendars are up-to-date, that messages are received and distributed, the office is kept neat, mail and packages are sent, and so on. This position demands a high level of multitasking, excellent people skills, and requires someone who enjoys working with all volunteers. This position can also act like a cheerleader for the campaign and by organizing appreciation events for the volunteers.

Over the more than sixty library campaigns we've helped train and run, we've come to understand that volunteering to lead or support a ballot measure campaign is very different from volunteering for a lot of other library organizations. Many people who work on campaigns enjoy that campaigns have an end date and that their involvement, while intense during the campaign season, will be over after Election Day. They are often activated by the fact that passing a referendum, bond, or other ballot measure creates needed financial stability or tremendous new leverage for the library. We know that many of them are not "power users" of the library. It is wonderful to see folks who have never volunteered before come out to support their community through their library's campaign.

In the same way that we recommend that all our campaigns plan to hand off their donor lists after the election to the library's Friends or foundation, we encourage all our campaigns to provide a pathway to other volunteer opportunities in those organizations, too. It's important to do that after Election Day, and to do it quickly. We suggest that your campaign committee leadership team have a very early conversation with Friends and foundation leadership about a post-election outreach plan, and then not worry about it until after the election. Your time and attention needs to be on supporting the volunteers who are doing great get-out-the-vote work for your library today.

NOTES

1. "Field Organizing," PDF (Washington: Democracy for America).
2. "Finance and Fundraising," PDF (Washington: Democracy for America).

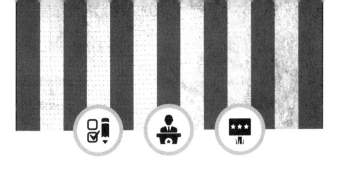

CHAPTER TWELVE

Theme and Message

E VERY POLITICAL CAMPAIGN HAS A THEME, AND CAMPAIGN messages are tied to this theme. However, there is a difference between your campaign theme and your campaign messages. Many campaigns don't understand this distinction.

Before you begin developing your message, you want to decide the answer to the questions, "Why the library, why now, what does the library do for the community?" This is because your campaign theme is a single succinct idea that can be used to communicate with different groups of voters about the campaign's overall identity and its vision for the community at large. Every e-mail, every flyer, every letter to the editor, every Facebook post, and every conversation about the campaign needs to return to the theme of the campaign. This theme shouldn't feel scripted or sound like an empty promise. It must have some kind of meaning that resonates with the voter. It should be rooted in what new outcomes will happen for the community if the library is funded.

EXAMPLES

Barack Obama's theme in the 2008 election was "Change" and it was a slogan that was attached to nearly everything published and shown to voters. The single word was prominently featured on his websites, his podium and background when he gave speeches, and on any marketing that came from his campaign. Donald Trump's 2016 theme of "Make America Great Again" was fundamentally one of change, but it was change brought by an outsider to the process. It was prominent across all aspects of his campaign. Even on days when he was accused of making up campaign promises off the top of his head, that same head featured a baseball cap with the slogan on it. He was able to reinforce his campaign theme in every photo.

In 2004 George W. Bush's overall theme was along the lines of "hope," but it was never officially adopted. Although his campaign never officially adopted a theme, they did consistently use variations of this ideology in their slogans "Moving America Forward," "Yes, America Can," and "A Safer World and More Hopeful America."

Whichever theme you choose for your campaign, the idea is the same. You should hate the theme by Election Day! That's because if, by the end of the campaign, you don't hate repeating the theme of the campaign, you haven't said it to enough people. You can bet that Obama was tired of the word "Change" by the end of the campaign, but you can also bet that there were plenty of Americans who hadn't heard it enough to believe it. For your theme to resonate with your community, they need to hear it enough times in as many different ways as you can deliver it.

THE MESSAGE

While your theme is high-level, a library campaign has multiple messages that are specific and targeted to particular audiences. While the theme is the overarching idea of the campaign, the message is developed to target a specific audience and is prepared for responses that you are most likely to receive on the campaign trail. You can even change this message as the campaign evolves over the course of the election cycle.

The best messages are the ones that show the values that the library shares with the community. They should go beyond the simple "Support your local library" and give voters a good reason to want to vote for the ballot measure. Your message should convey some emotion or be tied to the beliefs of the audience that you are speaking to. In any case, this message must always return back to the theme of the campaign and reinforce that ideology.

AUDIENCE

When Barack Obama spoke about change at campaign stops across the country, he delivered messages about change that were tailored to the audience he was speaking to. For example, when he was talking about change in Iowa, his message was about change as it pertained to agriculture. When he talked about change in Michigan, his message was about change as it pertained to the auto industry and manufacturing. In the same way, your campaign for your library should hold true to its theme, but develop messages to deliver to the audiences that you are speaking to. That means that if you are talking to the Chamber of Commerce, you're going to talk about the library's role in the local economy and business sector and when you talk to the school board, you're going to talk about the library's role in the education of the students in the area. This isn't always an easy task, especially for librarians who take on so many roles in a community and who are proud of the work they are doing. You won't get far talking to busy voters if you assume that everyone wants to hear everything about the library all the time.

This means that in order to build a good message, you need to understand the audience that you are talking to. That's why it is important before meeting with an organization or individual to do some research to find out what is important to them. If you can tailor your message to their work, mission, or needs it will resonate more. This takes time, of course, but it is an important step that shouldn't be overlooked. If a person or an organization is passionate about economic issues and you show up ready to talk about the education issues that you are passionate about, you aren't going to be able to meet them where they are. Instead, it is best to take some time and do your research. Write down some things that you know about the person or the organization, and the topics that are important to them. Then you can use your message to meet them in the issues that they care about and show them how the library can help them solve those issues.

This method works especially well with politicians like mayors and city council members. Often, these individuals ran for election on some platform. If you take the time to research their platform, you can talk to them about how the library can directly address their agenda and help move their agenda forward. For example, if the mayor promised safer neighborhoods, you can talk to the mayor about how libraries tend to create safe spaces and positive activities for high-risk populations and therefore has the potential to lower crime rates. This is all based on the idea that it's much easier to have a meaningful conversation with someone who already finds meaning in the topic of conversation. If you were to talk to a mayor about education when they only care about public safety, then it will be very hard to find a common ground from which to support the library.

YOUR MESSAGE IN 27 WORDS, 9 SECONDS, 3 POINTS

When developing the library campaign message, it's important to keep in mind the best way to convey this message. Because every library campaign is simply a long string of communication opportunities with your community of voters, it's important to develop a way to get their attention quickly and without losing it in the end. It is best to remember that no matter how much we wish voters were lining up to hear our message, the absolute reality is that they are not. In fact, they are waiting for our message to be delivered to them. It isn't pandering or dumbing down a message to frame it in simple sound bites that they can easily digest amidst the noise and static of a thousand other messages they are hearing every day.

One of the best methods for message delivery is through the "27–9–3 message frame," which is used by many progressive organizations in their campaign communications. In this approach, create an audience-specific message 27 words long that takes 9 seconds to make 3 simple points. For example, a basic 27–9–3 message about how the library ballot measure would support business development could read "If the referendum passes, our library can support economic development by providing meeting space, training, information, and personal assistance to start and grow a business across the counties." Likewise, if you are trying to stress the positive changes the library can bring by supporting student achievement if the measure passes, your 27–9–3 can look like "Our committee supports a strong, educated community. We are voting Yes for the library because literacy and learning opportunities should exist for everyone in our community regardless of age or ability, or the resources of parents and caregivers."

This method creates an opportunity for easy repetitions using clear and concise language. The added benefit is that your message can easily be picked up by many kinds of media. This is because the media will often look for an easy and short quote to use in the first paragraph of their political story. They don't want to use something longer than 27 words to make a point in their lead because many people won't read beyond that. A 27-word message is usually tweetable, shareable on social media, and often media channels such as radio and television are all looking for a concise quote which encapsulates your campaign and its message. Using the 27–9–3 approach gets your "foot in the door" and helps to "hook" your community of voters.

This method is also a great way to drill down to what you think is the key takeaway when meeting with organizations. We often meet with library campaigns that have a long list of talking points that they want to make with everyone they come in contact with. Having them practice the exercise of creating 27–9–3 messages that are tailored to the audience they are speaking to is a great way to get them to practice focusing on what really matters in the campaign—messages that resonate with voters. A great example is "If funded, our library can be an effective partner with [insert partner here] because we level the playing field, create a collaborative space, and serve the same populations."

EXERCISE

If you want to practice creating these messages with your campaign leadership team, it can be done very easily. First, have everyone work in groups of 3–4 and ask them to take a few minutes and brainstorm a list of organizations that they want to meet with. Next, ask them to take a few minutes and write down what it is that those organizations or individuals believe in. In this step, it is always okay to do the research and make sure that everyone knows as much about the groups as possible. After that, have them brainstorm as many ways that the library intersects with those individuals' or organizations' beliefs. Last, have them choose the best or strongest ways that the library supports those beliefs to create their 27–9–3 message.

Here are two examples of 27–9–3 messages to organizations that are often in many communities.

- **Chamber of Commerce:** *assumption*—they care about businesses and economy
  The library supports the local economy by providing access to market research databases, acting as an economic hub, and providing books that help people start and maintain businesses.
- **School board:** *assumption*—they care about education and student achievement
  The library ensures that students are successful through after-school homework help, books and resources that provide in-depth subject coverage, and access to high-speed Internet.

Expanding on the Message

Of course, you wouldn't simply walk into a meeting with these organizations and expect to deliver your 27–9–3 message and then walk out. Once you have built a clear and concise message that is relevant to your audience, you can build upon it to really drive it home. For example, you can go into more in-depth discussion about how the after-school homework help has been successful in advancing student achievement. But you want to make sure that you don't start talking about the economic impact for small businesses while talking to the education groups, and that's why framing these messages in this way helps to create more effective talks to organizations.

Repeating the Message

If you've spent any time watching political ads or paying attention to campaigns, you might have noticed that campaigns spend significant amounts of time and money repeating the message they've developed. Repeating a message to potential voters is one of the most important things a campaign can do. Repetition reinforces the ideas around why they should care and why they should vote. In fact, you know that your campaign is doing a good job of being repetitious if your staff and volunteers are sick of hearing the message. By the time the public is sick of hearing it, they will just begin registering the message. You have to remember that the public is continuously being heavily influenced and inundated by brand slogans through a barrage of repeating commercials on TV, radio, and print ads.

Corporate marketers believe that a consumer must see the same message dozens of times before it gets impressed upon the minds of consumers. In fact, some marketers believe that not only do consumers view thousands of messages every day, but they must see a message at least twenty-seven times over a short period in order to be effective.[1] This is because they believe that a person only really registers 1 out of 3 ads they come across and it takes, on average, 9 impressions for someone to take action.

Delivering the Message

The bulk of your campaign's resources will and should be spent on getting the message to the community. It's important to make sure that your message is being delivered in the most efficient and effective way possible, and as often as possible. The best way we know to make sure that your message sticks in the minds of the voters is by using the following criteria developed by the organization Democracy for America:[2]

- *Concise:* Your message is not an essay discussing the relative merits of the library and why it's important. Get to the point and get there directly.
- *Clear:* Don't leave any doubt about what your message is, whose side you're on, and that people need to be voting for the library.
- *Consistent:* Repetition is the best way to stand out in the minds of your voters. Repetition is the best way to stand out in the minds of your voters. Repetition

is the best way to stand out in the minds of your voters. Don't have multiple or differing messages that you are delivering. Everyone is on the same page and saying the same thing because consistency and repetition reinforce the message. Repetition is the best way to stand out in the minds of your voters.

- **Convincing:** Never deceive your supporters or potential voters. There is no quicker way to lose an election than to be perceived as untruthful. People already view elections and campaign promises with a critical eye. If your campaign is caught in a lie, there is no way to win their trust back. They will believe that you don't care about them enough to tell the truth. Be honest and sincere and that will show in your campaign.

- **Contrasting:** You need to draw a line in the sand on the favorable side of your campaign and it should lay clearly between you and any opposition. If people don't have a clear decision to make, they won't make a decision, or they may not vote at all. The library's funding or building project is a vision and a hope of the community. You can and should contrast that *vision for* the community with any opposition opinions that come up.

Message Box

The messages of a campaign exist for a reason. If the campaign was unopposed, or if everyone believed the same thing, we wouldn't need a message at all. However, that's not the case. While libraries currently have the advantage of being well supported at the ballot box, this isn't the case in every community or in every campaign. There is almost always some kind of opposition, and the message box is a tool that a campaign can use to appropriately address the opposition.[3]

The real advantage of a message box is that by using it, we will be able to anticipate the opposition's messages and be prepared to bring the conversation back to our message. The message box is a visual brainstorming exercise that lays out the potential messages from each side of the campaign. If done correctly, it will show what your library campaign says about itself, what it will say about its opponents, what your opponents say about themselves, and what your opponents say about your library campaign.

Here is what a campaign message box will look like:

What we say about ourselves	What they say about us
What we say about them	**What they say about themselves**

Spending time on constructing message boxes will help your campaign refine its own message even before your campaign begins. It will also help you understand the weaknesses of your campaign rhetoric, understand any strengths of your library's ballot measure plans, help you find opportunities, and help you defend against any threats. Having your campaign message thoroughly understood by your leadership team early on will help you plan your defense against oppositional attacks before you need it. It will also help you to see ways to bring your opponent's message back to your own.

You will be able to preempt your opposition's message if you know what they are going to say before the campaign begins. For example, the biggest oppositional message to a library measure is "no new taxes." In this case, you can talk about the return on investment in libraries for communities early on in your campaign and undercut the opponent's message. No matter what the opponent's message is, the golden rule is to bring it back to yours. This means that you should always try bring it back to the two "what *we* say about _____" boxes.

While the message box keeps the campaign on track and realistic, it needs to be continuously utilized. This tool becomes even more important if you switch to a new message, or if you suddenly start being attacked by a new or unexpected opposition. Because of this, it is great to take the committee leadership through the exercise and update it every week or as often as possible. When you do this, you might find that things have changed throughout the campaign when the opposition delivers their campaign message. Your message will be most effective if you have defined how to control the message or how the campaign will be defined if your opposition controls the message.

Stay on Message

Every campaign should pay attention to three things: repeating the message, staying on message, and repeating the message. We've already discussed repeating the message and that is easy enough, but the real difficulty comes when we try to stay on message while our opposition tries to throw us off (and they will). The worst thing that happens in a campaign is when a representative of the campaign who is unskilled in staying on message gets railroaded into straying away from the message. This is because the public and media and everyone around the campaign can only see, hear, and report on what the campaign says and does. If your campaign stays on message, the media and the public will respond by repeating your message.

The place where many campaigns fail is during question-and-answer scenarios. The opposition, the public, and the media often have alternate agendas to your campaign, and they are going to want you to respond to those agendas. They are going to ask questions that are designed to throw your campaign off its course to get what they want. No matter what, they can only get from you what you give them, so your campaign must be disciplined enough to not feel like it needs to respond to every question or accusation. A great answer is one that returns to the campaign message, a good answer is one that confesses that you don't have the answer right now, and all the other answers don't matter.

Testing Your Messages

The national data behind what the most effective messages are to voters about why they should support a library initiative is relatively thin. We don't have a set of messages that are most effective to the right audiences. While we wish we could give you a comprehensive list of messages that work, and the audiences that they work for, we can only offer some speculation. It's going to be your job to test variations of messages early in your campaign to see what resonates most with the voters. For example, the messages that get the most clicks through e-mail, the most donations, the most volunteer sign-ups, or the most pledges to vote yes need to be found in each community through a series of testing. You can do small tests for a few dollars on your social media or e-mail platforms (we'll talk about how to do that in those chapters), and then expand the most effective messages in other media forms like newspaper, TV, or radio ads.

Audiences and Messages That Might Work

While we don't have current data that models voter responses to library issues, and we don't know the most effective messages across many audiences, we do have some experiences that guide us and can help narrow down your testing. What follows are some examples of the audiences and messages that have worked for our library campaigns:

- *Business owners:* When speaking to business owners, think about ways that libraries help small businesses thrive. If you have stories about someone who started a business in your library or someone who got the resources that they needed in your library, then talk about that. If you can't identify someone who did, talk about how small businesses can get valuable information from your library and how libraries can help small businesses compete with larger businesses through information from your books and databases about market analytics, business intelligence, and supply chain information. Business owners also know about the concept of returns on investments, and this is a great demographic to target ads about how much money your library returns to the community for every dollar spent on it.

- *Parents:* Parents want what's best for their children. Many also want what is best for other kids. It's great to talk about the value of storytimes, after-school help, literacy, and so on that will help ensure that children have what they need to get ahead in life. It is very important that you talk about the *value* of things like storytimes and after-school help and not that you talk about *when* the next storytime or after-school study program happens. Remember, in campaign communications you are trying to get people to vote for the library, not to use the library.

- *Political moderates:* Moderate Republicans, moderate Democrats, and independents all value the library at about the same rate. When you're speaking to Democrats, make sure you are talking about the social benefits of libraries, and when you are talking to Republicans you should talk about the economic benefits and fiscal responsibility of libraries. For Republicans you can talk about how the library helps people get off social services and gives them economic freedom. For Democrats you can talk about how the library connects people to social services that help them get ahead.

- *Tea Party, libertarians:* These groups are the hardest to target to. In fact, we would recommend that the library exclude these groups from their targeting. Libraries don't yet have the data around what messaging we need to effectively talk to these voters. They are antitax and antigovernment, so the library already has two strikes against it for being a government agency that tax money is spent on. However, you also want to make sure that you don't inflame these groups or create an oppositional force within them, so don't directly attack or make negative statements about their ideologies. We have found that messages about transparency in the spending of government resources can quiet this group and move them from a vocal opposition to a silent opposition. Please see chapter 13 for a longer discussion of engaging these types of voters.

- *Homeowners and property owners:* People who own homes are often concerned about the value of their homes and the liveability of the community that they've purchased a home in. Speaking about the ways that the library improves a community resonates with this group. They want to hear that the library will make the community safer, will provide long-term benefits, and will help solve problems within the community. There is often a concern in this group about property taxes, but speaking about how much the library benefits a community and is a long-term investment that helps to protect their long-term investment is a strategy that works.

- *Retirees:* The American Association of Retired Persons has libraries listed in their criteria for desirable communities to move to in one's retirement years. Currently, a large block of voters within retirement age have a sense of nostalgia about libraries. Messaging to this group about some of those nostalgic ideas around books and reading is effective, but it is also important to gently speak about some of the things that a modern library can provide to them. This group is one of the fastest growing e-book segments, and messages about the services that libraries provide to seniors who want to learn the skills of the twenty-first century can resonate with them.[4]

- *Millennials:* Millennials who don't have children and aren't in school are one of the harder groups to target messaging to. Many of the voters in this group might not have grown up with libraries in their schools. Many of them grew up with finding all of their information on the Internet. However, this group does seek out experiences and social opportunities in communities and it values programming offered by the library. They also have concerns about employment, skill-building, and financial independence through self-employment. The library campaign can benefit from targeting this group with messages about building relationships, in-person services, and ways that the library provides services to start-ups and independent contract workers.[5]

There are quite a few other demographics that library campaigns can target. There are many companies that can provide market and consumer groups that a library can target for messages. For other ideas about market demographics, we recommend looking at market segmentation products like Mosaic, which classifies all U.S. households and neighborhoods into 71 unique types and 19 overarching groups and has in-depth descriptions about consumer behavior and interests for each group. No matter what demographic your campaign targets, make sure that it is built around an audience of voters and excludes nonvoters in order to save campaign resources.

NOTES

1. Cameron Herold, "The Most Important Rule in Marketing," OPEN Forum, 2012, https://www.openforum.com/articles/the-most-important-rule-in-marketing/.

2. "Developing Your Campaign's Message," PDF (Washington: Democracy for America).

3. Christine Pelosi, *Campaign Boot Camp 2.0: Basic Training for Candidates, Staffers, Volunteers, and Nonprofits* (San Francisco: Berrett-Koehler, 2012), 49–53.

4. Lee Rainie and Andrew Perrin, "Slightly Fewer Americans Are Reading Print Books, New Survey Finds," Pew Research Center, October 19, 2015, www.pewresearch.org/fact-tank/2015/10/19/slightly-fewer-americans-are-reading-print-books-new-survey-finds/.

5. Susan Manalli, "Millennials Among Us," Public Libraries Online, August 20, 2015, http://publiclibrariesonline.org/2015/08/millennials-among-us/.

CHAPTER THIRTEEN

Responding to Opposition

WHEN WE TALK OUTSIDE OF LIBRARY CIRCLES ABOUT how several libraries lose each Election Day, it is a surprise to civilians. "Why would anyone vote against the library?" they ask. They answer their own question when we turn it around to ask: "Why do you think people would vote against a tax for the library?" They tend to answer "The Internet," or "Taxes are high," or "No one uses the library anymore." And these are folks who love libraries asking these questions! When even the library lovers have fundamental questions about the relevance and currency of libraries, people opposed to raising their own taxes to fund the library certainly will have questions.

No matter how great your plan is and how well thought out your messages are, your library campaign is going to have its critics. It doesn't matter how much the library is loved; antitax and even anti-library groups will almost always have some voice in your community. There are most likely groups of people in your community who hold the opinion that the library isn't needed. There are people who think that the library should be run by volunteers. There are people who believe that the library is doing something malicious with their money. Finally, there are likely groups of people who just plain and simply don't want to pay more taxes no matter what it is for.

How do we stay on message in the face of our critics? While you should expect to always have opposition, you shouldn't always have to have a fight on your hands. There are ways to quiet the opposition enough so that they don't pose a risk for your campaign. You don't need them to love the library; you don't even need them to vote for the library, or even be totally quiet. You just need them to not get in the way or sabotage the campaign. Your goal is only to turn them from an active opposition into a passive opposition. They will personally vote against the library. It's oppositional organizing you want to avoid.

Before we begin, we should point out that our opposition-response techniques work for face-to-face encounters, social media, and for comments on blog posts or news articles. It's the way that you structure your response that is important and it works across all media platforms. In most cases, we want to make sure to note that you should never directly attack your opposition by calling them out by name or specifically responding to just them. That is, unless you are running a negative campaign, and running a negative campaign is something that we rarely recommend. This is largely because negative campaigns fuel your opposition's campaign as much as they will fuel your own. Instead of directly attacking your opponent, you should build a message that can be repeated often enough that their message simply gets buried. You can have your supporters post variations of the same counter-message or dozens of positive stories on a blog post until the negative comments are buried. Whatever you do, don't validate the opposition or fuel their anger, mistrust, or hatred by attacking them.

YOU SHOULD RESPOND AND YOU MUST PREPARE

Oppositional forces influence voter behavior in two ways: by organizing and activating "no" voters, and by suppressing the votes from "on the fence" voters. In communities with a reservoir of antitax sentiment, an organized opposition gives these voters permission to vote against the library. But opposition doesn't only empower "no" voters; the presence of an active opposition also creates a conflict between the library and the community. This conflict creates confusion about the library's plans among voters, especially among those voters who are not "believers" (see chapter 1). When a voter is confused about a ballot measure, they are more likely to "skip" that line on the ballot rather than to vote yes or vote no. The confused voter does not want to do something wrong, especially by accident. If they have seen a conflict between the library and some part of the community (the opposition), they will essentially wait that election out and hope someone else will figure out a solution to the conflict.

The mere presence of opposition isn't enough to kill an election for libraries. Unanswered and unengaged opposition will. Early engagement with oppositional individuals and groups is possible and we encourage you to do it. The goal is to keep them from causing confusion. If too many "soft" yes voters are confused and skip the ballot question, it can easily tip the vote into "no" territory. No one wants to see an active campaign against the library activating a bigger no vote, either.

SOURCES OF OPPOSITION

It's critically important to know who your opposition is and why they don't support the library ballot measure or the library itself. This is something that should have ideally been done during the surfacing phase of your campaign (see chapter 2), but new opposition can show up at any time. Luckily, we have something up our sleeve. Here at EveryLibrary, we have heard just about every possible oppositional message to libraries, from the most ridiculous to the most reasonable. We have some strong suggestions on how to overcome these messages, and we hope our approach will inform you about ways to confront any local variations on these negative messages. Here are some of the most frequently heard opposition messages that we have encountered:

- The library tax will be yet another tax that (homeowners/small business owners/residents) can't afford to pay.
- The Internet has everything that I could find at the library.
- I don't want to pay more taxes.
- We don't need a new library.
- The library can be run by volunteers.
- Libraries are irrelevant because I never use them.

What you also need to recognize is that some people will never change their view or opinion no matter what you say or do. Attempting to convince them otherwise will be a huge waste of resources and not something that your campaign can afford to do. It is far more important to go out and engage the people who are already on your side and get those voters to the polls in greater numbers than the opposition can. You can be much more effective talking to people who are on the fence than those who have already made up their mind.

The desire to respond to the opposition directly can be difficult to resist. Instead, there are ways that you can use the opposition to build your supporter base. You can actually turn your opposition's messages against them and use those messages to convince your supporters to get to the polls. You can use the public debate to educate the public about the issues and build greater support.

Listen

The first thing that you should always do when handling discussions from people who have concerns about library ballot measures is listen to them. Some opposition stems from fear or misunderstanding; you need to handle their concerns with respect and show a concern and understanding about what they are afraid of. Don't directly oppose their position because that will give them a sense of validation and they will remain actively opposed. Instead, you should listen and respect their opinion and not be afraid to ask meaningful questions. If the opposition comes from an ideological perspective about taxes or government, it is even more important not to minimize or invalidate their political position and turn the discussion into a debate. Once you understand the source of their opposition, you can start to address it.

Repeat

Once you know what their personal fears or political concerns are, the first thing you should do is repeat them. You should not directly counter their argument with an opposing viewpoint, since this will be perceived as combative and people will fight back until they feel that they have won. By repeating their concerns or fears you prove that you understand them and that you respect their ideals, and the repetition will be almost immediately calming.

- The library tax will be yet another tax that small business owners can't afford to pay.
  - I understand the great burden placed on small business owners. . . .

- The Internet has everything that I could find at the library.
  - The Internet is a great source of information . . .

- I don't want to pay more taxes.
  - I understand that taxes are high . . .

- We don't need a new library.
  - We know that people love the old library and everything that it provided to the community . . .

- The library can be run by volunteers.
  - That's an excellent suggestion and our volunteers are very valuable . . .

Question

Sometimes the opposition is unclear or has a poorly thought-out political framework, or what they are saying doesn't make sense in light of the facts. If you can't figure out what their fear is, don't be afraid to ask questions. You can usually get to the root of the issue by kindly asking questions and then addressing the issue that emerges from them. Most people will feel that you genuinely care if you are asking questions, and you can help move them over from active to passive opposition.

Get Back to the Message

Here is where that message box comes in and where you can see how useful it is (see chapter 12). Since you should have already brainstormed and anticipated many of the opposition's messages, you will be able to develop "and" statements to craft your counter-message. The "and" statement is what you use after repeating their concern. This is how you are working to solve the same issue that they are concerned about. This is how you show that you are actually on their side and that you both have the same concerns. It is very important that you use an "and" statement and not a "but" or a "yes but" statement. You should never use a "no" statement because you are not disagreeing with them. You are trying to show that you agree and that you are both actually on the same side.

- The library tax will be yet another tax that small business owners can't afford to pay.
  - I understand the great burden placed on small business owners AND that's why we provide so many resources that make being a small business owner easier.

- The Internet has everything that I could find at the library.
  - The Internet is a great source of information AND that's why we want to increase the community's access to it and add value to what you get from it.

- I don't want to pay more taxes.
  - I understand that taxes are high AND that is why it's so important to me to provide services to the community that help bring the cost of living down and the value of the community up.

- We don't need a new library.
  - We know that people love the old library and everything that it provides to the community AND that's why it's so important to us that we continue to provide the services of the old library and the kinds of services that you deserve in a modern age.

- The library can be run by volunteers.
  - That's an excellent suggestion and we love our volunteers AND that's why the library uses as many volunteers as we can to streamline our processes and free up our paid staff to provide the best services we possibly can.

Reinforce Your Message

You can reinforce your message by using examples of how you're achieving your "and" statement. These examples should be concrete and provable. You should never lie and say that your library provides something that it doesn't or something that you can't prove that it provides. This is also where that message box comes back into play. You can use your opposition's messages to research your examples so that you have them in mind before the discussion even begins. It's always best to give more than one example, but you should probably never offer more than three in order to avoid the appearance of an "I gotcha" moment.

- The library tax will be yet another tax that small business owners can't afford to pay.
  - I understand the great burden placed on small business owners AND that's why we provide so many resources that make being a small business owner easier. FOR EXAMPLE, we often have programming on hiring staff for small business owners and we offer patent and trademark classes to teach small business owners to protect their property.

- The Internet has everything that I could find at the library.
  - The Internet is a great source of information AND that's why we want

to increase the community's access to it and add value to what you get from it. FOR EXAMPLE, we offer high-speed Internet access along with databases that provide a level of well-researched and scientifically supported articles that you just can't find for free on the Internet.

- I don't want to pay more taxes.
  - I understand that taxes are high AND that is why it's so important to me to provide services to the community that help bring the cost of living down and the value of the community up. FOR EXAMPLE, we provide opportunities for teens and youth to volunteer and become engaged citizens and we provide storytimes for new parents to help the children with early literacy and get them ready for school.

- We don't need a new library.
  - We know that people love the old library and everything that it provides to the community AND that's why it's so important to us that we continue to provide the services of the old library and the kinds of services that you deserve in a modern age. FOR EXAMPLE, with a new library, we can provide for programming space to support our growing community and we can provide access to even more materials.

- The library can be run by volunteers.
  - That's an excellent suggestion AND that's why the library uses as many volunteers as we can to streamline our processes and free up our paid staff to provide the best services we possibly can. FOR EXAMPLE, we love having our volunteers take on roles that free up staff to work on higher-level tasks such as budgets, training, and working with high-level technology issues.

Equip Your Campaign Team

These counter-messages are your campaign's best weapons against the opposition. While these example answers work well, they are not formatted for your community of voters and you will need the right weapon at the right time. Everything that we have used here are simply common examples. In our experience, you will hear them. But you will need to do local opposition research and continuously revisit through your message box any other opposition messages that you come across.

Most importantly, you need to practice with your weapons to get back on message. This means taking some time with your campaign committee and volunteers to do role-playing games. It is enlightening and useful for the team when one person plays the opposition and one responds to their claims by getting back to your message using the correct format. Record some of the best responses, distribute them to your campaign members, and make sure that everyone has them memorized and is well trained on responding to the opposition.

WHEN THE OPPOSITION LIES

Sometimes the opposition lies. There is not a whole lot you can do about that. We have seen it happen in a number of library campaigns. The problem with lies is that because they are not based on fact, there is very little evidence to the contrary. But there are a few things that you can do about it in order to simply pacify the opposition until the campaign is over. Remember that you are simply trying to win the election and you don't need to discredit or prove the liars wrong, you just need them to be quiet until the campaign is over.

While you'll find that there are people in the community who are serious in their opposition to your library, there are a few things you can try to do to either get them to quiet down or get out of the way. Let's use a "porn in the library" example for a way to engage various techniques to address and mitigate the opposition.

One of the biggest lies that we have seen crop up around election time is that of porn in the library. Often, these library detractors will try to use examples of porn issues in other libraries, a lack of filters on the computers, and language and content in young adult materials to "prove" that the library *wants* to expose kids to porn. Of course, we know that there is no truth to this ideology, but there is typically very little you can do to disprove it. You are trying to disprove a negative and there's very little you can do about that.

One technique would be to simply use the same "Agree, And, For Example" format that we discussed earlier. In the example of the individuals concerned about porn we can use this:

Thank you for bringing this to our attention, we also want our children to be safe and secure while they are in the library so we take your claim very seriously AND we are going to do something about it. FOR EXAMPLE, we are going to look into a committee to seriously look into the exposure of porn to children in the community.

You can invite them more into the campaign to be a part of the solution. You can talk about how the library really needs the resources that the win for the library would bring in order to ensure that the library can protect the kids. With the money you can purchase better filters and take staff time to look at the collection development policy or form a committee specifically to protect the children. Of course, if you make these campaign promises, you will need to deliver on them if you win.

Another solution is to sidestep the opposition and form a committee to look into the issue. In this case, you might even invite the detractor to be a part of the committee. You can set the schedule of meetings and the timing of the outcomes of the committee to occur after Election Day. It is important to depoliticize this important policy issue by focusing on it after the election, when everyone can give the issue the attention it deserves.

You can also build a series of counter-stories or narratives to drown out the opposition. What this means is that you find people in your community who can tell personal stories about the library that undermine the opposition's main narrative. You will need to identify community members who can show up at meetings or write letters to the editor and tell a personal account of their experience that is "opposite to the opposition." In the case of porn in the library, you can have community members show up at meetings and talk about how their kids are not being exposed to adult material on the computers or that their kids found value in the books they read at the library, and that they could then have a meaningful conversation about the issue with their children. They can tell stories of being responsible parents who monitor their children in public spaces. If you use this technique, never mention or directly oppose or attack the person making the original claim. You simply bury their claim in great stories that tell a counter-account of their experience.

✪ ✪ ✪

WHEN THE OPPOSITION IS HUGE

Large national antitax groups like the Americans for Prosperity (AFP) are starting to come out against libraries on Election Days. It is a very troubling situation and one that needs attention from the entire library community. If the Koch Brothers are willing to fund anti-library direct mail and robo-calls into communities to further their antitax agenda, we've entered a new era in American politics. When the AFP comes out against a library, they can tip the election without referencing the funding or building plan for the library. They can defeat us because they know how to talk about taxes and libraries don't. Our vocabulary is poor. As we discuss techniques for overcoming opposition in a particular election, we also need to work on a new or renewed framework about tax policy and public policy in this country that supports the very existence of our institutions from a policy perspective. As an industry, we haven't talked about taxes in generations. We cannot remain inarticulate in the face of antitax rhetoric from the Koch Brothers and the Tea Party and expect to survive.   ✪

The last technique you can use is to simply ignore the opposition. Many times, if you ignore an opposition statement, especially one that doesn't come from a credible source or doesn't have a large enough audience, it simply won't gain enough traction and goes away. This is risky, but if you know enough about the detractor or how they are connected across the community, you can make an informed guess as to whether or not they can get enough support of their claim to become a problem. But if you lend or transfer to them the credibility of your campaign by engaging them as if they were legitimate, you can actually create their audience for them and draw more people into the fray, creating a larger problem for the campaign. Whereas, if you don't engage, the detractor may simply go find something else to oppose somewhere else in the community. This is usually because they are trying to build a name for themselves or play a "hero" role in the community, and they won't be able to gain that role if nobody steps up to be the villain.

One thing that you should never do is openly debate, criticize, or demean the person who lies. They can use your opening to debate to validate themselves and their claim. If you criticize or publicly demean them, they can make the claim that you are simply trying to put them down because they are close to "the truth." You will become the villain that they are looking for and they will make the case that they are the hero.

ACTIVELY ENGAGING THE OPPOSITION

EveryLibrary worked with the Kent District Library (KDL) in Michigan on their 2014 renewal of a 10-year, $20,000,000 operating levy. KDL Director Lance

Werner conducted an extensive series of in-person engagements with local budget watchdog groups well in advance of the ballot. Werner's discussion of his strategic process of choosing the messaging to the public about the library and the ballot measure as part of the information-only campaign and his description of how the library engaged an antitax group as constituents instead of adversaries originally appeared on EveryLibrary.org (http://everylibrary.org/library-tax-different-part-one/ and http://everylibrary.org/library-tax-different-part-two/).

In August 2014, the Kent District Library (KDL) passed its largest tax increase (45 percent or .88 mills to 1.28 mills) by the widest margin that it has ever achieved (57 percent). The millage [the amount of tax per thousand dollars of assessed property value] passed in 21 out of 26 municipalities. The August 2014 vote marked the first time that KDL passed a renewal and increase on the first try since 2000. I would be remiss if I failed to state that Kent County is among the most conservative counties in Michigan. Not only is it one of Michigan's most conservative counties, but it also has a robust Tea Party presence and is the home to Tea Party favorites like Congressman Justin Amash.

When I began my tenure as the executive director of KDL, I was warned by several people in Kent and Ingham counties that the odds against getting a millage increase passed in Kent County were steep at best. I was also warned that KDL would be lucky to get its renewal passed. I proceeded to venture forward despite the dire warnings and KDL's track record of achieving millage increases. I was confident that KDL would be successful because I knew something that the naysayers didn't know. *Kent County residents love their library.* KDL currently has 60 percent of the 395,000 residents of its jurisdictional service area as active cardholders. In a recent survey conducted by EMC Research, 93 percent of respondents in KDL's jurisdictional service area had a favorable to very favorable view of the Kent District Library.

The love of Kent District Library is based on many factors, including the incredible service provided by KDL's passionate employees. Our goal is to create a sense of family with our patrons and among our employees and volunteers. KDL's employee passion and dedication went a long way to strengthening the public's trust in our services. KDL staked a claim to being a state leader in early childhood literacy endeavors and as a popular materials library. Obviously, there are many other KDL offerings that garner library love, but the list would be too long for this narrative. I was fortunate to find all of this waiting for me when I began my directorship in 2011; however, the KDL leadership team and I agreed that there needed to be more.

At my first board meeting as KDL's executive director, I asked the board for authorization to create Michigan's most robust, KDL-specific digital collection. At our second board meeting, the board approved the project and we became Michigan's premier e-library. KDL was the first library in the state to offer e-magazines and streaming movies. As you might expect, KDL love grew exponentially. KDL circulated approximately 10,000 e-items in 2010 and 523,000 e-items in 2013. You might be asking yourself why I mention this. My reason is as follows: in order to be successful in millage campaigns, it is vital to demonstrate relevance.

While being able to effectively tell a library's story is critical, having a good story is equally important. We had many compelling things to talk about in regard to our services and funding issues. For instance, KDL cut $1,600,000 out of a $15,000,000 budget ($1,300,000 out of labor with no layoffs), and was operating at 2006 funding levels. Another talking point was that the average ROI per household in our jurisdictional service area is $1,100 of service for the $70 in property tax KDL receives each year. All of this sounds compelling, but it was not enough. We had to establish toeholds to get traction in our conversations with our taxpayers and to demonstrate that KDL wasn't an "ordinary" library system or governmental entity.

We knew three years ago that if KDL was to be successful in its millage endeavors, library love alone was not going to carry the day. Library love is the foundation on which millage campaigns must be built. The structure that sits on top of library love has numerous facets. One of the most critical is storytelling. When I started at KDL, we decided that it would be a good idea to gain recognition of KDL services and grow library love by seeking awards for the services that we provide. KDL sought and was recognized by the Grand Rapids Chamber of Commerce for their EPIC Award for Excellence in Business (KDL was the only governmental entity to ever be considered), the state librarian's Citation of Excellence, Lighthouse Recognition from the Michigan Quality Council (KDL is the only library ever to undergo this quality initiative), Quality Service Audit Checklist Excellent Status from the Library of Michigan, the Linda E. Anderson Award from Employers for Better Health, and was recognized as a *Library Journal* Star Library for the last 3 out of 4 years. All of these accolades helped KDL further reinforce its reputation locally as a well-run and valuable governmental entity and added credibility to our story. We were able to separate KDL from other taxing entities, creating the idea that *the library tax is Different.*

Differentiating library service and library tax funding from other types of municipal services and taxes is vital to success, particularly in a fiscally conservative environment where there is strong antitax sentiment. There are a number of tax watchdog/government accountability groups in Kent County. One of them is called the Kent County Taxpayers' Alliance. I had read numerous stories in the local newspaper about their challenges to many of Kent County's tax proposals. I had also been warned repeatedly that they were trouble and would launch a counter-campaign. They had previously engaged the super PAC Americans for Prosperity in their challenge to a Grand Rapids road tax. Needless to say, we were concerned. We had very little funding for our grass-roots campaign, and standing up to a super PAC-funded counter-campaign would have been devastating. Naturally, I received a call from them in April 2014 requesting a talk about our proposed millage increase.

Instead of trying to avoid them (which is what most other taxing entities in our area do), we made the choice to meet with them personally. It was a great meeting and we shared the truth. Instead of trying to obfuscate our plans, we decided to present them with all of our financial data and prepared to answer any tough questions they might have. We believe in transparency and accountability and this group was (and is) concerned with governmental accountability. Instead of engaging the Kent County Taxpayers' Alliance as adversaries, we engaged them as friends and constituents. They asked us tough questions and we answered them. Kudos to them for holding our feet to the fire. As a result of this meeting, one of their members graciously volunteered to help KDL with its millage campaign as a volunteer. Our volunteer worked tirelessly and went door to door on our behalf. He gave us new perspective and sound advice from a Tea Party point of view. There was never any effort to launch a counter-campaign. In fact, we had support from residents possessing diverse political views. KDL was represented as it should be, as a nonpartisan entity that works to provide service to everyone.

Our campaign was successful for the reasons mentioned above, but we also had terrific polling data, a wonderful informational campaign (including a strong KDL employee-based Speaker's Bureau), support from John Chrastka and the EveryLibrary super PAC, and despite funding concerns, a strong grassroots campaign. KDL also received a glowing endorsement from the Grand Rapids Press Editorial Board and wide support among county residents. As a result, KDL passed its millage increase in places that it had never passed before.

We also learned a lot of lessons. First, incredible, transformative service forms the foundation for all other activities (build library love). Second, accountability and transparency are critical (always be truthful). Third, it is not enough to engage in these first and second lessons; always work to tell the library's story (if a library is engaged in the first and second lessons, it is bound to be a good one). The fourth is the importance of treating everyone like a constituent (especially when there is a substantial likelihood of an initial critical reception). Finally, teamwork will carry the day.

Now that we have achieved our increase, the real work begins. We will fulfill our promises to our taxpayers.   ✪

OPPOSITION RESEARCH

It is at the dark heart of political campaigns where you find opposition researchers. More commonly referred to as "oppos," they are the part of the campaign team who dig up information about their opposition to use in negative messages or campaign attack ads. The people working on opposition research are looking to collect as much information on their opponents to feed back to their campaign as possible. A lot of times, this information can be used as a component of negative campaigns and it includes large amounts of biographical information as well as information about any kinds of previous legal issues, criminal histories, media coverage, and a wide range of other details. While it is mostly seeking negative information about the opposition, the research also helps put together a better picture of who the opposition is and what they believe in and often helps guide the messages of the campaign that aren't negative. Sometimes you might even be surprised to find that there is a way to ·find some common ground with an organization or individual who you originally thought would oppose the library.

The thought of opposition research in library campaigns can turn a lot of people off of it. However, this research can also help you identify new ways to bring the opposition in line with your campaign or otherwise engage them positively. So it's not always a negative practice. Sometimes you can use the results of your research to engage the opposition in a positive way to quiet them down or even bring them onto your side by connecting to them on issues that matter to them more than the library tax. For example, if you find that they are dedicated to helping people find employment or starting small businesses, you can talk to them about how the library does just that very efficiently and inexpensively. If you find out that they fundamentally believe in privacy issues, you can positively engage them by talking about the library's activities during the ALA's Choose Privacy Week. So always be on the lookout for both damaging information about your opposition and information that can bring about a positive change.

In the case of libraries, where there is rarely a clear or prominent individual or group in opposition to the library, and where there is almost never a planned negative campaign from the library side, this step is often overlooked as part of the preparation to run a ballot measure. However, there are occasionally instances when having an in-depth oppositional analysis would benefit the library. A strong oppositional newspaper can even save the campaign money later by allowing the campaign to understand who opposes libraries and why and preempt opposition messages with messages of their own.

It can be astounding what a good research team can turn up to discredit opposition. For example, you might remember the Mitt Romney "47 Percent" video that turned up late in the 2012 presidential campaign. In it, Governor Romney talked to a group of high-level campaign donors about how he was only concerned with 47 percent of the voters. While that is a correct approach to campaign marketing, and that comment was designed to reassure his donors that his campaign was spending their money wisely, the opposition used that video to put their own frame around it. This video had been online for a long time before it was discovered by a campaign researcher. It was used to further the opposition's frame that Romney was elitist and out of touch. It was one of the most damaging attacks against the Republican nominee. This piece of video would never have been found had it not been for a team of researchers scouring the Internet for things just like this.

WHO AND WHEN TO RESEARCH

Before your campaign officially begins, you should start thinking about who in the community might oppose the library. This can be a part of your library's surfacing process as discussed in chapter 2. Take some time and brainstorm a list of people and organizations that you feel might oppose the library. In most cases, you probably already have some ideas if you've been attending city council meetings or conducting your pre-campaign listening tours or have that one guy who comes to the reference desk in the library to complain about the government. Take note of who these people are or might be. Take a few minutes to brainstorm the people that you know about in your community who hold these views. The research that you do about them will give you a better clue about the likelihood that they will come out and vocally oppose the library. It is a good idea to be aware and ready for them as early as possible.

What should be understood is that these opposition forces are often people or groups in a community who believe that they are acting as government watchdogs or who hold strong antitax or antigovernment beliefs. We have never come across someone who proudly believes that they are a terrible person or a bully. Doing this research will help you understand more about why it is that they hold the views that they do and help you find ways to address their legitimate concerns about the library before it becomes a problem the week before Election Day.

Sometimes these groups of people are not a formal organization, but are just a loose affiliation of people who have something as simple as a group on Facebook or a blog. We have seen opposition folks come together and form a group in the comments section of a pro-tax and pro-library campaign editorial. It truly doesn't matter if your opposition comes from well-organized groups like the local Tea Party, the Americans for Prosperity, or libertarian organizations, or if it comes from a lone actor, rogue community member, or someone with an antigovernment Facebook group. You should know about them before your campaign starts, and the first step in your oppositional research should be identifying these kinds of people and groups.

Once you have identified who in the community is most likely to oppose the library, the real research begins. You will start by putting together a time line of the organization or the individual. In the case of an individual, this is going to be like a mini-biography and you will start with the date they were born, work your way through their education, marriage/divorce, children, employment history, if they are a regular voter, and so on. For an organization, you will similarly work your way through its founding, funding, key events, key members and employees, and so on. You can use Google to start your research and look through social media posts, find out if the organization is listed in the Internal Revenue Service, is in good standing with the state's attorney, or use rating sites like Guidestar or even Yelp to find more information. Spend time looking up histories of giving with sites like DonorSearch (www.donorsearch.net) or InsideGov (www.insidegov.com) to see if the individual gave previously to nonprofits or political campaigns and use sites like FollowTheMoney.org (www.followthemoney.org) or OpenSecrets (www .opensecrets.org) to do the same for organizations. Find out if the individuals are part of a group or organization, or were in the past, and find out what partnerships the organizations have with other groups in the community. If you can find their social media pages, you might be able to find posts or comments that can assist your campaign, or maybe they mention somewhere online that they support taxes for things that align with the library, and this runs counter to their current antitax or antigovernment messaging.

THE OPPOSITION WILL DO RESEARCH TOO

While the library might not do opposition research simply because there is often not a strong or well-organized target, you can bet that there are people in the community who are looking to target the library. These are typically people who are antitax or antigovernment and much of their research is about that. A single person is almost definitely better equipped to conduct research on the library because the library is a large target and the public is armed with Freedom of Information Act (FOIA) requests. In fact, we have seen a number of campaigns hurt or destroyed by just one lone actor with an FOIA request or a camera. We have also seen a number of groups and individuals abuse the FOIA system to hamper the library and create doubt and uncertainty in the community.

The Freedom of Information Act ensures that the public has access to everything the government does. Whether you agree with the act or not, it does mean that at any given time, a member of the public can make a request for information, often called an FOIA Request, and get access to any and all e-mails or sources of other information that deal with that subject. If the library director is using the library's e-mail address to conduct campaign business (which is illegal), the director could not just lose the campaign for the library, but he could also lose his job and put the jobs of his employees at risk. No library employee should send e-mails from his or her personal e-mail account during scheduled work time (or it becomes FOIA-accessible) or send e-mails out about the business of the campaign from a library e-mail account. But the public can also use the FOIA to request phone records, spending receipts, and any number of other activities that the library does on a daily basis. That's why everything that is done in the library must be kept fully separate from the campaign itself. Make sure that you are not doing any of the following:

- Making calls about the campaign from a library phone
- E-mailing about the campaign from a library e-mail account
- Using a library resource like a computer to make social media posts for the campaign
- Holding meetings in the library to discuss the campaign on paid time
- Printing anything for the campaign from library printers

✪ ✪ ✪

One of the worst things a library can do in the few years before a campaign is to put books in the dumpster. We have seen far too many campaigns destroyed by what is simply a standard practice for many libraries by someone working for the opposition. It is almost standard practice in some areas to rummage through dumpsters to find discarded books in order to destroy a campaign. All it takes is one citizen-journalist to start a huge controversy by simply taking a picture of books being thrown away. There is nothing that kills a campaign faster than the idea that the library is wasting public money or donated materials, or throwing away "perfectly good" books when there are "illiterate kids in Africa that could use them." If you are working in or around a library, you know that books get thrown away for a host of legitimate reasons. Even though the books "look fine" from the outside, if they have been in contact with other moldy materials, have interior pages that are soiled or removed, or have misprints that make the books unreadable, they can't be donated and need to be discarded. Even though you have a valid reason to discard a book, never let anyone see it. Not only have we seen campaigns destroyed by this public myth that throwing a book away is akin to book burning (no matter what the condition of the book), but we have seen whole careers destroyed by it. Always keep discarded books away from the public eye. ✪

The library is going to be under intense scrutiny. In one of our campaigns, the library was accused of wasting taxpayer money—and not deserving any more—by keeping the lights on all night. Seemingly ridiculous or innocuous things like a late shift for the cleaning crew are sometimes brought up by the opposition. We have seen members of the opposition complain that staff are clearly paid too much because a member of the opposition noticed that an employee was driving a car that was just "too nice." Likewise, someone might complain that a staff member lives in too nice of a home or in an "expensive" neighborhood. Of course, since the voters' taxes pay the librarian's salary, you might hear that the librarians were seen reading at the reference desk when they should have been working. As we've mentioned, the librarian is the candidate. Part of the library's own training needs to be about preparing its staff for the kind of scrutiny that they will be under during a campaign, and how to be humble public servants in the face of this scrutiny. It is better to help them anticipate that the opposition may be researching them than for them to be suddenly confronted by an opposition message.

CHAPTER FOURTEEN

Earned Media

G ETTING THE ATTENTION OF LOCAL MEDIA OUTLETS about a ballot initiative or other library-related issue will not necessarily be difficult, but will require a bit of legwork and patience. At heart, the task is facilitated by relationship-building. These relationships will need to be built on trust and mutual respect as well as a strong understanding on your part of the local media ecosystem. This means that you will need to have strong relationships with all of the local players in this media ecosystem. That ecosystem can encompass local bloggers with big readership, people with large social media followings, and of course the local news media in print, digital, television, and radio. If you're planning your campaign early, it is never too soon to start building up relationships with the local media players.

Earned media generally means editorial, opinion, or news coverage in the papers, on TV and radio, and on blogs and social media that the campaign didn't pay for directly but instead received for free. Paid media, which we will discuss in chapter 15, includes both traditional and new types of paid advertising. Earned media for local library campaigns are significantly different than how earned media work for national and state candidates. The early analysis of the role and value of earned media between Hillary Clinton and Donald Trump in 2016 shows that Trump "out earned" Clinton by about 30 percent in this category.[1] Of course, Trump was a unique candidate not only for what he said to earn that coverage, but also for how singularly focused he was on creating free coverage for his campaign by being willing to say just about anything from the stump. We don't advise our library campaigns to attempt to mimic Trump's tone, tenor, and topics, but the importance of earned editorial, opinion, and new coverage of your campaign in your local media cannot be overlooked.

GET FAMILIAR WITH LOCAL PUBLICATIONS AND REPORTERS

Before you start contacting media outlets, make sure that you know as much about them as possible. You will want to know how much coverage they have given the library in the past and how often your library is mentioned in the local media. In order to do that, you can set up Google alerts for mentions of the library, use Twitter's advanced search for regional twitter feeds, read the comments in the local papers, and click on links to the highest commenters. You should also scour the local newspaper and its website, and ask your neighbors about any locally focused blogs and magazines they read. Look for reporters who have covered library issues in the past or who are covering community issues or city government, but also take the time to look for stories on related issues like education or literacy and make note of who wrote them. Many local papers and blogs operate on a small staff where a writer's beat can range widely, but there will often be just a few names that you will see frequently writing about budgets and other related issues. These will be the people you want to contact.

If you want to automate this process and you have a large enough budget, you can hire a company to handle your media for you. Companies like Meltwater or PR NewsWire can manage monitoring your media mentions for you and they can manage your press releases and get them into the right hands at the right time. However, the drawback of this method is that you won't build very strong relationships with your local media outlets, and having that relationship may save you some headaches later if you need to add your personal touch.

It also helps if you have those relationships in place when you want to be interviewed or get called onto the radio or local television. If the interviewer knows you well and has a strong relationship with you, they are more likely to give you a better interview. Likewise, if you have a strong relationship with a reporter, you might get them to assist you. After all, while it is your role to give good tips to the media and maintain a good relationship with a media outlet, they may give you the courtesy of tipping you off to a story that is potentially damaging to the campaign. You might have enough time to prepare a statement, or lessen the damage before the news hits the stands.

Be sure to start this process well in advance of Election Day. You want to have time to get on the radar of whoever is the local information maven and establish your relationship with them as early as possible. Don't be afraid to reach out, ask questions, and share other library-related news with them to get them up to speed with your library. There are many excuses in libraries to cultivate this relationship such as Library

Card Sign-Up Month, summer reading, Banned Books Week, National Library Week, or High-Five a Librarian Day. If you don't have a good reason to draw media attention, feel free to make one up. Have a celebration in your library, announce a new service or program, or "announce" some of the services or collections that people might not know about but which have always been available. Whatever you do, it is about building up that relationship with the media people in your community.

DEVELOP YOUR PITCH

Especially in larger markets, writers are generally stretched thin and tend to be busy, so before you reach out, you need to know exactly what you will say. Don't waste their time or yours by not knowing what to say when they walk in the door. Spend an hour or so and write it out. This will help ensure that you stay on message and that you don't accidentally say something that could be damaging to the campaign. Most reporters will ask for a pitch in writing anyway. That way they can refer to it as they put together their story. Many bloggers will want the same thing. Be concise and to the point and omit unnecessary details. You need to tell them exactly what you want them to cover, and why it's important.

Begin your pitch with a personalized line about why you're reaching out to that reporter or blogger specifically. Some of the bigger-name information sources often receive dozens of pitches a day, many of which are impersonal or irrelevant to their content. It's important to think from their perspective and ensure that when you approach them you have a viable story to share. Many of these individuals aren't interested in reprinting your opinion; instead, they're looking for a story that affects their community and will grab their readership. Make clear that you understand their schedule and what they are writing about and have a good reason to contact them. Then tell them what they need to know: what is happening and why it matters. Finish with what you would like them to do, whether that is attending an event or interviewing a source. Make the next step obvious and actionable. If you can avoid it, never leave a reporter without a call to action for their readers, whether it is to find out more information, visit the library, sign a petition, and so on.

HAVE THE STORY READY TO GO

The more resources you can provide to one of these people, the more valuable you'll be to them. To put together a story, give them more than one opinion or voice. If you can arrange to have other contacts, from different perspectives, ready to comment, you'll make their job easier and increase your likelihood of coverage. Depending on the issue, this could be a local librarian, a city council member, or a patron. Children always make great sources for the campaign and the media and public respond really well to pictures of children and quotes from children. Don't forget to have a good photo for them or an opportunity for a good video. Remember that most media is digital now so they can use things like videos and recorded audio, and they will need pictures if not for the article, then for the social media posts.

RESPECT THEIR SCHEDULE

Most reporters, especially at newspapers, spend their morning conducting interviews and gathering information, while their afternoons become a frantic race to write their stories before their deadlines. On the other hand, many big bloggers or online personalities have second jobs or might be stay-at-home parents with erratic schedules. In either case, whether e-mailing or calling, your outreach should be done in the mornings since it will give reporters a longer lead time and the local social media folks time to respond. Reporters will be neither willing nor able to speak to you when they're up against a deadline, but other media can be more flexible. Keep in mind that many reporters have to drop whatever they're working on to cover breaking news—a sudden fire, crime, weather event, and so on—so you may not be able to get them the first time you reach out.

BE PERSISTENT BUT RESPECTFUL

E-mail your pitch first and give the writer two to three days to respond before following up with a phone call. If they ask you to call back, wait a respectful amount of time before calling back. If you're up against a particular event—an upcoming vote or meeting—you can be more persistent, but keep in mind that reporters and some of those not on a news cycle have a multitude of competing priorities. Some of the most successful bloggers are stay-at-home parents and have a lot of duties at home, including sick children, after-school sports, and much more.

You will be best served if you view your media outreach as a relationship-building process. Writers are far more likely to put together a story on your cause if they can tell that you understand and respect their work and can provide clear and compelling resources. Be a help, not a hindrance.

KINDS OF EARNED MEDIA

There are quite a few different kinds of earned media and each deserves to be treated as it is. Finding the right media format for your message is a big part of any media release, so you should take the time to understand each kind of medium and its particular cycles as well as its particular reader/viewer/listener audiences.

Online Media

Online media are currently the new normal for most people's information sources. Pew reports that in 2016, fully 62 percent of American adults view their news coverage on social media.[2] Earned online media can come in many forms such as blogs, tweets, videos on YouTube or Vimeo, Facebook posts, and much more. It seems that the rules for engaging online media are changing every day. Online media companies and personalities are quickly coming and going. Some of the media outlets are serious and informational, while others are fun and entertaining, but each should be taken seriously and the library's spokesperson should match the tone of the outlet. For example, Hillary Clinton, during her run in the 2016 presidential election, went to take part in an interview with Zack Galifianakis on his fictitious interview show called "Between Two Ferns" that is broadcast on the College Humor website. In this interview she matched the medium and played along with Galifianakis.[3] This helped earn her many days of front page online news spots and tens of millions of views by a younger demographic.

While this national coverage is not what a local library campaign seeks, it is a good example of successfully embracing the digital opportunities that are available. If there are local bloggers, vloggers, or people with big local social media followings, it is always a good idea to reach out to them. You might find that someone runs a strong local Facebook group or is outspoken on sites like NextDoor or is a prominent "mommy blogger." If you can identify these folks early, you can build up relationships with them and they will inform their mass following about the library. We always recommend that you spend an afternoon and look for local groups or people with prominent followings on social media. Also take the time to ask your staff and ballot committee or volunteers about what kinds of opportunities might exist there. Your own personal media and consumption, reading habits, interest in social media or social networking sites, and your favorite columnists are personal and not representative of the wider community you are trying to reach.

Print Media

While many people are lamenting the loss of printed newspapers, in many communities there are local papers that are still well read and widely circulated. A lot of times these print news sources are read by an older demographic, but there are some papers that cater to younger community members. The benefit of getting into one of these papers is that sometimes other papers and media sources use these print media outlets to pick up news stories of their own. It's more often the case that news moves from the print media to the digital and it rarely moves in the other direction. A paper won't waste valuable ink and paper space on a press release that has already made its rounds on the Internet. You probably know which newspapers are in your community, but if you don't, all it takes is a quick trip to the local market to pick up what's there in the newsstands and then some quick searches on the Internet to find the contact information for the reporters.

To get into the print media market you need to especially understand their schedule. Unlike bloggers, the print media market has deadlines that reporters have to make or they won't get into the paper before it's printed. Make sure, whenever you're talking to reporters from any print outlet, that you ask when their deadlines are and give them the information they need far ahead of that deadline. You don't want to miss an opportunity because you didn't get them information in time, and you don't want to destroy their trust by getting them information so late that it makes them have to rush to get it into the paper.

Some local news outlets run weekly or monthly "reader opinion polls." We often see a question in the early days of a campaign about the library ballot measure. It's an easy question for the paper to poll on because it affects everyone in town. While the poll is nowhere near scientific, it's a non-story if the library wins. But if you "lose" an opinion poll it is negative earned media. We always recommend that our campaigns monitor their local news outlets and encourage volunteers to make their first "vote yes" for the library in any opinion poll.

Local Radio

Radio is an interesting medium because it tends to have a very specific market. In fact, you can often find local radio channels that cater to very specific political parties and ideologies. Besides political talk radio shows, there are also radio stations that are primarily entertainment and others that are primarily news. Your campaign can get its information into any of these categories, but each category has a different set of requirements and the decision about what gets on the radio is often made by the program director and not by the on-air personalities. Take the time to build up a relationship with these directors so they are more likely to give you better slots on the shows. Some morning talk radio shows start at 4 or 5 a.m., and while there are some people up at that time, their audiences are generally larger during the high-commute hours. You want to get the most for your airtime and the program director is the key to doing that.

You should remember that there are quite a few shock jocks and on-air personalities who are purposefully abrasive, aggressive, or confrontational. If you are planning on going on these shows, spend plenty of time researching their views and learning about how they engage with their audiences. These kinds of personalities like to have surprise guests or they have callers who are just as abrasive as they are. Mentally prepare yourself for this kind of interview if you are going on it. One technique is to prepare with a friend who will help you write some tough questions and answers and you can practice answering them while speaking. Just remember that while having written answers is great for practice, a radio show will not be happy to have a guest reading answers.

Lastly, and this should go without saying, radio is dependent on sound. Don't make the mistake of having talking points that depend on visuals like pictures or hand gestures or video. Radio also doesn't handle lengths of silence for any period of time. This is called "dead air" and it is one of the deadliest sins you can commit on radio. That's yet another reason to practice answering questions and quickly responding. The interesting thing about this is that even though there is a dependence on sound, listeners can hear when someone is smiling. Try this if you don't believe us. Holding your mouth in a smile makes a clearly different sound to the listener and if you are trying to get people on your side, you want to maintain this positivity even in the crosshairs of an aggressive radio host.

Television

While radio is always dependent on sounds, television is highly dependent on visual aids. This is a great time to show off anything in the library that is visual or otherwise wouldn't make for good radio. If you have a new art installation, or a fun and engaging program, or if your library has a bike repair station, or a seed library that you can bring into the station, these are all visuals that would work on television more than on any other earned medium. That's also because a television studio can come to the library to get recordings of content, but this doesn't always happen as easily for many radio stations unless it is a large event.

You should remember that these broadcasts are dependent on ratings and if you want to get invited back, you should be sure that you are talking about something that they would care about or something that is exciting and tells a compelling story. So if the television station is coming to talk about the bike repair station, the library might consider holding an event or program during that time to attract people that they can interview or so that the camera crew can get some good footage for later broadcasts. Make it exciting and interesting for the viewers with a good amount of action and activity and movement. Lastly, cameras can be intimidating, so you want to make sure that whoever you put in front of the camera is comfortable there and is engaging and fun to watch. There's nothing more uncomfortable than watching an interview with someone who seems terrified to be in front of a camera or who isn't engaging or entertaining.

WHAT IS NEWSWORTHY?

Before you ask a news reporter or online medium to engage with your campaign, you should make sure that what you're presenting to them is newsworthy. Many of us engaged in a campaign think everything should be big news to everyone, but that's because the campaign is something that we already love and believe in. To everyone else, and to the media consumer, it is just more noise. Your press releases need to stand out to get the attention that you need and to ensure that you aren't wasting the time of local press with a bunch of information that they don't care about. In order to ensure that what you are putting out is newsworthy, test your story against these four characteristics of a newsworthy story:[4]

- *Timing:* Your story should be fresh and new. It should have some sense of urgency or a time limit. Try to find some new angle that hasn't been reported on yet. Especially in the age of immediate information sources, your news has to be current and up-to-date. If you're trying to report on something that happened a week ago, it is too late and it is no longer interesting. Likewise, if it's something that is happening a month from now, it's also not engaging. People care about events only when they are happening in the next day or two. That's also why your biggest spends for paid media come in the last month and week of the campaign. Sooner than that, and nobody cares because they have other things to think about.

- *Significance:* What is the size and scope of the news story? How many people does it affect and how much does it affect them? Because the media are dependent on clicks and ratings, they want something that has the largest and most profound effect on the greatest number of people. They are often looking for something that stirs controversy or conflict, or upends the preconceived notions of as many people as it can. If you are talking about something that only affects a few people who are already in the know, then you aren't going to get the coverage that you're looking for. Try and think of angles that make your news story relevant to larger groups of people in a dramatic way or that make people rethink how they feel about something. Controversy in a campaign isn't always bad. Because the campaign was (for all intents and purposes) broke, the recent Trump campaign was dependent on controversy to stay in the earned media market. They worked hard to find more controversial things for Donald Trump to say. A library campaign probably shouldn't follow this model casually, but one library campaign did when they threatened to burn all the books if the campaign didn't succeed.

- *Distance:* The closer a story is, the more the people will care about it. The adage that all politics is local is very true, and it's true for news as well. This shouldn't be a surprise to you, and it shouldn't be a problem in your campaign because your campaign is local. If your library serves a small population and is a long distance away from the biggest major news source, this could pose a problem if you're trying to get your story in those papers. Instead, focus on what's local in media outlets that serve the local population.

- *Human interest:* Libraries have an opportunity to excel at human interest stories. These stories are the ones that appeal most to the emotions. They typically evoke positive emotional responses like joy or empathy. The benefit of these stories is that they often have a longer time line and they don't necessarily need to directly affect a large group of people, although the emotions of the story of just a few people will tend to captivate the emotions of larger groups of people. For example, there was a library that helped a young child who was born without a hand to print one on a 3-D printer. The news didn't hit the market until months later and it only affected a few people. But many people were moved by the story. These are great stories for your library and your campaign to collect to tell on the campaign trail.

* * *

"A VOTE AGAINST THE LIBRARY IS LIKE A VOTE TO BURN BOOKS"

The Troy, Michigan, public library was set to close in June 2011 following two unsuccessful votes in February and November 2010 that would have stabilized funding for the library. When polled, the citizens of Troy overwhelmingly said they were willing to increase their taxes to fund the library, but voter turnout in both elections was very low and was dominated by an antitax group called "Troy Citizens United." This antitax group regularly mobilized voters against any tax on the ballot, including ones for the library. With the fate of the library in the balance, in May the city council provided a small amount of funding that would carry the library until the next regularly scheduled Election Day on August 2, when a .7 mill five-year levy would be on the ballot.

The campaign to save the Troy library at the ballot box then became unlike any other we've seen. When the folks from Troy Citizens United came out publicly to again oppose the millage on antitax grounds, they were joined in their opposition by a new committee called "Safeguarding American Families." This committee's position was that they wanted the vote to fail so they could throw a book-burning party when the library closed. And they took their book-burning party plans to front lawns, the news, and social media around town. Their campaign went viral nationwide immediately.

Safeguarding American Families printed yard signs that said: "Vote to close Troy library Aug. 2nd, Book burning party Aug 5th." When the signs were taken down or torn up, they replaced them with new ones. They placed an ad in the local newspaper looking to hire entertainment for their book-burning party. Their Facebook page was called "Book Burning Party" and their Twitter account pushed the hashtag "#BookBurningParty" hard. Folks in town were outraged and the library reeled. The image of a book-burning party in town galvanized the voters, the media, and town leaders.

Mercifully, the book-burning campaign was a deliberate campaign to catch people's attention and not the platform of a legitimate group in town. Right before the August vote, Safeguarding American Families unveiled its final message: "A vote against the library is like a vote to burn books." The "Safeguarding American Families" committee was the brainchild of Leo Burnett, a national advertising firm with offices in Troy. They said their goal was to change the conversation from taxes to libraries. Their tactics succeeded when voters woke up and turned out. The mill levy passed with 58 percent of the ballot. The entire $3,500 budget was donated and Leo Burnett won advertising industry awards for the campaign. Given the amount of coverage the campaign received nationally, it may be hard to pull off a book-burning theme again for any library. Some people have labeled the whole campaign a hoax, but it was really the best kind of earned media. It changed minds and influenced voter behavior by changing and dominating the conversation across multiple media channels.

Leo Burnett produced a recap video at https://vimeo.com/35758683 that tells the story.   ✪

WRITING A PRESS RELEASE

Typically, a campaign announces information to the media in the form of a press release. These are great opportunities to educate and assist reporters in writing a story for them. You are taking the time to provide the materials for the reporter and, in fact, often the reporters will simply copy and paste directly from the press release into their news article or into the script for their news reporters or radio personalities to read on air. However, writing a good press release takes a little practice.

Just like any campaign message, your press releases should be clear, consistent, and concise. They should rarely exceed one page and should be well checked for typos, punctuation, and grammar. Be quick to get to the point of the article with a lead in the first sentence or paragraph that sets up the rest of the story. Even if your campaign is writing quickly during a time of crisis, take the few extra minutes to edit the release to ensure that it is easily read and used by reporters. A word lost here and there could significantly change a story to one you don't want to tell, so check it after you think it's been checked well. Have a good number of quotes throughout the release from reputable sources that the media can contact for follow-up and confirmation. A captivating or intriguing title for the release will help ensure that the reporter uses a title that is good for your campaign. Make their job easier and you can get the results you want. While it is falling out of fashion in some areas, you can end your press release with a series of hashmarks such ### in order to signify the end of the release.

LETTERS TO THE EDITOR AND GUEST COLUMNS

Letters to the editor (LTEs) are a great way for your campaign to get into the news cycles. These letters are primarily a print media tool. Even if the newspaper has gone online, they still usually post letters to the editor. Another one of the things that your campaign can do is have your volunteers spend time writing and submitting editorials after canvassing or phone banking events. Volunteers can work together to write a letter and have one person submit it. Some newspapers allow for longer letters to be posted as "guest columns" or editorials. It is important to talk with your local media outlets about how they would like to receive letters or editorial submissions as well as their own publication schedule. Your campaign team needs to know the process to put it to work in your earned media strategy.

To do this kind of earned media right, your campaign needs an internal process that identifies willing and capable volunteers to write, submit, and monitor letters to the editor and guest opinion columns. You will likely have volunteers who are not interested in doing door-to-door or phone work but who are good writers. Put them to work early in the campaign brainstorming topics for letters to the editor and guest columns. Topics should cover a wide range of community needs that the library ballot measure will address like early childhood, school partnerships, business development, livable communities, property values, senior services, special or unique collections, civic pride, and responsible taxes. Your LTE team can identify people within the committee to write the letters as well as people from the broader community whose name on a letter or guest column would get some notice. One way people can support the library campaign is by agreeing to sign a letter or byline a column. If your committee can help them write it, that will enable them to stay on message.

Pro-campaign LTEs should be part of your regular marketing schedule. We recommend pre-writing enough unique letters to submit one per week per news outlet in the three months before your Election Day. If you have a committee volunteer who is responsible for managing the writing and submission of LTEs and guest columns, it always works better. Your campaign should also designate someone to review local LTEs for anti-library and antitax sentiments. It depends on the town, but we always encourage our campaigns to actively answer negative letters to the editor with pro-library letters of their own. One truth about local politics is that in the absence of a response, the readers have no reason to assume that what was written isn't true. We discuss more about responding to the opposition in chapter 13.

Quick Tips for Writing Letters to the Editor

In a letter to the editor, talk about who the writer is. Use phrases like "I moved here because . . . ," "I have been a resident for 20 years . . . ," "I am a member of (a group) . . ." or "I am a parent of. . . ." Identify why the library is important and valuable to the whole community and then highlight how it is used by a specific group to solve a problem. The LTE can address issues like civic pride, but focusing on a concrete reason for voting yes makes a better letter. End the letter with an invitation to join the writer—and the majority of the community—in voting for the library. Be sure to include the specific date of the election and the name or number of the ballot question.

Earned media are a great way to get your campaign messages out into the community. Even though earned media are a low-cost way to get your messages out, they aren't free. It costs your campaign time to plan and release stories to the reporters as well as the time it takes to conduct interviews and show up for media events. It also take volunteers away from doing other business of the campaign like fund-raising or voter contact. If your campaign is short on time and short on people, then it may consider running paid ads in the community to put the campaign message in front of the public.

NOTES

1. Mary Harris, "A Media Post-Mortem on the 2016 Presidential Election—MediaQuant," MediaQuant, November 14, 2016, www.mediaquant.net/2016/11/a-media-post-mortem-on-the-2016-presidential-election/.

2. Amy Mitchell and Jesse Holcomb, "State of the News Media 2016," Pew Research Center's Journalism Project, June 15, 2016, www.journalism.org/2016/06/15/state-of-the-news-media-2016/.

3. Clare Foran, "Hillary Clinton's Appearance on Between Two Ferns Wasn't Brave," *The Atlantic*, September 23, 2016, www.theatlantic.com/politics/archive/2016/09/hillary-clinton-between-two-ferns-zach-galifianakis/501383/.

4. "What Makes a Story Newsworthy?" What Makes a Story Newsworthy? www.mediacollege.com/journalism/news/newsworthy.html.

CHAPTER FIFTEEN

Paid Media

P AID MEDIA CAN BE EXPENSIVE FOR A CAMPAIGN, BUT IF they are used properly they can be very effective at getting your message out to new audiences. In order to have effective ads that use your campaign's funds wisely, you have to take the time to do careful planning and research into your media market. There are professionals who can run your advertising campaign for you and while it is true that professional-level services are an added cost, these professionals can also negotiate lower spends with companies and help you determine where your money will be best spent. Some can even help you create your content so you don't have to create content yourself. This is another money vs. time tradeoff for your campaign. You'll have to make the decision about which you want to spend on your paid media.

Of course, your campaign does not have unlimited funds, but if it did you would pay for ads across all forms of paid media in your community. Paid media can come in many different forms such as billboards, radio and television ads, online ads (as we discuss in the chapter on Facebook), magazine and newspaper ads, and many more. Each one has its own benefits and its own drawbacks. There are different audiences for each kind of media and people respond differently to each one. Making decisions about who you want to reach, why you want to speak to them, and how to best do it is part of your campaign's paid media plan, which needs to be developed before you start paying for ads.

OBJECTIVES

Just like any other plan, it's important to understand what you are trying to achieve. You are going to want to set goals for your media buys and understand what you get in return. Typically this means setting a goal for how many voters you want to reach throughout the campaign. If you want to try to reach each voter 7–10 times throughout the campaign, then you need to understand how to measure those metrics. When you purchase media they are usually measured in CPMs (cost per thousand impressions) or GRPs (the sum total of the ratings achieved for a media schedule). You want to make sure that you get the most out of each with the least costly spend. Setting an objective can help you with that.

If there are 1,000 people in your community and you want to reach them 7 times throughout the campaign, then that is 7,000 impressions or 7 CPMs. When you are purchasing your media buys, the number of impressions should be your goal. If you are working with a professional, they can help you correctly size your media buys so you don't over- or underspend. A good professional understands some of the confusing language in buying media. For example, if you aren't working with a professional, then you should understand that if you are buying GRPs and you want everyone to see a television ad 7 times, then you need to purchase 700 GRPs since the general rule of thumb is that 100 GRPs means the average TV viewer will see a commercial once. Of course, this also means that heavy television watchers will see the ads more often than people who don't watch much television. In any case, understand that you should have everyone in your community see an ad seven times throughout the last month of the campaign and make that number your objective in your paid media plan.

AUDIENCES

Of course, with any message, it's not going to be effective for all demographics and you should tailor each message to your ad audiences. For example, putting an ad about the great social services offered by libraries on a conservative talk radio show might not suit your campaign goals. Take some time and think about what kinds of people watch or listen or read the various outlets that you are going to be placing these ads in and then tailor messages to them. Most of the time a good marketing professional can help you make these decisions.

Be careful with these professionals since they might be coming in with out-of-date views about libraries. Our coauthor Patrick once tried to purchase outdoor ads on billboards through Comcast and the specialist Patrick was working with refused to let him put ads on anything but bus terminals, since he believed that only poor people used libraries. The messages Patrick was creating weren't directed at low-income communities, but at building support in the high-income communities. Patrick wasn't looking to grow library users, but was looking to grow the number of library supporters. Those are very different things in a campaign. Because he couldn't buy the media that he wanted, Patrick wound up having to drop the whole project.

BUDGETS

If you don't have a budget, you don't have a paid media campaign. You need to make the decisions about what you want to spend on paid media before you start contacting professional marketers or before you contact advertising firms to run your campaign. A lot of times, they will help you adjust your budget, but they won't talk to you unless you have some budget ideas in mind. For example, when we purchased podcast ads for EveryLibrary through Midroll, we simply gave them a budget and our objective and they were able to create a campaign for us that would reach the right audiences the right number of times. If you contact a newspaper or television station, they can tell you a lot of the same things but they won't be able to make any decisions without a known budget.

PAID MEDIA PLACEMENT

There are many different markets for your messages, and understanding each one will help you make decisions about them. The following list is some of the more traditional media placements that your campaign can purchase and some general information about each one. However, this list is not meant to be comprehensive.

NEWSPAPERS

Many people are lamenting the loss of the newspaper. In our experience there are large segments of the population that still rely on newspapers for their daily information in many of the towns and cities that we have worked with. You can often find newspapers in coffee shops and waiting rooms in almost every city, and there are still many Americans who read their paper over coffee in the morning. The real benefit of newspapers is that they are fairly targeted and know their audiences. They can place ads on fairly short notice with a quick turnaround. You can also place ads of varying sizes throughout the paper. Know going in that you are competing for space and attention against a large number of other advertisements. Of course, unless they are a weekly paper your ads will have a short life span. This can be okay if you are addressing an issue quickly in your campaign. Likewise, if your Election Day is a crowded ballot, ad space may book up early. Plan your buys in advance with your newspapers' sales reps. You don't want to be priced out of your own market by waiting too long.

MAGAZINES

Ads in magazines, unlike newspapers, have advantages like a much longer life span but do come with their own disadvantages. The big advantages are that magazines tend to have a much more specific audience than newspapers and the printing is done in a much higher quality. But since most magazines have a national circulation and a higher cost for ads, you will be spending a lot of money to reach people who simply can't vote in your local election. The exceptions to this are some of the local magazines around broader subjects like parenting or local attractions. You also won't be able to get a quick turnaround in a magazine, since they tend to go to print a month or so before they are released to newsstands. Unless you have a really strong local magazine, we don't recommend paying for ads in magazines very often.

DIGITAL PLACEMENTS AND SOCIAL MEDIA

There is a wide range of digital media platforms that your campaign can use to place ads in front of voters and that are extremely precise in their placement, but they are not always useful unless done well and on the right platforms. There is also the added inconvenience of rapidly changing platforms, tools, and functions. Even though there are these drawbacks, it is extremely important to have a robust paid digital campaign. It's so important that we have dedicated chapters specifically to e-mail (chapter 21) and Facebook (chapter 22). But what about the other platforms?

Using other digital platforms for campaigns can be highly effective if done correctly. We do believe that e-mail and Facebook are the two most important ones, but that is due to the current prominence of Facebook. If you have a community with a large Twitter, LinkedIn, or Instagram population, then you might consider running ads on those sites. Online video is a great medium because it allows for visual aids as well as strong and appealing emotional pleas. There is a lot of potential for creative content that drives home the messages of the campaign.

RADIO

Radio can be a great place to put persuasion ads, but it is difficult to use for immediate call-to-action ads. Most listeners are driving or taking part in some other activity while they are listening to the radio, so if you want them to sign a pledge or petition for the campaign it can be difficult. The great thing about radio is that you can make changes fairly quickly by just sending them an updated recorded ad or an updated script. Short, targeted radio ads are attainable for even the smallest campaigns we work with. Because like-minded people tend to listen to specific stations, your ads about the benefits of the library can be targeted to their slice of the community. You can even reach listeners who speak languages other than English fairly easily in some markets. Those stations are experienced in translating their customers' ads into their own languages.

TELEVISION

The fact remains that television is one of the largest media vehicles in the country. The average adult watches more than five hours of television every day. This is great news for national library campaigns, but anything local is going to be a little more limited unless there is a local television station. This is because television broadcast ads often span a geographic area that is much larger than the local voting population for a library campaign, and any paid ad that reaches a nonvoter is just wasted money. This problem is compounded for small campaigns because television ads can also be very expensive and waste more resources. Whereas, in larger campaigns with a good local station, a well put together television ad can generate a lot of attention for the campaign.

OUTDOOR AND ENVIRONMENTAL ADS

There are many different opportunities for outdoor advertising besides the billboards and bus stations that we previously mentioned. You can find outdoor advertising on subways, taxis, trains, and buses. You often run across outside advertising on cafe table tops, front windows, yard signs, bumper stickers, and much more. We have seen campaigns put ads on everything from coasters in bars to the mats on the trays at McDonald's or attached to pizza boxes the week before Election Day. The best thing about these types of ads is that with some of these ad placements, people spend longer lengths of time with them than they do with TV, radio, or print. A well-done environmental ad can leave an impression on a viewer because there is, essentially, no way to escape it.

However, across all outdoor ad placements, the ad impression length is fairly short and averages around 2–3 seconds. This is especially true of billboards. This means that whatever is on the billboard has to be quick and to the point. Traditional billboards require a longer lead time to design and produce an outdoor ad, and get onto their display schedule. New all-digital billboards have very quick turnaround times for design and placement. In fact, new media companies like Blip Billboards are springing up around the country to compete with established outdoor advertisers to allow people to buy ad time on their digital billboard inventory with same-day turnaround and for very short increments of time. The biggest drawback with outdoor advertising for a campaign is that building audiences for the messages is a little more difficult since such a wide range of people see them. However, you can do a few things to anticipate this, such as placing ads about the business benefits of libraries in the local business district or benefits to the community's children and families on billboards near schools, playgrounds, or parks. For outdoor ads, the audience is almost always based on geography.

DIRECT MAIL

The decision to use direct mail can be one of the toughest in a campaign. There is often a great amount of pressure to use it from consultants and campaign managers. Profit margins for the direct mail industry are exceptionally high and therefore the direct mail industry itself pushes direct mail on political campaigns as a solution to mass messaging. In fact, while there are some benefits to a well-run direct mail campaign, we often warn against it for most local campaigns for many reasons. This is primarily because understanding a direct mail campaign well enough to implement it is a tough proposition. The library industry is inexperienced in using direct mail as effectively as it could. Doing direct mail correctly in a political campaign for libraries is difficult at best and is impossible and a waste of money at worst.

Our lukewarm opinion of direct mail may be the most highly controversial view in this book. Direct mail is one of the most accepted and widely embraced tactics in political campaigns. In our view, a library campaign should first allocate its limited resources to social media advertising and focus its time and energy on direct voter engagement techniques like door-to-door canvassing and phone banking that produce better results on a per-contact basis. For those campaigns evaluating a recommendation to use direct mail heavily in their GOTV efforts, we will talk about when and where it works, and when and where the campaign should be cautious about using it.

WHEN AND WHERE TO BE CAUTIOUS

The cost of direct mail is extremely high on a per-impression basis. We have seen campaigns where the consultant or campaign manager fees are half of the campaign budget and the other half is the cost of the direct mail. Each piece of direct mail can cost a campaign around $1.25–1.50 to print and mail. This price is often increased if done through a consultant who typically makes a margin off each piece of mail that the campaign sends. If your campaign has a consultant who is pushing for multiple pieces of mail and is requiring you to do it through his company, we recommend that you have a discussion with him about up-front versus hidden fees. The only reason to invest heavily in direct mail is for the benefit of the campaign.

As we've stated throughout this book, there is no message about libraries that resonates with all voters. This means that if you don't know who you're talking to, then you don't know what to say. In the case of direct mail, campaigns often send a blanket piece of mail to all the voters in their district, town, or precinct. This kind of blanket messaging almost never convinces enough readers to take action. The amount of work of either gathering your voter data or paying for the data to make it effective also increases its cost.

Direct mail has a very high read rate, but a very low action rate. You will often hear from consultants who talk about how much they love direct mail because so many people read it. While this is true, your campaign doesn't just need people to read your mail, it needs people to be persuaded or have their minds changed or be convinced to show up at the polls to vote for your library. There is a dramatic drop-off between the number of people who read direct mail and the people who are persuaded to show up to vote in favor of the library because of it. In fact, most of the research about direct mail shows that the number of people who made decisions based on direct mail is less than 2 percent.[1]

WHEN AND WHERE TO USE IT

There are ways to use direct mail effectively in a campaign. While we are very cautious about the use of direct mail, it is never something that we completely write off, either. It should be used sparingly, only where necessary, and with the right data and message to make it effective. If you have those things, you can increase the effectiveness of the tactic.

You should always try to reduce the costs of direct mail. Don't feel obligated to accept your consultant's price, and feel free to spend some time shopping around for any cheaper printers. You might be able to find a local printer who is supportive of the library campaign, and where you can negotiate costs you can find some more savings. If you can save just $100 on direct mail, you can reach 10,000 people on Facebook or pay for pizza and beer for 10 volunteers who are doing phone banking for the weekend.

Direct mail should be part of a larger voter contact plan. If the first time that people hear about your campaign is through the piece of direct mail, then there will be no return on investment for your direct mail campaign. The money would have been better spent on ongoing persuasion tactics over a few weeks. But if you use direct mail to voters who you know have been touched multiple times throughout the campaign, then you will get a higher yield of voters.

Sometimes the local geography makes direct mail necessary. There are some turfs that are just unwalkable or uncallable due to the lack of connectivity, the distance between houses, rugged or rural terrain, or a high density of gated condos or apartments that the volunteers can't canvass. In these kinds of areas direct mail is a necessary tactic for voter contact.

If your campaign has great data, then direct mail can be used to the best of its ability. The great thing about direct mail is that you can highly target voters with specific messages that only they care about without contacting the ones who don't care about that message. This can be a difficult thing to do right. However, if you know that a household is home to middle-class liberal parents with primary school-age children, then you can craft a message that caters to them about the future of their children.

Direct mail is the most effective when it is highly emotional. That's why your opposition has an advantage in direct mail. They can send out an antitax, antigovernment, or fear-based piece of mail and hurt your campaign. The truth is that voters respond to highly emotional, negative or attack messages through direct mail at a higher rate than persuasive, factual, and level-headed messages in the mail.

The absolutely most effective way to use direct mail is to use your volunteers to help. If you have a large corps of volunteers, they should check the voter files for people that they know. Your campaign should order some informational postcards about the campaign and then your volunteers will come together the weekend before the election and write personalized messages to each of their friends, family, and colleagues urging them to vote yes for the library. These kinds of personalized notes from familiar and friendly names have the most potential to engage and persuade voters. It isn't automated, but because it is personal it elevates direct mail to a whole new level.

NOTE

1. Sasha Issenberg, *The Victory Lab: The Secret Science of Winning Campaigns* (New York: Crown, 2012).

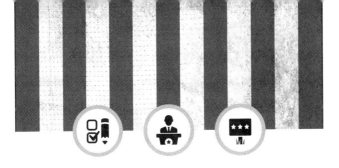

CHAPTER SIXTEEN

Voter Data

S INCE PRESIDENT BARACK OBAMA WON THE PRESIDENCY in 2008 with a data-driven rather than hunch-driven voter engagement campaign, we have seen a dramatic shift in the way that political campaigns use data to win. In fact, we have seen political data become big business in politics, with hundreds of data firms rolling out various combinations of data sets that try to tie consumer behavior, social media, demographic data, and more together to try to predict voter behavior. This voter/consumer data is as deep as it is wide, and when attached to "enhance" voter files, it has the potential to be the defining factor between a win and a loss in many elections.

In the same way that it's used on the national scale or in big state contests, this voter/consumer data can be bought and used to win local library elections. This data can be used extremely effectively in campaigns facing opposition since, in almost all cases, the individuals and groups who oppose library tax measures are only rarely well funded or highly organized. They are typically a loose cadre of individuals, and the library campaign's access to funding and strong organization coupled with good data is what wins elections in the face of most opposition. Even in campaigns where state, regional, or national antitax or antigovernment groups are anticipated to come out against the library ballot measure, having and using your better voter data earlier in the campaign can inoculate you against late messaging from the opposition. If you reach voters first and communicate with them with an understanding of what their own interests are, you can commit them to your measure. Opposition won't bump them off.

OVERVIEW

All of the commercially available enhanced voter data sets start with the same basic information. Each local election authority, usually a county clerk of elections, maintains a list of registered voters for that jurisdiction. The enhanced voter files all start with that publicly available voter file and build new data enhancements around each individual voter. The basic voter data from your local clerk of elections will include the voter's name, address, and occasionally a phone number, the voter's history of when they registered, and if they cast a ballot or not in each election going back to that registration date. In states where party registration, age, gender, alternate address, and now e-mail address are collected, this will also appear on the basic voter file. Then firms attach other openly available information like census records, home value, consumer information, and languages spoken in the household to each voter record. By attaching consumer data to each voter, the same kind that's used in big business, data companies can paint a broad picture of a voter that includes spending habits, income, donation habits, home ownership, and even what kinds of magazines they subscribe to. Most recently, there are large companies like Acxiom that can attach social media accounts to individual voters just through their name and address to find out what kinds of interests or "likes" each voter has.

These kinds of voter files are commonly referred to as "enhanced voter files." Enhanced voter files are not what you get from your board of elections. While you may feel that the basic voter file will work for your campaign, we encourage all our campaigns to purchase or otherwise acquire enhanced voter files. We believe that library campaigns need more data for targeting voters because libraries have so many different aspects of service to consider. Better voter data will help you make decisions about strategies so you can spend your money more effectively. In larger campaigns, the campaign should spend the extra money on these enhanced voter files and some kind of data management system in order to help save money during the campaign.

Lastly, these enhanced voter files are useless unless there is some understanding about the voter behaviors of the various demographics. That's why there are many companies that conduct political polling. These companies are trying to make sense of the data and create models so that all of this data becomes meaningful and useful in order to better target messages and direct campaign strategies.[1]

By using all of this data, the campaign leadership can help set strategies and tactics that specifically target individuals with the best possible message to activate them to vote for their candidate or cause. This information can guide campaigns to make decisions about when and where each tactic or message should be deployed for optimum effectiveness, how many people in each data set need to be contacted, and how many times they should be "touched" to have the message resonate with them. People who are further away in ideology from the cause or candidate would need to have more campaign resources, and different campaign resources, spent on them in order to persuade them than people who are already likely to agree with the candidate or cause, for example. By understanding the audiences of different TV networks or shows or various print media, a campaign can connect the right message with the right audience for maximum effectiveness. A strong data team can also educate the campaign about who should get direct mail and who should get an in-person visit or a phone call.

This kind of work has become a multimillion dollar business for third-party organizations. These political shops are the ones that feed the data to the Republican National Committee (RNC) and the Democratic National Committee (DNC), organizations that have spent millions to develop extensive databases of essentially every American voter. However, we have also seen the Koch Brothers–funded PAC, Americans for Prosperity, build one of the biggest private political data platforms rivaling, and in some ways surpassing, those of the DNC and RNC. This voter data advantage is especially startling considering the AFP is the only well-established national organization in the country that has funded fights against libraries in places like Illinois and Kansas. Even though we have seen the Tea Party come out against libraries in a number of campaigns, they are not yet as well organized, nor do they yet have the data to fight against libraries in a more organized way.

The creation of library-centric voter data is one of the primary activities that EveryLibrary is taking to help libraries win elections. As an industry, libraries need to stay ahead of these kinds of trends and build data sets that will help bring down the cost of library campaigns and can be readily used in a campaign to create better strategies and tactics. EveryLibrary is currently building the nation's largest database of library supporters. We are working on national polling and we are positioning the organization as the national clearinghouse on data for library elections. There is still a lot of work to be done. We always encourage campaigns to return IDed voter files to us, or send us their polling results so that we can add that information to our national database. ✪

DATA FOR LIBRARY CAMPAIGNS

There are many options to source data sets in a campaign. The costs vary based on the depth and scope of data that you want, but all of your data should start with getting an enhanced voter file. Much of the enhanced voter data is available at a reasonable price through companies that sell the data. When you're looking for a company to purchase the data from, it is sometimes easier to get it from companies that primarily work with progressive (or liberal) causes. Even though conservatives support libraries fairly well, the progressive-focused firms appear to have better voter data at more reasonable prices. We won't recommend a specific vendor for enhanced voter files here because they are changing so rapidly. If someone on your campaign has a close association with the local Republican or Democratic organizations or leading politicians, there is no prohibition against the library campaign team asking for voter data. There may be a local consideration, however, if the campaign is perceived as overly partisan (though in some communities it works the other way).

If you have taken our advice about campaign management software and are using platforms like NationBuilder or EveryAction, you can almost always get the voter file put directly into your database for free, and in a way that works best with those platforms. Then you can simply purchase data add-ons from the approved third-party vendors that work with those platforms and all of the data gets automatically put into your database correctly.

There are companies that offer voter files that rank voters by their likelihood to support various "causes." While there are no national studies for library issues or the likelihood of supporting library issues (yet), there are many others that can help guide your messaging. For example, the company L2 provides enhanced voter files that are also enhanced with data from a company called Haystack DNA that ranks voters on a scale of 1–100 by their likelihood to support things like education, affordable housing, right to work, and so on. So, by knowing that a voter supports education, you can direct messages to them that reinforce the idea that libraries are education hubs, for example.

If your only option is to get the voter file from your local board of elections, please know that it will not come formatted for any platform. Any work to add consumer enhancements to your voter file will have to be done by you by hand on Excel or other similar data management tools. A properly filed library campaign committee has a right to purchase voter data for its jurisdiction. Some clerks will still want to deliver the file on paper. We highly recommend paying for at least an Excel sheet. But in some communities where the library ballot measure is contentious, we've seen clerks slow down or otherwise obstruct committee access to the data. They know how powerful it is for the campaign to know its voters. Don't let anyone stand in your campaign's way.

No matter how you get the enhanced voter files, they need to contain a few key pieces of information in order to be especially useful for a library campaign.

- *Name and addresses of the voters:* This information comes in all voter files, but it needs some assurance of accuracy, so try looking for your own name or the names of a number of your friends and family and check their addresses to make sure it's accurate. One of the most effective ways to check its accuracy is to look for the names and addresses of deceased residents. Often, this information takes a while to make it to the voter file, so it's one of the first things you can check to see how up-to-date the file is. In any case, the name and address are always by far the most accurate and consistent information in a voter file.

- *Party affiliation:* Depending on state laws, voter files from the board of elections may come with party affiliations. Because different messages resonate with different party affiliations, it is often helpful to know what party voters belong to. People with progressive-leaning affiliations may be more influenced by social good messages and people with conservative-leaning affiliations may be more influenced by messages around self-determination. If someone is registered as a Tea Party or other third-party conservative, you might, for example, want to consider messaging them about the kinds of freedoms and self-determination that libraries offer citizens.

- *Phone number:* Many times a voter file from the board of elections comes with voters' phone numbers. However, these numbers are notoriously inaccurate because the clerk has no obligation to update them. Not only have people moved away from landlines and over to cell phones, but people's cell phone numbers change with some frequency. One of the things you want to make sure of when you purchase an enhanced voter file is improved accuracy of phone numbers. When you are doing your phone banking these accurate numbers are going to be very important.

- *Voting history:* One of the most important data points is the voting history of everyone in the file. While no public record of "how" anyone voted is in the file, there is a record of "if" they voted in each election included in the file. Based on their frequency of voting, your campaign can start to distinguish between who to target first and where to spend the most funds. That's because the community members who consistently vote in every election are the ones who your campaign targets first. They will vote in your election, and you need to inform and persuade them. After that, your campaign should target the people with a history of voting in similar election cycles as the one your library's campaign is in. For example, if someone only votes in a presidential election, and your campaign is for a special election, you might consider saving resources by not contacting them since they are unlikely to come out and vote in a special election. The voter history can also include "flags" for voter ballot preferences like "permanent vote by mail" or "absentee last election." We'll discuss the impact of these voter preferences on your campaign strategy in more detail below.

- *Household income and consumer data:* Many commercially available enhanced voter files include consumer data, and there is a strong debate in the political science field about whether or not knowing that someone bought a Subaru or lives in a $300,000 house has any effect on their voting behavior. However, we believe that you can target voters based on their consumer behavior if you are targeting specific messages that are tailored to their behavior. If you know that someone subscribes to a craft beer magazine, for example, and your library has beer-making demonstrations, you might let them know about that. Whether or not that has a significant impact on their voting behavior, as we said, is still up for debate.

- *Family life:* Because libraries are typically branded as family-friendly destinations and because parents are one of the strongest demographics who demonstrate strong support for libraries, knowing if there are children in the household can dramatically affect their voting behavior. The campaign manager in Kern County developed specifically targeted direct mail to households with families that talked about better futures for the community's children, with strong results.

- *Age:* Knowing a voter's age can be useful to build messages or strategies that better target those demographics. In many communities, older voters don't use Facebook or e-mail as often as an information source but are more likely to have landlines and answer their phones or answer their doors. Younger voters might be more likely to respond to text messages from the campaign and rely on Facebook more heavily.

WHEN IS IT ELECTION DAY FOR A VOTER?

The landscape of exactly when Election Day is for each of your voters is changing rapidly.[2] While your library could be on the ballot the first Tuesday of November, in many states and for a lot of voters that day is becoming more like Tabulation Day than Election Day. As of this writing, only three states offer 100 percent "vote by mail" (Colorado, Oregon, Washington) for all elections. If you are in those states, "Election Day" for any given voter is the day they decide to fill in their ballot and drop it off or mail it in. That can be anytime within the statutory window for that election. Seventeen additional states offer 100 percent vote by mail on certain types of elections. This count will change after the 2016 election cycle. This means that how the vote was conducted for your last local or federal election may not be the way the vote will be done in this election. It is vitally important to know and understand the process of casting a ballot for your specific Election Day very early, and to plan your voter ID and get-out-the-vote efforts accordingly.

Thirty-three additional states offer some time of early voting that is either conducted in person or by mail, and is either on an election-by-election choice of the voters or through a voter request to become a permanent vote-by-mail voter. Even in the thirteen states that do not permit "at will" early voting and require voters to request absentee ballots with an "excuse" (Alabama, Connecticut, Delaware, Kentucky, Michigan, Mississippi, Missouri, New Hampshire, New York, Pennsylvania, Rhode Island, South Carolina, Virginia), the number of voters requesting those ballots is on the rise. The shift to early voting or to permanent absentee mail-in ballots is only beginning to be understood by even the major political campaigns. For library campaigns, it means supporting a longer, more engaged, more robust GOTV effort. In many vote-by-mail states, clerks of election are required to offer daily updates of the voter file that show who has and has not yet returned a ballot "as of yesterday." Your campaign should subscribe to these daily voter file updates in order to know who on your list of pre-identified favorable voters still needs to vote, and who you can now stop contacting because they have already voted.

While there is more data work to do each day, "chasing the ballots" like this saves you from wasting volunteer time on door-to-door and phone work. Even a last direct-mail postcard can be better targeted by knowing who has already voted. If your state does not require clerks to proactively disclose the early-voting daily voter file, they still maintain it for inspection. Even the smallest campaign that may not have the resources to chase the ballots still needs to review and understand the absentee flags in the voter file and plan on engaging those voters well ahead of when ballots are made available. You do not want absentee voters to be unaware of the library issue when they vote.

KEEP IT FRESH

Even the best voter data is only good the day you acquire it or purchase it. It starts to get stale immediately. A local campaign like yours isn't as concerned as a national or statewide campaign about folks moving or dying, but you should be as concerned as they are with keeping your voter file up-to-date. Anytime a volunteer or campaign team member contacts any voter, the nature of the contact and what was learned about the voter's attitude and beliefs needs to be recorded and updated in the database. We discuss community organizing systems in detail in chapter 18, but even if you are still using 3 × 5 cards to track each voter contact, you and your volunteer team need to update each voter record with every touch or action. The goal for how you use your voter files is to know what enough of your voters think and how they will vote before the polls open. Having that insight builds confidence among your team if you are ahead, and acts to clarify everyone's focus if you are behind going into Election Day for your library.

NOTES

1. "American Economic Association," https://www.aeaweb.org/articles?id=10.1257/jep.28.2.51.
2. "Absentee and Early Voting," National Conference of State Legislatures, October 25, 2016, www.ncsl.org/research/elections-and-campaigns/absentee-and-early-voting.aspx.

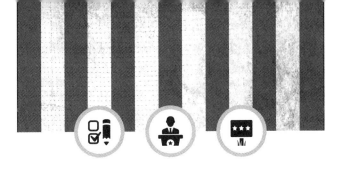

CHAPTER SEVENTEEN

Polling

W E RECOMMEND POLLING BEFORE EVERY CAMPAIGN. Your polling data will let you know if you should even spend the time and money running a campaign. We have occasionally seen a library poll so low that they need to spend a year or two building trust with the community, improving their surfacing strategy, and resetting public opinion before re-polling and considering a run. If you are polling 5 percentage points below what you need to win an election, you are going to have to fight hard to win that election. Typically a campaign can have a decent chance of winning within 2–3 percent of the needed votes. However, you should realize that the more your library measure is below the threshold for winning an election, the more resources it will take to win, and the harder you and your campaign committee will have to work for the win. On the other hand, we often see libraries polling far above the needed win number. In those elections, it is yours to lose by making mistakes, not thinking you have to campaign, or not taking some new opposition seriously. No matter what your polling results are, you will have to work for a win.

WHY POLL?

By conducting a professional poll a campaign can find out about the public's perception of the library and which demographics most strongly support the library, as well as learn about why each demographic supports or opposes the library tax measure. In many cases your enhanced voter file isn't useful unless you know what that data means, and the way to find out what the data means is through a good poll. If your campaign doesn't know that parents in your community are the least likely to support a library tax because of their perceptions about a school tax, then targeting parents isn't going to help your campaign. However, you simply won't know that if you don't do polling. We have seen campaigns lose because they didn't do polling and had incorrect preconceived notions about the public's perception of the library. Based on a hunch instead of on data, they went on to spend limited campaign funds on messages that didn't resonate with voters or wasn't targeted to the right voters. If your campaign leadership team or the library's support organization conducts a poll before your campaign, then you can better understand how to use enhanced voter files to target messages more effectively.

WHAT IS A POLL?

Many Americans are familiar with the concept of public opinion polling. Essentially, these polls are a research survey that measures the public opinion of the community to be affected by the results of the local election. They are designed to provide insights into the ideas and beliefs of the local population by systematically questioning them and then extrapolating generalities with a narrow set of confidence levels. In the 2012 and 2016 presidential elections, Nate Silver's organization FiveThirtyEight rose to prominence in the national media by correctly calling the presidential elections by modeling a wide range of data, focus groups, polls, and surveys. FiveThirtyEight used multiple polls conducted by multiple firms to create a statistical model of voter attitudes and likely voter behaviors. But FiveThirtyEight wasn't a polling firm that created and fielded specific questions for specific campaigns.

HOW TO CONDUCT A POLL

In order to ensure the most accurate polling data, we always recommend working with a professional pollster. We never recommend that the campaign committee develop the poll on its own. Conducting a poll is a time-extensive process, and without some really good experience and expertise crafting questions and interpreting answers you can gather some very bad data. The library itself is not the organization that fields the political poll, either, because questions about voter attitudes are fundamentally about finding ways to persuade voters. Your campaign committee or a local 501c3 library support organization are the right types of organizations to put a political poll into the field.

FINDING A POLLSTER

We work with quite a few pollsters that we like to use and recommend to campaigns. We are hesitant to list our favorites in this book because polling companies can change pretty quickly. If you'd like more advice about hiring a pollster or want to know who we recommend, we'd love to talk to you about that. But, you can also do a fairly quick Google search and find many of the polling groups that are out there. Some of our recommendations for finding a pollster are as follows:

1. Make sure that they have a history of polling.
2. Request sample polls from other library campaigns.
3. Request a proposal to see what tools they use for polling.
4. Ask if they do verbatim polling (verbatim polling means they track everything the public says, word for word. Sometimes interesting information comes out here that is just good for the library to know, but it's not necessary).
5. Ask if they do phone, e-mail, and in-person polling (with focus groups). This often gets the best data set for larger campaigns. But some pollsters just do phone surveys and that can be okay as well, but not as complete.
6. Pollsters who have published their data in professional and peer-reviewed journals are often more accurate and respected.
7. Find a pollster who isn't necessarily biased in support of or in opposition to libraries.
8. Find a pollster who can show you plain English reports that anyone in your campaign can understand and interpret.

If at all possible, we recommend against automatically working with someone who works with your nearby local government(s) to conduct the poll. Close proximity to your town or city leadership can introduce some strange biases in the results of the poll. Since so much of your work will depend on the accurate outcomes of the data, the poll needs to be as accurate as possible. Finding an outside, objective polling firm is the first step in collecting actionable data.

WHAT TO ASK IN A POLL

In political polling, there are two kinds of polls: neutral ones and push polls. Neutral polling is done by academics, think tanks, and consultants or news organizations. Neutral polls follow reasonably rigorous methodologies to try and ascertain voter attitudes about candidates or issues. These polls are either snapshots of the electorate or tracked polls that can gauge changes in voter attitudes over time. Campaigns regularly hire professional pollsters to field these polls. Depending on the proctor, they are more or less unbiased polls. Key factors in determining the veracity of the results include disclosing the methodology for selecting and stratifying respondents, the method for fielding the poll (who asks the questions and through what channel), the timing relative to external events, and the relative bias in the questions themselves. A neutral political poll can be proactive about a candidate or issues, or it can look into how voters perceive their opponent or the other side of an issue. A well-built neutral poll is actionable for a candidate.

Then there are the "push polls." These polls are not intended to legitimately gauge voter attitudes but instead are designed to move a message or influence the perception among the recipients. Push polls are designed to field questions that first give information (which may or may not be fact-based) and then ask about attitudes. The results of the poll are often less important than the message being pushed by the campaign. In some cases, push polls are designed to introduce a candidate or concept to the electorate and are fielded as marketing instead of research. While one can question the ethics of political push polls, the efficacy of the technique is hard to ignore.

Library services are like the proverbial elephant that, when touched by a group of blindfolded individuals, yields surprisingly different perceptions of just exactly what is being touched. It is rather rare for library users, even power users, to access all of the programs, services, collections, and even facilities the library provides. The regulars at the children's department are not likely regulars for homebound delivery services. And while you may recoil at the thought that even your good users don't know the tail is attached to the trunk, nonusers haven't seen any part of the elephant since it was a baby.

We do not advocate that libraries adopt the "dark side" of push polling in their planning and assessment work, but certain techniques from both neutral and push polling can make sense when planning a tax measure and talking to nonusers. A well-built planning and assessment survey should include questions that take a page from push polls and include information about the breadth and depth of library work, and not just laundry lists of services. We believe that framing the question, especially to nonusers, can solicit more actionable results in the end.

Paul Harstad is a leading political pollster with a wide breadth of successful national, statewide, and local candidates who also does nonprofit and library polling. He has developed two key polling questions that can shine a bright light on the likelihood that voters will support the library on Election Day. The Harstad Questions ask people to express how willing they are to be taxed at a certain rate for the library. Then they are asked to consider cuts to the library's services in several categories as well as the impact of those cuts on library service populations. Finally, respondents are asked to rate how troubling each of these cutbacks is to them personally. It is very telling to find out not just what the voters' tolerance for a tax is, but also how compassionate they are for the populations that would be affected by cuts if the measure does not pass.

CHAPTER EIGHTEEN

Website and Digital Platforms

T IS IMPORTANT TO REMEMBER THAT YOUR CAMPAIGN WEBSITE is not what will win your campaign. A digital strategy is also not what will win your campaign. A campaign is won through hard work and multiple voter contacts. However, a strong digital presence can serve another purpose. It's more than likely that your library campaign won't have an office. But with a strong website combined with one of the political digital platforms, or by using many of the tools that are available online, your campaign will have an online central location to do the work it needs to do in order to contact voters to win the election.

The platforms that we are going to introduce you to were originally developed to help political campaigns win elections using connected "big data." Because they are so new, the platforms go by a few different names but are commonly called "community organizing systems" (COSs). Library campaigns should harness the power of these political platforms. COSs have become so ubiquitous that you probably have already interacted with a large number of them. If you signed a petition at Change.org, signed up to support any major party candidate, or donated to a cause you have interacted with these kinds of platforms. These kinds of platforms are used by national political parties, local candidates, and various social issues. When we talk about the voter-data systems being built by the Koch Brothers and how their independent platform is bigger than the two big parties' platforms, we are talking about these systems. The widespread use of COSs is what drives political messaging. It is also what activates the public to show up at the polls, sign petitions, write letters to the editor, volunteer, or give money.

We believe that your campaign should invest in a strong community organizing system. There are a large number of platforms that you can choose from. These include the progressive EveryAction, the conservative Red Stampede, the open source CivicCRM, and the turnkey resource NationBuilder. In no way is this a complete list, but they are a good cross-section of the kinds of platforms that are available to you. There are benefits and drawbacks to using each of these and while we aren't endorsing any one over the others, EveryLibrary uses NationBuilder for our political work. This is because we believe that libraries are a nonpartisan issue, so that eliminates partisan platforms like Red Stampede or EveryAction. We don't use CivicCRM because it requires some level of programming and technical knowledge to set it up for a campaign, and we understand that many campaigns don't have those resources. Because of this, NationBuilder is the one we will use as the example throughout this chapter.

We're not going to go into too much detail about the mechanics of using these platforms because they are changing so often. NationBuilder has very good training videos on Vimeo and YouTube that can help you learn about some of the latest features. EveryAction has fantastic customer service. So, instead we are going to include a discussion of the overall philosophies and some of the tools that are available to you through these platforms here.

VOTER FILE

The biggest strength of these platforms is the database behind them. For almost all of them, your campaign will receive the voter file for free from the company and it will be formatted specifically to the requirements of the platform. This voter file is the basis for all of your campaign work and needs to be as accurate and up-to-date as possible. By using these platforms, your voter file will be kept up-to-date for you, easily searchable, and quickly accessible. You can attach almost unlimited data to each voter profile such as tags, voting history, likelihood of voting yes or no, contact history, social media information (if you get their e-mail addresses), and any contact history. Your campaign can even buy enhanced data from third-party vendors that can incorporate everything like consumer data, more accurate phone numbers, voters' likeliness to support various causes, and a whole lot more.

OTHER WEBSITE PLATFORMS

There are quite a few other platforms that are easy to use to build a public-facing website, but they lack the capabilities that you will need to rally support and track voters across your voter universe. While we don't recommend it, if you are comfortable giving up many of these capabilities you can use other platforms like WordPress, SquareSpace, or Drupal to make a home page for your campaign. These platforms are also very cheap to use and you can train almost anyone in a campaign to update them. There are occasions when you can get away with using one of these simple website builders. However, a fear of technology or an unwillingness to learn how to use community organizing platforms is not an acceptable excuse for not using them. In any case, if you do use one of these more basic sites, you will have to use a wide range of third-party tools to manage your campaign like Excel, EventBrite, VolunteerMatch, PayPal, Google Maps, SurveyMonkey, Hootsuite, a financial management system, some kind of e-mail platform, and somewhere you need to do work with your voter file. Wouldn't it just be easier to use one platform to accomplish all of these same things?

THE CAMPAIGN WEBSITE

Building your campaign website is fairly straightforward, and you don't need a whole lot of content if you aren't using a blog feature. In fact, you can build a strong campaign website with just a few pages set up through NationBuilder or one of the other community organizing systems. We have seen campaign websites built without these features on other platforms and win, but they often wish they had made it easier for themselves by using the model that we are going to lay out for you here.

- *Home Page:* The home page of your campaign website should be short and sweet. It needs to include the title of measure, key dates, and clear calls to action. You might include a few paragraphs for persuasion below this about why the library is so important to the community or some messaging around the campaign theme as we discussed in that chapter. This is the first page that people will see, so it should be easy to navigate and not overwhelm visitors with too much information.

- *About the Committee:* Your committee members are the face of the campaign and the community is going to want to know who is behind the campaign. This kind of page can help alleviate the discourse in the community that the library is just being funded as a temple built to honor the library director or other politicians if the committee is made up of community members. But even if the committee does include the library director or politicians, it is always a good idea for the campaign to be open and transparent. The community might also be interested in knowing who they can contact to get their questions answered about the campaign. If you can have some contact information like e-mail addresses associated with the profiles on the committee page, that is a good idea. However, committee members should be trained about how to respond to any opposition e-mails they receive from this page.

- *Vote YES for [measure] Pledge Page:* This is where you will put the name and text of the ballot measure. It can be followed by a persuasive piece rooted in the community's need for a well-funded library or why the ballot measure needs to pass. One thing that is very important to have on this page is a way for visitors to "pledge" to vote yes for the initiative. In NationBuilder, when someone pledges to vote yes, it is recorded in your database and you know that this is one less person that your campaign has to persuade. You can also use your pledges as a source for potential endorsers, volunteers, or donors since they've already taken the time to identify themselves.

- *Facts and Endorsements:* This is where you can put more information about why you believe the initiative is important. For example, this is where you might have the statistics on the library's size, annual budget, or usage rates, or any data that is comparable to other libraries in the area. You want to make sure that these numbers are accurate and are not exaggerated in any way. There have been more than a few campaigns that have been lost because the library inflated numbers and was caught with FOIA requests. Take the time to check and double-check all of your numbers here for accuracy. You can also include a persuasive explanation or endorsement of the library's official ballot measure information. This page can also include a call to pledge to vote yes or it can be another pledge page in NationBuilder.

- *Volunteer:* Most community organizing platforms will help you manage your volunteers. They often include an easy-to-manage page where people can sign up to volunteer for the campaign. On this page you should write a compelling piece about why it is so important to volunteer for the campaign, and then list some of the volunteer roles and tasks that are important to the campaign.

In the community organizing platforms you can create a form that people can check to identify what tasks they would be interested in taking part in.

- *Donate Page:* Make it easy to donate to your campaign. The more clicks or hoops that people have to jump through in order to donate, the more people will drop off from donating. Make it as easy as possible while also following all the laws around compliance in collecting donations to political campaigns. Know and understand the laws of your state. Using one of these community organizing systems will make it easier to collect and report campaign donations.

- *News:* This is the blog version of what the campaign is doing and where you can share any big news or write articles for sharing on social media. You can have the announcements of your endorsements here or report on any media coverage and important happenings. One of the most powerful things about the blog is that you can write articles that address concerns from the opposition and tell stories of impact about the library here. Then you can share them on social media and boost the posts on Facebook to the specific audiences that will care about them. No matter what you write about in your blog, each post should always end with some kind of call to action such as a call for donations, volunteers, vote yes pledges, and so on. Don't let people who take the time to read a blog post walk away without taking some action to engage with the campaign.

- *Events:* Your campaign will most likely have fund-raisers, rallies, and so on. If you are using a community organizing platform, it will be easy to create events here the same way you would use a platform like EventBrite. One of the best parts about these integrated websites is that anyone who RSVPs for an event is automatically marked off in your voter database. You can make the assumption about the people who show up that they are willing to take more action for the campaign. These platforms allow you to tag attendees and then send them follow-up e-mails for more engagement and calls to action.

THE BACK END OF THE WEBSITE

While the look and functionality of the public face of your website are important, the real power comes from what happens on the back end with the voter file and the data that your campaign collects. Your campaign should have a lot of data about your local voters by Election Day. You will need to know who is donating for reporting purposes, who is volunteering so you can follow up with them, who is voting yes or no for the ballot measure, where people live, their phone numbers, and so on. There is really just no end to the data, and having it all in one place for each individual voter is going to make your life a lot easier.

Voter Profiles

While the campaign management capabilities of NationBuilder are great, the real power of the platform is how it connects all of the data through the action pages. By understanding everyone's connections to your campaign, you can keep people engaged in your efforts and understand their needs. NationBuilder creates an individual profile for a user around his or her e-mail address, connecting the data it collects to that profile. This profile can be tagged with interactions that will allow you to communicate with a community member in a way that engages her and helps her understand how the library connects with her needs or interests. The tags are the most important aspect of the user profile and are what make a profile useful for later interactions. These profiles can also include public information such as home addresses, phone numbers, and social media accounts.

Turfs

These platforms typically include a very strong geographic information system (GIS). Since voter files include addresses, you can use the GIS to map your voters and create turfs and lists by their geography. These platforms often let you free-hand draw lines around clusters of voters and group them for things that are dependent on geography like canvassing (which we discuss in chapter 19). You might also find some interesting trends about who is more likely to vote for the library based on their geography and the data in the voter file.

E-Mail

The primary way that an organizing platform connects you to the voter online is through e-mail. NationBuilder acts as a very sophisticated e-mail platform by using a tagging system, so you can send better e-mails to your voter universe and only send them to the individuals who you know will care. Unless you spend a lot of time and energy on your e-mail lists in Constant Contact or MailChimp, many people will get blanket e-mails about your latest newsletters, events, or activities that don't apply to them. That means a higher drop-off rate, a lower open rate, and fewer people engaging with your library through e-mail. The tagging system in NationBuilder allows you to send targeted e-mails to community members whose profiles have been tagged with specific interests. You can add these tags yourself, let users add them, or let NationBuilder generate them through a user's interactions with the site.

Contacts

You can keep track of all of the contacts that your campaign makes with voters. In the following chapter we are going to talk about canvassing and phone banking, which are two of the most important activities of your campaign. This is where a community organizing platform becomes indispensable. It is almost impossible to track all of your campaign contacts in an Excel spreadsheet unless you have someone on the campaign team who is amazing at using Excel. But by using these platforms you can have volunteers record when they contact a voter and the voter's response to the contact. These contacts can be recorded as e-mail, phone, or face-to-face or even social media. You will save money by understanding who you contacted, how they plan to vote, and who needs to contact them because you won't contact the wrong people or spend resources contacting yes voters multiple times.

DIY Digital Platform

We encourage all our campaigns to use a robust COS system. But some campaigns feel that they lack the time or experience to use a system like NationBuilder. Unfortunately, we know from a few of our campaigns that a homegrown or do-it-yourself (DIY) digital platform for web hosting and navigation, event management, donor management, volunteer engagement, and voter ID and follow-up is often more work and a larger cost than choosing a turnkey solution and taking the time to learn the system. The library campaign is often a short window in time and often ends the day after the election. It is important to remember that you are not creating a long-term advocacy campaign or setting up a new permanent support organization like a Friends group or foundation when you are building your library ballot committee. Quick and effective beat ownership and editability every day on the path to the ballot.

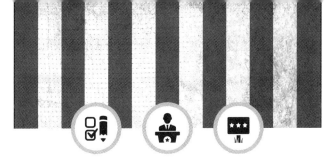

CHAPTER NINETEEN

Canvassing and Phone Banking

D IRECT VOTER CONTACT IS THE GREAT EQUALIZER between campaigns. A campaign can have all the money in the world to afford print, television, radio, social, and digital advertising, but if it lacks a dedicated group of volunteers who are willing to put themselves out as personal representatives for the candidate or the ballot measure, then the campaign is missing the most effective way to activate, motivate, convince, and turn out voters. This voter-to-voter contact is called the "ground game" because it happens at the precinct or neighborhood level, and is very personal by its nature.

Elections at all levels of government are won and lost with the ground game. Issues are decided in the halls of Congress because one side brought out more constituents than the other through one-on-one persuasion. In the 2012 presidential campaign President Obama's reelection efforts focused on certain key precincts in certain swing states to field door-to-door canvassers and phone banks to reach specific voters where they lived about issues they cared about. The Republican National Committee deserves a lot of the credit for supporting Donald Trump's Electoral College win by targeting key precincts in specific Rust Belt swing states with person-to-person contact that created the margin for victory. In every other area of campaign tactics and techniques, we encourage our library campaigns to look at the big campaigns for inspiration, but to be realistic about what they can accomplish. With the ground game, however, a library campaign can be just as effective as national and statewide campaigns. Here is why.

Two of the most effective "ground game" tactics in a campaign are phone banking and canvassing. These tactics are not only effective, but if they are done by volunteers, they are also inexpensive and provide a great way for your campaign to utilize volunteers who are hungry to make a difference. But remember, as we discussed in earlier chapters, volunteers are not free. These tactics will require a higher level of expenditure of other resources, namely your time and people. If your campaign is well funded, there are professional services that will do your phone banking and canvassing for you. If you have more people than money, we have some insights and advice for putting them to work. In any case, using these ground game tactics properly can be challenging without the right tools or understanding.

CANVASSING AND PHONE BANKING THROUGH CAMPAIGN HISTORY

Modern canvassing has a long history, with records and accounts of canvassing for politics that date as far back as the elections of the Roman Republic. Canvassing has been a foundational tool in the political process and has been widely used by candidates and causes since the eighteenth century (depicted in humorous election paintings as far back as 1755). Canvassing creates voter support, identifies yes voters, persuades the persuadable, and reaches voters who are otherwise difficult to reach. There are stories of corruption and bribery throughout the history of canvassing, largely due to its extraordinary effectiveness in persuading and turning out voters to support a candidate or cause. While there was a significant drop in the use and effectiveness of canvassing in the 1990s, there has been a recent revival of interest in canvassing due in large part to many of the newest digital tools that make it much easier to manage both volunteers and data. Currently canvassing has become one of the most popular ground tactics to reach voters.

The history of phone banking is not nearly as glamorous as canvassing (there are definitely no paintings celebrating phone bankers), but it has still been an effective tool for voter ID and GOTV activities. Phone banking can be done by live callers or robo-calls. It reached its peak in the 1990s at about the same time as door-to-door canvassing declined, but since then it has seen a drastic decline in effectiveness with the advent of the Internet and cell phones. Phone banking is seeing a decline in use driven largely by the shift from landlines to cell phones by many households. Many campaigns have replaced phone banking with social media and e-mail outreach. But with a good enhanced voter file, savvy campaign managers still rely on phone banking as another way to reach potential voters. In fact, we have seen a 2016 example of effective phone banking when the Koch-funded Americans for Prosperity political action committee successfully used a robo-call to defeat an initiative to build a new library in Plainfield, Illinois. You can hear the robo-call on our website at action .everylibrary.org/fightthekochbrothers.

FEARS AND MISCONCEPTIONS

Before we talk about how to best conduct phone banking or canvassing, let's address some of the most common fears and misconceptions that people have about these activities. Often, when we talk to campaigns about the necessity of doing voter outreach through these tactics, we get a wide range of responses about why doing on-the-ground voter outreach simply won't work in their area. While we respect and understand these concerns, we need to address them so that we can manage expectations and fears. In fact, you can easily manage the fears of your volunteers if you work with them to think through the possible risks and then train them to handle those situations as they arise. A well-trained canvasser should have the tools and knowledge they need to feel confident while they are working.

The top misconceptions and myths about door-to-door work and phone banking for libraries need to be discussed:

- *People don't like it when you knock on their doors.* The biggest objection we hear from campaigns when we talk about door-to-door canvassing or phone banking is that people just don't like it when someone knocks on their door or calls them on the phone. However, as hard as it is to believe, unless you have a bad or aggressive attitude, or you are selling vacuum cleaners, people truly want to hear from their neighbors about the issues that they care about. To be honest, door-to-door work only irritates people about as much as any other voter outreach method. Social media ads and e-mail solicitations are also perceived negatively by some voters. TV ads in certain swing-state media markets reach a saturation point that causes people to turn programs off. None of those techniques would be dropped due to those concerns by any significant campaign. In our experience, nearly all of the voters you contact will truly feel like they are getting decent and honest information. If you're doing it right, you won't waste too much of their time. People will also feel included in the democratic process and won't feel like they are being excluded by a government initiative. As there are in any voter outreach initiative, there will be exceptions. But in general, you will find that most people will be in a range of positive to neutral responses and you will weather just a few cynical or negative individuals.

- *You can't call people on the "do not call list."* There are probably many people in your voter file who are on the "do not call" list. It is not well known or understood, however, that political calls are exempt from do not call laws and political campaigns are exempt in the law.[1] This means it is perfectly legal to call people on the federal do not call list. Calls for political purposes—including donations, political polling, or on behalf of a campaign or a candidate—are permissible activities. Think of it this way: the politicians made these laws and the politicians rely heavily on phone banking to win their bids for election. There is no way that they are going to outlaw calling the public for political purposes. That's good news for us!

- *Knocking on the doors of strangers is unsafe.* While it is true that there are risks associated with canvassing, there are very few instances of canvassers having dangerous or unsafe interactions with people in their turf. We would even go so far as to argue that we've seen more unsafe interactions between staff and patrons inside the library than outside of it. Does that mean we should simply go carelessly out into the streets? Of course not. But with some good planning and risk management strategies you can ensure that the safety of the canvassers is the highest priority. Here are some good general rules for ensuring canvasser safety:

  1. The most effective way to ensure your safety when canvassing is to simply stay aware. If you are vigilant you can often spot loose dogs or a car that is driving too fast hundreds of yards down the road. Recognize the potential for danger and proceed with caution.
  2. Do not argue. On occasion you will knock on the door of a person who is unreceptive to your message. When you encounter someone who is combative, simply end the conversation and go canvass another part of your turf.
  3. Rattle gates before entering a yard and be on the lookout for dogs. Assume every mid- to large-sized dog is a potential danger unless specifically told otherwise by the dog's owner.
  4. Worst-case scenario, if you do find yourself being chased by a loose, aggressive dog, don't try to outrun it. Just find the nearest spot to get away and regroup. Try to pull yourself up into a tree, jump over a wall or fence, or if necessary, into the bed of a nearby pickup truck. When

being chased by a dog, it's definitely better to ask for forgiveness than permission.

5. Never go inside a house, even when invited. Always stay on the doorstep.
6. Trust your gut and don't knock on a door or enter a yard you feel uneasy about.
7. Canvassers should always carry a cell phone with them.
8. Only the essentials should be taken with you when canvassing. Leave any valuables in your car or hidden from sight.
9. And last but certainly not least, it's always a best practice to go canvassing in pairs and have each individual canvass opposite sides of the street. There will be times when this is not an option, but it should be the goal, particularly for any new canvassers.

■ *You are not allowed to knock on doors that are marked "no soliciting."* We are often asked if volunteers are allowed to knock on doors marked "no soliciting." While you need to know and follow local ordinances, there are generally few local laws that prohibit political canvassers from knocking on those doors. In our experience, we have found that most people with those signs on their doors don't even remember putting them there, and "no soliciting" signs don't often mean that the person is less receptive to campaign messages. In fact, we once worked with a canvasser who would knock on every single door, no matter what. Through his charm and positive personality he would always get a great response from whoever answered the door. This doesn't necessary mean that your canvassers should knock on doors marked "no soliciting"; it just means that they can. It will be up to you and your campaign to make that decision. Weigh the pros and cons and discuss the comfort levels and quality of your volunteers to make that determination.

■ *It's okay to leave campaign literature in the mailbox.* No you cannot. Don't ever leave campaign material in a mailbox or anywhere near a mailbox. Mailboxes are completely off limits. It is illegal to leave materials in a mailbox, and we don't condone behavior that is a federal offense. If you are going to leave campaign materials when voters are not home, we always recommend leaving them on the door (door-hangers) or on the mat at the foot of the doorway.

■ *You can convince the opposition to see your side.* One of the most impor tant things a competent campaign manager needs to help his volunteers understand is that it is always best to politely walk away from anyone who is committed to voting no. This can be really hard for passionate volunteers, and many of them will want to engage with no voters in a belief that they can convince them to change their mind. In very few cases will these doorstep or telephone debates change the minds of the voters. In every single case, it will take valuable time away from finding more community members who will vote yes. Debating with a no voter can often do the opposite of persuading by solidifying their oppositional stance. A doorstep debate can sometimes drive them to publicly and vocally campaign in opposition to the library. Teach your volunteers that people have a right to vote no about the library, as long as they vote no quietly.

There are three reasons for doing canvassing and phone banking: to identify potential yes voters, to convince those who are undecided to vote for your library initiative, and to convince everyone who is committed to voting yes to show up on Election Day and cast their vote. In order to do this work properly, you will need to know who to talk to, and you will need the right scripts to make it happen. Of course, you are also going to make sure that your volunteers are trained to find those people and use those scripts to maximum effect.

WHICH DOORS, WHICH PHONES?

A group of voters who you want to contact in a similar way in a campaign is called a voter universe. You can have voter universes that are made up of political party affiliations, propensity for voting, consumer data, geographic locations, or by the kinds of tactics that you want to use to contact them. There are many philosophies on building a proper voter universe and you can read more about them in chapter 16.

However, for phone banking and canvassing, there are a few more subtleties that can help you better target voters and most efficiently use your volunteers' time. Within each of these voter universes, you are going to have to "cut the lists" into more manageable segments. Often these segments are called "turfs" and a volunteer becomes responsible for managing his or her own turfs. It's best to have volunteers who live in a turf to contact other people within that turf because people enjoy hearing from their neighbors more than from a stranger. Turfs also need to take geographies into consideration. For example, a canvassing turf shouldn't be intersected by a physical boundary like a river or a freeway. You want your turfs to be easily walkable by volunteers in a logical way. It also doesn't make sense to have a turf where houses are far apart if you can use a phone bank more efficiently for those areas instead.

Likewise, using a phone bank in an easily walkable area doesn't make much sense either when the phone banking resources could be better used in more rural areas.

HOW MANY VOLUNTEERS DO I NEED?

It doesn't take as many volunteers to canvass or phone a city or town as you might think. A trained canvasser can talk to about 30–40 households in an hour in an urban or suburban setting. A trained phone banker can call around 40–50 numbers an hour. If you have 10 volunteers do a 3–4 hour shift (you shouldn't have them do more than this), that's 10 volunteers × 30 contacts × 3 (or 4) hours and that equals 900–1,200 contacts in a day on a low estimate. If you do a few shifts in a week, or maybe a few over the weekend, voter contact numbers add up quickly.

CUTTING TURFS

Professional campaign managers rely on data tools to cut turf and make phone lists. Fortunately, many of these sophisticated mapping and segmentation tools are also available for small and mid-sized campaigns. We recommend that you use one of the many community organizing systems like Nationbuilder or EveryAction. Those web-based tools will allow you to easily map territory, cut turfs, and build lists. Take the time to use their training guides and videos before starting to use your data. If you aren't using one of those platforms, we have some advice on ways to cut turfs using tools that are freely available.

VOTER FILES

To create canvassing turfs and phone lists, you will need to start with a good voter file. As we discussed in chapter 18, you can get a free voter file with your EveryAction or NationBuilder platform. But if you aren't using those, your campaign should request the voter files from your local clerk or board of elections. It should be delivered to you in an Excel or CSV format. When you request the file, ask the clerk to include the voter history from the previous six to eight elections in your jurisdiction. This voter history will show if the voter did or did not vote in each election. In most states, partisan ballot choices and absentee status are also included in the file. This public record voter file is adequate data for most phone banking and canvassing.

However, if you want to have better data connected to your voters that will help you build a more complete voter universe, we recommend spending some extra money and purchasing an enhanced voter file from a private company. There are quite a few companies that sell high-quality enhanced voter files that include more up-to-date phone numbers and even cell phone numbers. If you do go the route of buying an enhanced voter file, ask to see some sample data before you purchase to ensure that the data is accurate.

CREATING A WALK LIST

Creating a walk list from a turf cut isn't terribly difficult if you aren't using a geocode-enabled platform like NationBuilder or EveryAction. If you need a free turf-cutting and mapping tool, you can do it using Google Maps with Mapcustom izer.com or other available online applications. Once you create a turf on a map, print the names and addresses of the houses that are in that turf, add columns for yes, no, maybe, or left a flyer, and give it to your canvasser. No matter how you do it, the key for your voter ID and persuasion walk lists is to record the results of voter interactions by your canvassers. For each household that they connect with, canvassers need to record whether or not the voter will vote yes or no, or if they are undecided, and whether or not they left a flyer at the door if no one was home. These data points need to be added back into your voter file for two key reasons: so that you don't knock on the same door twice, and you know which houses need persuasion contacts later in the campaign. The community organizing systems make this process much easier.

CREATING A PHONE LIST

Creating a phone list is often easier than making maps, but the problem with many voter files provided by county clerks of election is that the phone numbers are notoriously inaccurate and out-of-date. This is where an enhanced voter file from a reputable company will come in handy. Many enhanced voter files include both landline and cell phone numbers, which improve your rate of connecting to voters. Once you have the voter file, the actual creation of the phone list is easy.

There are a couple of different methodologies to use to create the phone list. The first is to simply break up the phone list and hand out those lists to your volunteers to start calling. While this is a quick and easy way to do it, and it is effective for some areas, you might want to take a more strategic method. One approach is to create turfs for phone lists like you did with the walk lists discussed above. This way, you can have volunteers call their own neighbors, which can be a much more effective and convincing call than a stranger calling. For example, if your volunteers can call someone and say, "Hi, my name is ____ and I'm your neighbor on (street) . . ." they will be more likely to get a positive response. For small campaigns, ask your volunteers to highlight the people they know on the voter file and call those people. This is a great way to ensure a quality conversation with the community by your volunteers.

VIRTUAL CALL CENTER

Often, the biggest impediment to successful phone banking is the lack of a location to run it. There are other tools that let your volunteers manage their own canvass and phone lists remotely. Several cloud-based call center services like Callfire and Five9 let you upload your phone lists and scripts to a server and have volunteers call from their own homes using their own cell phones or landlines. NationBuilder has a few third-party tools that integrate with it to do remote phone banking using your live voter data. This is a fast-growing industry, and companies are popping up across the political spectrum to help candidates and issues do better campaigns. We recommend taking some time and researching the ones that are out there.

CREATING SCRIPTS

Every phone bank and canvass starts with a good script. Volunteers need a script in order to start a conversation. A good script helps them learn the specific messaging that you want voters to hear. During training, volunteers need to be trained on the script and practice the script. But as volunteers become comfortable with it, you should give them permission to not read the script verbatim unless they need to. In fact, it's usually better if they don't. Voters wants to hear from a real person and not someone who sounds like a robot or a political shill.

Creating the scripts isn't terribly difficult. According to the Wellstone Center, a leading candidate-training organization, there are just four kinds of political scripts and each script will be used at a different time in the campaign.[2] These four common types of scripts are volunteer recruitment, voter ID, persuasion, and GOTV. The volunteer recruitment script will be used a few weeks before the campaign kickoff by high-level volunteers or staff. The voter ID script will be used early in the campaign to identify who in your community will vote for your library. The persuasion script will be used to follow up with anyone who wants any further information. The GOTV script will be used the last few days before Election Day to ensure that your yes voters actually show up at the polls to vote for your library.

While Wellstone only discusses these four kinds of scripts, many campaigns also use a fund-raising script. A fund-raising script is not considered a campaign script because it is not directly related to winning a campaign. That's because it is often illegal to use a voter file for direct fund-raising appeals. We discuss the fund-raising script and list development for fund-raising in chapter 10 on fund-raising.

BLIND ID OR NOT

There are two kinds of voter ID scripts: ones in which you identify yourself as part of the campaign or not. You might get different results from either one. This data can be especially skewed for a candidate if people want to hide any racial, gender, religious, or other bias from a canvasser or a caller. The fact is, sometimes people lie to hide the fact, or overcompensate for a perceived bias. This is generally referred to as the Bradley effect, which is a theory that proposes that some voters who intend to vote for a white candidate would nonetheless tell pollsters that they are undecided or likely to vote for the nonwhite candidate to alleviate that perceived bias.

The Bradley effect comes from a campaign in 1982 where Tom Bradley, the mayor of Los Angeles, ran as a candidate for the Democratic Party to be the governor of California. Bradley was a black man and his rival was a white candidate named George Deukmejian. The polls leading up to the election, and in fact, the exit polls during the election, had pinned Bradley as the clear winner of the election. However, the actual results of the election proved that Deukmejian was narrowly the winner. Many campaign experts believe that this discrepancy was due in part to the white electorate not wanting to admit their racial bias and therefore lying to pollsters about who they actually voted for.

One of the ways to mitigate this effect is to not identify yourself as part of the campaign in your voter ID scripts. This is called a blind ID. However, many pollsters have begun to suspect that in most recent elections, this bias in the data is not as pronounced as it once was and that pollsters don't need to take steps, like a blind ID, to account for it.

VOTER ID SCRIPT

A voter ID script is used by volunteers early in the campaign to identify potential yes voters. There is generally nothing fancy or too informative in the script. It quickly asks a few key questions of the voter: if they know that the library is on the ballot this next Election Day, what issues they care about, and how they will vote. The goal is to get through as many people on the voter file as possible and record their answers so that the campaign can identify any trends or see if it can reach its vote goal. It is critical to capture data on each voter contact and their response. Definite yes voters will need to be contacted again closer to Election Day to ensure they vote. Definite no voters should never be contacted by the library campaign again by phone, in person, by e-mail, or on social media (if possible). You don't want to risk them coming out against the library on Election Day because you reminded them. The voter ID script is most powerful in identifying "unsure" or "maybe" voters while also understanding what issues in the community they identify with, so that future contacts for persuasion can use that information to the campaign's advantage. Knowing this information about voters early in the campaign will cut down on costs of persuasion and GOTV later in the campaign. Of course, with Election Day just a few months away, even the voter ID script should include an element of persuasion in it.

❯ SAMPLE VOTER ID SCRIPT

Hi. My name is _____ (*full name*) and I live in Springfield. I'm a volunteer for the Vote Yes Committee for OUR new library. We're calling our neighbors who usually vote about the opportunity to build a new library in Springfield. Are you planning to vote again on November 7th?

If YES: Great. The current library was built in 1960. The referendum on the ballot will authorize building a new 21st-century library for Accomack County. Can we count on your YES vote for a new library?

If Voting YES: Thank You! I will add your name to our list of YES voters. Do you know where to vote on November 7th . . . ?

    <record outcome in database>

_____

If Not Sure: Can I answer any questions about the plan for a new library? Can I send you a brochure about what a YES vote will do for Springfield? Thank you.

> *<record outcome in database>*

_____

If Not Voting or Refuses to Answer: If you decide to vote on November 7th, please remember that a new library in Springfield County helps with education, jobs skills, and community enrichment. We're voting YES for the Springfield County Library. Thank you for your time. . . . . Good-bye.

> *<record outcome in database>*

_____

Plans to Vote No: Thank you for taking the time to talk with me. Good-bye.

> *<record outcome in database>*

_____

Hostile response: Thank you, I'm sorry to have bothered you. Good-bye.

> *<Hang up><record outcome in database>*

Alternately, the voter ID script can be used to collect and record some additional polling data that will help you refine your campaign messaging. If done very early in the campaign process, this approach can yield some actionable results. Likewise, if you run into trouble with your messaging, fielding a version of this voter ID script can help you reset it.

❯ VOTER IDENTIFICATION (ID) SCRIPT
The purpose of this script is to identify the preferences of your targeted voters.

Hi, may I speak to (***name of next voter on list***)? My name is (***name of volunteer***). We're doing a brief survey of voters in the district to identify the most important issues to voters.

(If voter hesitates, remind them that you only have three questions and it will take less than a minute to complete the survey.)

Q1. From your perspective, do you think that the (city, county, local gov) is on the right track or the wrong track?

1. Right track	3. Not sure
2. Wrong track	4. Refused

Q2. If the following were on the ballot and the elections were held today, what issues would you most likely vote for?

1. Police
2. Schools
3. Fire Department

4. Library
5. Roads
6. Refused

Q3. We'd love to know what the most important issues affecting the (*city, county, local gov*) are to you? What are the two biggest issues facing our community that will determine how you will vote in the upcoming election?

PERSUASION AND GET-OUT-THE-VOTE SCRIPT

These scripts are used to contact voters who have been identified as potential yes voters. These are people in the community who are undecided or potentially (although very infrequently) in the soft no category. However, the persuasion script is never used to try and persuade a definite no voter. In fact, calling no voters to try to persuade them to change their mind most often reinforces their no and encourages them to take action in opposition to the campaign. But a good persuasion call first identifies the issues that the voter cares about, and then relates some information about the library that addresses that issue. For example, if a voter is strong on education, the persuasion call will discuss the ways that a library addresses education or student achievement in the community. If the voter cares about business development or community growth, tailoring your campaign message to highlight elements of the library plan that address those topics is appropriate, smart, and hopefully persuasive.

The get-out-the-vote (GOTV) script is the reminder to the yes voters to show up at the polls and cast their vote in favor of the library. This script should also only be used for the infrequent voters. That is, the campaign shouldn't spend time or money on the voters who always vote in every election. They will almost definitely show up to support the library. Instead, by contacting the infrequent or new voters, you can push up the votes for the library and unless someone is calling the no voters to remind them to vote, this is what gives you the biggest edge in the election.

❯ SAMPLE GOTV (EARLY VOTING) SCRIPT

You need to know the early voting and absentee voting rules of your state.

Based on the rules, you should design a voter engagement plan to get them to vote early.

The purpose of this script is to educate identified supporters on early voting options and turn them out early.

Hi, may I speak to (*name of next voter on list*)? My name is (*name of volunteer*). I'm calling as a volunteer for (*name of campaign*). We have you on our list of committed supporters for the library. We wanted to call today and let you know about early voting options.

Give a BRIEF overview of what the rules for early voting are.

(*Name of voter*), would you be interested in voting early so you can avoid long lines on Election Day?

If YES: That's great. The early voting period goes from (*give date ranges*). Would it be okay if we call or send you an e-mail for a reminder?

If NO: (*Name of voter*), you know the lines at the polls can get long on Election Day. We want to make sure that you have the opportunity to make voting as easy as possible. Please let us know if there is anything we can do to assist you in voting.

❿ SAMPLE VOTER PERSUASION SCRIPT

The purpose of this script is to call "undecided" voters and persuade them to vote for the library. The goal is to engage with voters and find out their objections and handle them as effectively as possible.

Hi, may I speak to (*name of next voter on list*)? My name is (*name of volunteer*) and I'm calling on behalf of the campaign for (*name of library*). We're talking to our friends and neighbors about our campaign. Are you familiar with our ballot initiative?

If they are familiar, ask them: Can we count on your vote on (*election day*) for (*name of library*)?

IF YES: Thank them. Get their e-mail and ask them to volunteer and say good-bye.

IF NO or UNDECIDED: Ask them what their concerns are. Try to address them. If you can't persuade, thank them for their time. (*Record objections on your call sheet.*)

If they are not familiar or undecided, ask them:
Well, I'm volunteering for (*campaign*) because I believe the library (*use their previous answers from the voter ID to address their concerns in the community and why or how the library can solve them*). I'm also supporting (*library*) because I believe (*volunteer's 27–9-3 belief statement*). That's pretty important, wouldn't you agree? What are some things you wish you could see changed in our library?

Try to engage the voter and let them talk. Record their answers on your call sheet. If there is little response, go to the next question.

Okay (***voter name***). I just wanted you to know that we are out working hard, listening to voters' concerns. Based on the feedback we've gotten, voters are excited to see (***library improvement statement***). Can we count on your vote for our library on Election Day?

If YES: That's great. May we get your e-mail so we can keep you posted on campaign events and volunteer opportunities? Thank you again for your time. Have a great (***day/evening***).

If NO: Ask them what their concerns are. Thank them for their time. (***Record objections on your call sheet.***)

If still Undecided: Thanks so much for your time. We hope we can earn your vote in the upcoming election. Have a great (***day/night***).

VOLUNTEER SCRIPT

The volunteer script is a lot like a persuasion script except it can be built off of the voter ID script. This is because when someone responds enthusiastically about supporting the library initiative, they can be followed up with a question about whether or not they would like to volunteer. Of course, it shouldn't have to be said, but anyone who is undecided, or a decided no for the campaign, should not be asked to volunteer.

❯ SAMPLE VOLUNTEER RECRUITMENT SCRIPT
There will be a multitude of reasons to engage volunteers in your campaign.

The biggest reason people never volunteer is because nobody ever asked them to. The purpose of this script is to call people who are identified donors and supporters and ask them to come out and volunteer for the campaign.

Hi, may I speak to (***name of next prospective volunteer on list***)? My name is (***name of caller***). I'm calling on behalf of (***name of candidate***). He/she asked me to call you about an upcoming event at the campaign. (***Provide details of the event and the specific actions you'll need from volunteers.***) Would you be willing to come down to Campaign Headquarters and help us?

If YES: Thank you so much! Okay, if you don't mind, let me get your e-mail and I'll send you all the details and follow up with you two days prior to the event. Thanks so much for your help.

If NO: I totally understand your busy schedule. Would you be interested in other volunteer opportunities? (*If YES*): Can I get your e-mail and I'll keep you updated on upcoming volunteer opportunities. Thanks so much for your time!

GETTING ORGANIZED FOR A WEEKEND CANVASS OR PHONE BANK

If you are ready to organize a weekend canvassing or phone banking for your campaign, there are a couple of things you can do to make sure that it's as successful as possible. You will want to be organized and ready when your volunteers walk through the door. Nothing will sabotage a weekend with volunteers more than poor planning and skipped steps. If the volunteers think that you're unprepared, they won't take their role in the campaign seriously. To help you get organized, here are a couple of things you can do to make sure that you have the most successful weekend possible:

- *Ensuring Volunteers Show Up:* Most importantly, you want to make sure that you have volunteers for your weekend. There's nothing more sad than a fired-up campaign team in a room all alone. That's why you need to take the time and effort to make sure that volunteers are ready to go and committed to a weekend of work. If someone committed to a weekend of canvassing or phone banking a week ago, they might change their mind, make other commitments, or otherwise pretend they forgot on the day of the event. In order to help commit your volunteers, you will want to be in constant communication with them. No matter how you communicate with them, it is your job to be enthusiastic and excited and appreciative that they are on board and part of the team, so any communication you have with them should convey that. Because volunteers tend to commit to things early or over a span of time, it's important to reconfirm everyone at least 3–4 days before the event. You can do this through a phone call or an e-mail, but a phone call is always best. Then, the night before the event, send out a reminder e-mail or (better yet) call them to confirm that they will participate. If you don't hear back from your volunteers, do not count on them to be there.

One extra tip is to ask your volunteers to bring a friend or two to volunteer with them. Volunteers like to have someone familiar with them, and it is easier to build your volunteer list and to build a community around your campaign if people already know each other. Often, volunteers are more likely to show up if they commit to bringing someone with them as well.

- *The Night Before:* The night before the event, you will make sure you have all of your supplies ready for your volunteers. Don't let volunteers show up in the morning while you are still prepping the event. Don't waste their time like that, and it's never good for them to show up early just to see a stressed-out campaign manager running around the office because the printer won't print the walk lists. Do it all early. Here is a list of some of the supplies you should have ready to go the night before the event:

  - Clipboards
  - Printed walk lists/call lists
  - Pens
  - Notepaper
  - Printed scripts
  - Chairs and tables for phone bankers
  - Cheap cell phones (for anyone who doesn't want to use their own phone)
  - Drivers for canvassers
  - Gas card (for volunteers who are driving)
  - Badges (or something that IDs volunteers as part of the campaign)
  - Log-ins to database for data entry
  - Plans set for meals if necessary
  - Drinks and snacks throughout the day

- *The Day Of:* On the day of the canvassing or phone banking event, make sure that you are ready to give the volunteers the best possible experience. This means that all the volunteers should be greeted and thanked with a positive and enthusiastic energy as they arrive. Offer them coffee or a snack if you can, and have them start to meet with each other and talk. It is your job to make introductions and small talk with volunteers so they feel immediately engaged. Sometimes it's also good to have pleasant music playing so that the room doesn't feel cold or isolated. Once everyone has arrived, they should start to get comfortable with what's happening that day. The first step is a round of introductions. Many campaigns start with a round of introductions where each volunteer briefly talks about why they volunteered or why it is that they believe in the library initiative. After this, it's time for them to break into groups of three to practice the scripts that they will be using throughout the day. Once again, let them know that they can go off script as long as they touch on the major points and they remain brief in their contacts. By having groups of three people, two volunteers can role-play a canvasser and contact and go through the practice of knocking on a door or calling. The third volunteer can watch and help constructively critique. If you have a lead volunteer, this is a great place for them to take charge of the group and lead the exercise. After everyone has run through the script a few times, it is time to talk through what to expect for the day. During this time, review any safety tips, remind them not to argue with anyone who is voting against the library, remind them to be polite and courteous, and remind them how important it is to get the data back from them at the end of the day. Make sure they understand how to fill out the data sheets and how to turn them in or how to fill in the data if the volunteers are doing that themselves. Once everyone is comfortable and ready, it is time to get started! Hand them their walk/phone lists and get them going. But your job as the canvassing manager isn't done. Throughout the day you need to check up on them. Text your canvassers and make sure they are okay. Celebrate any big wins from your phone bankers. Of course, it's up to you to set the attitude throughout the day, so keep up your positive and thankful energy and keep your volunteers engaged. Make sure people are getting their breaks and any meals or drinks that they need. After the day of canvassing and phone banking is over, it's time to celebrate! This is a good time to order some food and drinks for everyone. Bring everyone together to eat and drink and talk about successes and failures. Address any concerns that came up throughout the day. You can have them enter data while they are celebrating if they weren't updating data along the way. The day of canvassing and phone banking should be a great shared experience that volunteers can come together around. Swapping stories and laughing are a great sign that your volunteers are coming together. If this isn't happening, it's up to you to engage them and try to get them to reach that level. As people leave, don't forget to thank them for their time and ask them to recommit to the next event. You can also ask what would make their volunteering experience better so that you can grow and learn as a volunteer leader.

In our experience helping over sixty library campaigns scope out and field effective phone and canvassing programs, we find that the one thing that most irritates voters is not the message or the contact itself, but it is the tone and personality of the caller or door knocker. One of the best lessons we learned from our grandparents is that you can often get away with anything you like in life as long as you do it with a smile. When training your volunteers for a door or phone shift, evaluate your volunteers and make sure to reassign any who are in a bad mood, overly aggressive, or just have a bad attitude, to another role in your campaign. You will want to send some of your most positive, outgoing, enthusiastic volunteers out canvassing to ensure that you get the best possible response from the public. Train your canvassers that it is okay to smile, laugh, and take the time to enjoy talking to the public and the canvassing experience, even in the face of opposition.

NOTES

1. "National Do Not Call Registry," National Do Not Call Registry, https://www.donotcall.gov/faq/faqbusiness.aspx.
2. "Tips for Effective Voter Contact Scripts," Wellstone, www.wellstone.org/sites/default/files/attachments/Effective-Phone-and-Door-Scripts_0.pdf.

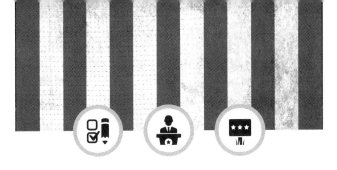

Campaign Events

C REATING AN EVENT FOR A CAMPAIGN CAN RAISE AWARE-
ness of your campaign, raise funds, identify supporters, and potentially
get your campaign the kind of media coverage that it needs. It can also
be a harrowing experience if it isn't well run. There are a wide range
of events that your campaign can take part in, from fund-raisers to rallies to house
parties. Each of these can be effective in helping your campaign get the resources
it needs and help it to win.

CAMPAIGN KICKOFFS

In many communities we have worked with, the library campaign launches with
a press release and social media boost but doesn't have the power of a campaign
kickoff event behind it. In 2016 two of our campaigns featured two very different
kinds of public "launch" events for their "yes" campaigns. The yes committee for the
Mid Continent Public Library hosted a rally on the steps of Independence Square
in Independence, Missouri, not far from the library's headquarters and very near
the Harry S. Truman Presidential Library. Speakers at the event included campaign
cochair Dr. Bridget McCandless, Independence Mayor Eileen Weir, State Rep. Rory
Rowland, and Rachel Gonzalez, the nation's youngest delegate at the Democratic
National Convention.

A special guest included Harry Truman (portrayed by actor Niel Johnson), who shared about Truman's love of reading and his early education obtained through using the public library. The rally garnered solid media coverage early in the active get-out-the-vote period. Yard signs, stickers, and campaign information were passed out. The campaign was able to flex its organizing skills and test its messaging from the podium.

The other campaign kickoff was by the Yes, Helen! campaign committee at the start of their GOTV period. The campaign leadership team arranged and hosted a daylong ice cream social and fund-raiser at a historic Dairy Queen a few blocks from the library. While it didn't have the traditional campaign event trappings, it served to organize volunteers, activate donors and voters, and distribute campaign support materials rather effectively. Both kickoff events had volunteers collecting e-mail addresses and signing people up to be volunteers. Both also had an official volunteer photographer assigned to capture great pictures of families, groups, and neighbors posing with campaign "yes" signs and generally enjoying themselves. All of the subsequent media coverage was shared on social media, but the campaign-friendly pictures were a real asset throughout each campaign. The size and scope were less important than the energy and organization that went into the kickoff event.

RALLIES

Rallies and other public events during a campaign are a great way to impress upon your community how important libraries are and leave a positive image in the minds of voters and politicians about the level of support that a library has. I'm sure you remember some of the powerful images that have come out of marches on Washington, parades, and public protests that have stayed with us for years and have been ingrained into the psyche of American voters. In the same way, these kinds of rallies and demonstrations for libraries can be a great way to imprint some images of American support for libraries in the minds of voter and politicians.

There are many different ways to organize a demonstration and many different tools that you can use. Although you might really have an image in your mind about a rally as a protest against something or as a mass march in your community with signs and slogans, try to think critically about what kind of demonstration would be most effective with the audience that you're trying to reach. For example, you can hold a press event or demonstration on the steps of city hall if you want to get the attention of local politicians. In order to get your point across, you can use many different tools like music, poetry, theater, voices, humor, or anything else that makes a noise and helps people take notice, but it is generally best to tie something in relation to libraries to your demonstration. For example, our colleagues at the library advocacy organization Urban Librarians Unite have been putting together a 24 Hour Read-In demonstration to raise awareness for their cause for several years. Each year it builds new equity among local politicians and earns a lot of media coverage for their library budget ask.

It's not always about the number of people that attend an event; it is often about having the right people at the event and having the right people see the event. We have seen libraries create a demonstration at a city meeting with anywhere from 2 to 200 people. All of the decisions about what kind of event you will be having, where you will have it, who will attend, and so on will be a part of the planning process. It depends on what kind of event will work best for you and the resources that you have. There is no one event that's better than the rest.

HOUSE PARTIES

House parties are a great way to encourage volunteers to raise funds, ID activist supporters, and educate the public. These events are used primarily by organizations that use grassroots campaign tactics to build support like progressive causes, the Tea Party, Americans for Prosperity, and candidates. Both Hillary Clinton's and Barack Obama's guides to creating house parties are accessible guides and are easily found on the Internet for reference. Creating a similar set of events for your library campaign can be a significant help in building the resources your campaign needs.

House parties are typically just a gathering of people at a volunteer's house where people can be educated about the campaign. These people can be friends, family, neighbors, coworkers, or anyone else that you can think of who might be interested in getting involved in supporting your library. The specifics of what happens at the house party are up to the volunteer who can provide food, invite guest speakers, play a promotional video provided by the campaign, or hold other activities that can boost awareness and involvement. These don't need to be complex or high-end events, and in fact, some of the most successful house parties are some of the simplest. A modest afternoon tea or coffee with friends and family often works just as well as an elaborate catered dinner party. The most important thing to remember is that the organizer is responsible for collecting any of the funds raised and/or any data collected about attendees and getting it back to the campaign.

One of the best things about a house party is that it is something that volunteers can do on their own. That's why both the Clinton and Obama campaigns published their house party guides online. They wanted people to take the initiative and create these events to take part in the campaign. Your library campaign can do the same thing by creating its own house party. At the end of this chapter we'll provide you with a sample house party guide that you can adopt for your campaign.

FUND-RAISERS

A fund-raiser is typically thought of as a formal event to solicit donations from key people in the community. These fund-raisers can be extravagant events with dinner, dancing, and special guests with big-name local sponsors. But they can also be smaller, less formal community gatherings. In any case, a fund-raiser that makes money instead of losing money takes a good amount of time and energy to organize, but one that is organized well can return a lot of resources back to the campaign. Because fund-raisers take up so much time and energy, they should be done early in the campaign. Later you will have a lot of other activities that need to get done and spending time planning a fund-raiser, especially if it's unsuccessful, can drain your campaign at a critical time.

At EveryLibrary, we regularly host fund-raising events to build equity for the organization, to raise our profile in certain cities or with groups of donors, and to have a good time with our donors. We want people to invest in our work in order to feel a sense of ownership about our success. If they already believe in our mission, we want them to enjoy their experience as donors, too. We sometimes joke about the need to put the "fun" back in fund-raisers, and we encourage our campaigns to look at their fund-raising events in a similar way. Working a campaign is hard. People want to have fun as well as be effective advocates and campaigners. You can build campaign resources through the money raised and by activating people who care.

GETTING ORGANIZED FOR EVENTS

Just like anything else in the campaign, there should be a well-written plan that keeps people on track and shows that the details and risks have been properly examined. There should also be someone in charge of the event, goals, deadlines, and so on. If there isn't a plan and there isn't someone in charge of the plan, don't think that there will be an event. Luckily, setting up an event plan is relatively easy. Here are some of the key things to think about.

GOALS

No matter what kind of event you are planning, you need to start by identifying what you want to accomplish. By determining your goal, you can help narrow down the kind of event that you should create. If you are trying to raise money, then you need to hold a fund-raiser. If you are trying to raise awareness, you might want to create a rally or a kickoff. If you are trying to build a cohort of volunteers and campaign insiders, you might try hosting a house party. Each of these campaign tactics is extremely effective, but they are only effective with measurable goals. That's why you should set a goal before you begin. These goals should be things like 25 new volunteers, 100 new identified supporters or yes voters, $1,000 raised for the campaign. Having a realistic goal from the beginning will help you get set up for success from the beginning.

However, no matter what resources you are trying to build for the campaign, make sure they are realistic. That means don't try to raise $100,000 in one large event at a conference center when there are only two volunteers who are working on putting it together. Sit down and think critically about what you can realistically achieve with the resources on hand. Also think about what resources you can spare if the event is a failure. Will your whole campaign be ruined if this one event isn't successful? Sometimes it's worth the risk if the rewards are high enough or there is a large enough chance for success. But unless a campaign is well situated from the onset, the first events are typically smaller and slowly build up to larger events as resources add up, or there are a series of smaller and more manageable events throughout the campaign.

BUDGET

Every plan should include a budget. This budget should be a line item of everything that is needed to create a successful event. It should include everything from event staff, marketing and invitations, space rental, catering, entertainment and guest speaker costs, transportation, security, utilities, to insurance. Most importantly, your budget needs to consider your fund-raising goal and ensure that you raise more money than the event costs. There's nothing worse than a fund-raiser that missed a detail in the budget and then made the decision to sell tickets too cheap to raise any funds. Of course, always be sure to budget something extra for unforeseen expenses to help avoid this situation.

Some fund-raising events can be "break-even" events by design. If the goal is to start a relationship with a new community of donors, it may be worthwhile to price an event so that you lower the barrier to participation while capturing information about who the donors are, what they believe, and how to contact them in the future. However, we caution our campaigns to plan event budgets in a way that allows them to either make money or have items, venues, and overhead donated by campaign supporters. The budget for the event needs to eventually support effective voter identification and get-out-the-vote work more than the amenities of the event.

VENUE

Often your venue is going to be the most expensive part of your event. Always try to get a space donated and don't be afraid to ask for discounts. However, don't try to build your event around your venue; instead, determine what kind of event you want to create and then find the most appropriate venue for that. If you are planning on having a band play or a guest speaker but your venue doesn't have a stage or sound system, for example, then you will need to find a new venue. Also take things like parking, handicap access, liquor permits, food preparation areas, and legal capacity into consideration. If the venue only holds 100 people and doesn't have a food permit but you need 200 to be profitable and you want to hold a dinner, then you will need to find a different venue or make adjustments to your event.

SPONSORSHIPS

Never be afraid to ask for sponsorships and in-kind donations. These sponsorships can come in the form of money, food or drink donations, or marketing. Many times, local small breweries will donate beer to events if they can just so they can get the word out about their beer. Sometimes you can even find big-name liquor companies to hold tastings at your event and they will provide a few extra bottles for guests. We have had food companies provide samples in goodie bags that guests can take home. Since it's a library measure, you might find a publisher willing to give copies of a latest book to guests. There are also usually many local companies or wealthy individuals that would love to help pay for the venue, but they won't do it unless they are asked. A big part of getting sponsorships is just asking for them.

RESPONSIBILITY

An event won't happen unless someone is in charge of it and held accountable for ensuring it happens. While there can be a committee that is working together to create the event, one person should be in the lead position as the event organizer. The rest of the people in the committee are the ones who are responsible for ensuring that the event has the resources that the organizer needs to be successful. Often an event organizer will rely on her connections in the community to raise the resources. It's a great idea to have the committee comprised of people like wealthy donors, business leaders, or local celebrities.

AUDIENCE

Who is the target audience for your event? Is this event geared towards a specific group like business people, local politicians, parents, or young professionals? In short, you must decide whom you will invite to your event so that you can make sure that those people get asked to attend it. Events should typically not be an open call for everyone in the community. You are going to want to target your supporters or the kinds of people whom you want to ask to support your library campaign. Even if it is a general fund-raiser, you will need to know who can afford the ticket price and spend your resources targeting them to ensure they are aware of the event and will attend it.

EVENT ACTIVITIES AND EVENT ACTIVISM

There is a wide range of activities that can happen at an event. This includes basic things like entertainment with a live band or DJ, hiring a local speaker, showing a video or short film about your cause, dancing, eating, drinking, marching to city hall, and so on. But at these events you can also try to get guests to take a little more action. For example, at some kinds of events you can ask them to write an editorial to the local newspaper or sign on to a letter to the local politicians. If the event is larger you can bring a computer, and if there's Wi-Fi you can use an online petition platform to get them to sign on to a petition. Don't be afraid to turn an activity into activism.

MARKETING AND INVITATIONS

Don't think that you can skimp on resources for marketing your event or inviting people to it. You need to spend significant time and energy convincing your supporters that your organization and event are worthy of their time and money. Sit down and don't just think about who should attend but create some guest lists, research your community to find people of influence or power or money, send out your invitations early, and spend money on ads in social media or newspapers, or whatever you need to do to make sure that people are well aware of the event. We've seen great events fail because nobody attended them because the campaign skimped on the budget for letting people know that the event was happening.

Your campaign events need to be marketed across all your campaign communications channels, but the marketing needs to support the event goals. We encourage all our campaigns to create three kinds of posts for an event that should be syndicated across their web and social media: the teaser, the invite, and the recap. Like with e-mail marketing, the teaser sets up what problem the event is intended to solve and shares the RSVP as a call to action. The invite itself needs to point to an RSVP that includes a ticket or sign-up (see below). The recap post is the campaign's chance to share stories, pictures, and a new call to action for the campaign one to three days following the event. Every event is marketed as successful, even if it fell a little short of your expectations.

SIGN-UPS AND SALES

You need to make sure that it's as easy as possible to sign up for the event or to purchase a ticket. If you're selling tickets to the event, make sure that your process for buying tickets is set up before invites go out and try to buy a ticket yourself as a test to make sure it goes through effectively. If there is a process for signing up, make sure it works and that the sign-ups are getting recorded somewhere. It is a terrible thing to have a hundred sign-ups and then not be able to find them later when the event happens. There are many great online tools to use to organize your sign-ups and sales such as Eventbrite, Meetup.com, Facebook, or even just a simple Google form. Of course, if your campaign is using one of the more sophisticated campaign platforms like NationBuilder or EveryAction, there are built-in event and ticket sale features there.

REMINDERS

Make sure that people are reminded that the event is happening. The week before the event you should try to send out some kind of reminder to everyone who said they would attend. Then send out another reminder the day before the event. This helps ensure that people don't make other plans or just plain forget that the event is happening. It's especially important to send out reminders to everyone who is helping to put the event together to remind them of their roles, duties, and responsibilities so that there are no surprises later.

SETUP

Whoever is responsible for the event should ensure that everything is ready to go well in advance of the event itself. You don't want people disorganized or find out that critical things are missing the morning of the event or just hours or minutes before it. If you can, try to set up the event the day before or at least as early as possible and go over the whole day's activities with your volunteers well ahead of time. If you want to take them through a run-through of the event, that's always a great extra step that can save some headaches later. Sometimes volunteers catch a critical missing piece because they are looking at it with fresh eyes.

DATA

Raising money at fund-raisers is always great, but your campaign should also collect and use information about attendees and RSVPs. A big part of your event should focus on collecting information from guests to aid the campaign. Most guests at a fund-raiser or rally will probably be in favor of whatever action you are recommending to benefit the library. They are also people who have demonstrated a deeper level of support for the campaign by taking action by attending the event. That makes them one of the best groups of people to ask to volunteer for the campaign, and you can take them off your voter ID roster and save your campaign resources by not having to contact them later for voter ID or persuasion. That's why you should have some mechanism built into your event to collect names, addresses, phone numbers, and e-mails from each guest or attendee. At the very least you want enough information to check them off the voter list, but preferably, you also want to have a way to contact them by e-mail or phone to remind them to vote for your initiative or let them know about other events later.

FOLLOW-UP

One part of the event that is often forgotten is the simple follow-up. A nice thank-you note or e-mail can help remind people of the event and keep your campaign in their mind. It also helps to cultivate more donors or volunteers later because people tend to want to work with or help people who are thankful for their time and energy. You can also send out requests for feedback or a solicitation for suggestions because people also like to feel that they are being heard or have bought themselves into the "insiders" club where they have a direct line to the campaign.

HOUSE PARTY GUIDE

In the fall of 2016, EveryLibrary invited our donors and supporters to host a series of house parties in advance of Election Day to share the #votelibraries message and build awareness for our national library advocacy campaign. Our House Party Guide is reproduced here for you to use and adapt for library ballot campaign or other advocacy work. See http://action.everylibrary.org/houseparties.

A house party is a great way to connect with other library activists, neighbors, coworkers, and friends and educate them about why libraries are so important for communities and about how important it is to fight for libraries of all kinds. We are all working together to help libraries reach their full potential to help communities, and one of the most effective ways to help libraries succeed is by throwing a house party to support libraries through EveryLibrary.

What Is a House Party?

House parties are gatherings of people who come together to learn more about the fight for America's libraries and the ways that EveryLibrary can work to support libraries in order to ensure a healthier, more vibrant, and more desirable community. But the most important thing is to have fun and get everyone to join in the fight by signing up to get involved in EveryLibrary's work to support libraries.

People just like you can host a house party and you don't need any special skills because we'll show you what you need to do. All it takes is a little planning and organization and a passion to support libraries. The best parties are the simplest and they don't need to be complicated or overly planned. Some house parties are nothing more than potlucks where people can connect and learn about EveryLibrary and find ways to work together to support libraries. Typically, all you need are food and drinks and some sign-up sheets to collect everyone's information, but you can also do a lot more!

Why Host a Party?

House parties are important because they help us build the resources we need to win. People are more likely to sign up to support libraries or make a donation if they're encouraged to do so by their friends, family, and colleagues. These parties provide an opportunity to connect and build national voter support for libraries through our work at EveryLibrary.

What Else Can I Accomplish?

If you'd like to do more or if you're a more experienced community organizer, EveryLibrary can help you take even more action to build national support for libraries.

We would love to see house parties take the time to phone bank to raise the money and build the support that we need to win. If you're interested in phone banking, we will supply you with a list of phone numbers to call. We'll even give you the scripts you need to be successful. Phone banking can be used either for fund-raising to support EveryLibrary's work, to ask people to join our e-mail list, or to sign the pledge to support libraries on one of our petitions at action.everylibrary.org.

It's also important that we talk directly with the public about the importance of libraries. That's why we encourage you to take the time to encourage your attendees to write letters to the editor in your local papers. These letters can talk about the importance of libraries, how libraries had a profound effect on you or your attendees, or how libraries improve communities.

How Do I Host a House Party?

Select a Date

- Check for local library campaigns to see if there are any in your area that might make your friends more excited to attend your house party, as well as potential conflicts. If there is a local library campaign, let's talk about how you can support that campaign too!

Choose Your Venue

- Most house parties will take place in someone's house. However, the location will help determine how many people to invite. You can invite 5 people or 500; whatever makes you feel the most comfortable is the right number.

Invite Your Guests

- Set a goal for how many people you want to attend. Remember that not everyone you invite will be able to attend, so invite about double the number of attendees you actually want to show up to be sure to hit your goal.
- You can invite local librarians and library staff, Friends or foundation group members, your family, friends, coworkers, people you know through civic or community groups, members of your religious community, and your neighbors. Cast a wide net to ensure you get anyone who might be a supporter.
- The best way to get people to attend your event is to pick up the phone and call them. There's just no substitute for a personal phone call. But definitely use e-mail, social media, and any other method you can think of to reach out to your networks.
- Ask them to RSVP so you can get a firm headcount for your event. You definitely want to reconfirm everyone's attendance a few days before the event, and remind them you're getting ready for them. That will make every attendee feel special and more likely to attend your house party.
- If you like, identify a few friends to act as cohosts and to help you spread the word and invite the people in their networks to attend if you've got space to fill.

Preparation

Plan your agenda. Here's a possible agenda for your party. But don't worry, these are just suggestions—you know your attendees best, so customize the agenda until it works for you.

- Introduce yourself, and share some reasons why you believe that libraries are fundamentally important in American communities and share ways that your attendees can support libraries through our Action.everylibrary .org website. It's from this page that you can encourage your attendees to sign up to support libraries or make donations.
- Make sure that there's plenty of food and drink so that your guests will have a great time.
- If you have good Internet access and a place to show it, you might show the latest video about the work that we're doing from our executive director, John Chrastka. If you're hosting a house party but don't want to show the video, we highly suggest you watch it because it includes a great overview of our work and excellent talking points for you to know about the fight for libraries in the United States.
- Take a few minutes and brainstorm how you and the attendees can work as part of the campaign for America's libraries. You can work together to set goals and responsibilities for what you can do in your area. Specifically, think of ways that you can all work to get more people in your area to sign up to support libraries or make a donation at action.everylibrary.org.
- Take action! Get your attendees involved by asking them to write a letter to the editor, phone banking, and directly asking their friends and family to sign up to support libraries or make a donation at action.everylibrary .org. If you're interested in having your guests phone bank for you, we will send you the call lists and the scripts you need to teach them in order to be successful. Please send us an e-mail so we can get those supplies to you as quickly as possible. Just an hour of phone banking with ten people can reach hundreds of Americans.
- Use a sign-up sheet to get information and have your guests fill it out to collect contact information such as e-mail addresses. The most important goal for your party is making sure we can continue to engage your guests and get them involved so we can continue to take action on behalf of libraries.
- If it makes sense for your party, feel free to ask your guests to support EveryLibrary by making a donation. Guests can make donations online to our campaign for libraries at action.everylibrary.org. Larger one-time donations are fantastic for our campaigns, and smaller monthly donations make sure that we can continue our work in the future.
- Remember that the costs associated with the party must come from donations or your personal funds.

After the Party

- It's not over! Make sure you send thank-you notes to everyone who attended. Or, if you give us their names and addresses, we would be happy to send them a thank-you postcard on your behalf.
- Don't forget to make an "ask" to your guests, whether you're asking them to host an event of their own, donate, or volunteer. If your guests made the commitment to come to your event, they might be willing to make more commitments to you, the campaign, and libraries across the country. Make the ask, because the chances are that your friends will say yes.
- Report back to us about your plans, successes, and even any failures! We want to hear from you to make these as successful as possible.

We want to thank you so much for your support. Just getting this far means a lot to libraries across the country. Please take the next step and host a house party before election day! ✪

CHAPTER TWENTY-ONE

E-Mail

E-MAIL ADDRESSES ARE STILL THE GATEWAY TO THE INTER-net for most voters. Using e-mails is the best way for your campaign to establish and maintain a long-term relationship with your supporters, donors, and volunteers. If you haven't started collecting e-mail addresses, start now to set your campaign up for more success later. Building an e-mail list takes time and effort, so starting as early as possible to identify and collect names and e-mail addresses will give you a significant communications advantage. Given how integrated certain channels like Facebook and Twitter are in the lives of voters, some may argue that social media are taking the place of e-mails as a campaign communications tool. Others could argue that campaigns should shift over to text messaging to reach millennials and younger voters. We don't see the argument about the platform or channel as a zero-sum one. We know from experience that having an extensive list of e-mailable supporters, donors, and volunteers is another critical pathway to get people to act on behalf of the campaign.

Implementing an effective e-mail strategy for your library campaign has the potential to dramatically improve the likelihood of a successful election. However, creating a plan for the way that a campaign uses e-mail is often over-looked, leaving campaigns with an ineffective strategy and a lowered success rate. An effective e-mail plan will set the guidelines to allow you to efficiently communicate your message with your electorate. After all, as we discussed in previous chapters, campaigns are essentially nothing more than a strategized method for communicating with voters.

The 2008 election was one of the first to truly capitalize on the power of e-mail. Many of the PACs that were working on issues on both sides of the aisle were raising millions of dollars through small donor contributions through e-mail lists. Some of the best-written e-mails would raise hundreds of thousands of dollars nearly overnight. Volunteers were often identified, engaged, and put to work through e-mails. Campaigns were able to get their message out to voters who cared and were passionate about their beliefs and were able to influence the national dialogue. Rallies and political events were organized and announced through e-mails. Invitations to engage with the campaign at a higher level through social media went out through e-mail lists. Most importantly, voters were motivated to go to the polls on Election Day. Of course, all of this can only happen in your campaign if you fully utilize the power of e-mails. This chapter will help you lay the foundation for a successful e-mail campaign.

EVERY OPPORTUNITY

Your campaign information-gathering plan needs to be strategized in such a way that every opportunity to gather e-mail addresses is taken advantage of. This means that everyone in the campaign understands how important e-mail lists are. The culture of your campaign should include the goal of gathering e-mail addresses at its core, and no opportunity should be missed to ask for these addresses.

Throughout your campaign, from surfacing through Election Day, there are hundreds of opportunities to add people to your e-mail list. Volunteers can bring sign-up sheets with them while they're canvassing. They can sign people up while phone banking. Every rally or political event should include an opportunity to gather e-mails. E-mail sign-up forms should be included on any social media pages where possible and all of the websites used by the campaign. You can even reward people with small giveaways like bumper stickers, yard signs, or buttons if they sign up for the e-mail list. This is your chance to get creative!

However you collect them, the most important thing you can do is maintain your e-mail list. Keep it up-to-date and refresh it as often as possible. If you are continuously asking the same people repeatedly for the same thing, they will tire of hearing from you and will drop off your e-mail list. Your campaign list needs to be refreshed continuously with new e-mail addresses and implemented to create new supporters.

ENGAGEMENT

Your first e-mails are going to be the least productive in terms of open rates and click-through rates. But don't give up! By most accounts, a good open rate (the percentage of people who open your e-mail) is only around 20 percent. Of that small percentage, the vast majority of people (around 69 percent) won't thoroughly read your e-mail. Instead, they'll just skim it. In fact, they will probably spend an average of 2–7 seconds looking at it. That's okay; sending an e-mail is essentially free and that's exactly why we want the largest possible e-mail list for your campaign.

You should realize that the way that people are using e-mail is changing. For example, more and more people are using their mobile devices for e-mail reading. People are receiving three times as many e-mails as they were in 2007. People are becoming more wary of spam e-mails and therefore more cautious about the e-mails that they open. Even with all of these barriers, you can drastically improve your open rates and lower your drop-out rates.

How do we improve those numbers? By building familiarity with the committee and the library's ballot measure with frequent, relevant contact.

SUBJECT LINES

The first thing you need to do is grab readers quickly with an exciting or catchy title in the subject line. This is what takes hold of your readers and encourages them to open the e-mail in the first place. We have seen effective one-word titles that intrigue the reader and we have seen effective titles that are longer than we'd ever consider using ourselves. You shouldn't be afraid to put something personal or controversial in the title to catch their attention. If it's a bad title, nobody will open it so there won't be any harm. If it's a great title, everyone will open it and the body of your message better be just as great, because now the pressure is on.

To write an engaging subject line try to use words that encourage action, or that give the reader a sense of what they will get if they open the e-mail. These are called value words and give the reader a sense of what the value of opening the e-mail will be. Ask yourself, what would make the reader care enough to open my e-mail and what will they get from opening it? Then build your subject line from the answer to those questions. For example, instead of just sending a weekly e-mail entitled "Newsletter" or "Campaign Update," use a title of one of the articles in the newsletter as the subject. It also helps if the subject is something exciting and emotional. For example, if you want to explain how libraries help entrepreneurs in communities, don't just say "Newsletter," but instead say "Find out how libraries make businesses stronger."

STAY ON MESSAGE

No matter what, the primary rule for the body of your e-mails is that it needs to reflect the tone and feeling of the campaign. It needs to authentically reflect the campaign's message. Your readers will come to expect a certain tone and message from the committee, and if your e-mail veers in one direction or another it can be jarring to your voters, and you have the potential to lose their faith that you are the same campaign that they signed up to support in the first place. It's often helpful to have either one writer for the committee, or if you have a team of writers, make sure that they all review each e-mail to ensure that it meets the criteria of satisfying this rule.

WRITING E-MAILS

People often ask what constitutes good writing on the Internet. Generally most campaign consultants agree that good writing is just good writing no matter where it is. A well-written e-mail is vivid, clear, gripping, and concise. It avoids jargon and isn't stiff or overly formal or confusing. A good e-mail can be personal and usually doesn't use large, impressive words with a lot of syllables; instead, it is accurate yet simple to read. It also doesn't assume that your readers know details that they might not know. This is your chance to tell your story, and a good story takes the reader with it.

URGENCY IS KEY

It's also important to remember how little time people will spend on your e-mail. After you catch them with a strong title, make sure that the first few lines are engaging and gripping and have a sense of urgency. Draw people into your story. This often means that you lead with your ask. Tell them why they should be reading your e-mail and why it matters. If there is a sense of urgency, tell them what is so urgent and why early in your e-mail. You can capture that moment for them in the first paragraph by naming a crisis or an opportunity to become engaged and involved and why it matters to them. If you can't immediately identify a sense of urgency, you can always try to give a deadline or a time of action to help. If there is no urgency, or you have nothing to ask for, then why are you sending an e-mail? What's so important?

What Did They Accomplish?

Show the reader how their actions can create change or can affect the election. Tell them what the outcomes will be if they engage this e-mail. For example, in an advocacy campaign you should tell them what signing a petition will accomplish, how calling a senator will help, or what you will do with their money once you have it. In a ballot campaign, tell them what their actions do to help support your committee and their library on Election Day. This is important because people want to be a part of the action, they want to know that what they're doing matters and that it says something special about them as a person to be engaged. How are they the hero for supporting your library campaign? Give them that opportunity to be a hero by taking an action for your campaign.

Bullets and Fewer Words

Lastly, here are some pointers to consider for e-mails. In understanding that people spend little time on your e-mails, help them scan it for what is important. Use bold fonts and italics when it's something important, but only when it's important. Write short paragraphs that boil down to the essence of what you're trying to say without too much extra verbiage. Fewer words are always better. If you can say it with a picture or reinforce the message of your e-mail with a picture, take that opportunity. Using bullets and short numbered lists is a great way to help people identify key aspects of what they need to know quickly and efficiently. Finally, get someone to review it, then review it again, then test it in an e-mail to yourself to make sure that formatting comes through and then review it again before you send it to your whole list.

How to Send It

There are quite a few platforms to send e-mail from. Two of the most common are Constant Contact and MailChimp. We don't promote one over the other. Preference is a matter of opinion, and we've seen effective campaigns run on either one. This is because both platforms offer many of the features that you're going to need to test for the effectiveness of your campaign, including open and click-through rates and A/B test percentages (see below). They are all relatively easy to use and have many other features. For example, almost all of them allow you to create mobile sign-up forms, web forms, and social media forms to push out to your constituents. It's generally easy to upload Excel spreadsheets of e-mail lists or take lists from other websites like Eventbrite and upload those e-mails into them.

Each of these commercially available e-mail management tools also comes with preformatted templates. Choose one that is clean and attractive to you and the committee and then dedicate yourself to always using that template. It is often less important which template you choose (or design yourself) than it is for you to always use the same template. Consistency creates familiarity, and familiarity increases open rates and engagements. We also recommend making a small list of trusted campaign insiders to use as an "e-mail draft review committee" to review the format and look of early campaign e-mails. E-mail programs like Gmail, Outlook, Yahoo, and Hotmail can sometimes wreak havoc on even the nicest templates. Less is often more with layout and design, too.

IS YOUR E-MAIL EFFECTIVE?

It is easy to tell if your e-mail is effective and if not, then what needs to be changed. For example, through your e-mail management system, you should be able to see how many people opened your e-mail and if the number is high, then you probably had a good title. If the number of people taking action is low, then you probably need to work on your ask. These are just some of the most basic indicators of effective or ineffective e-mails, but they are the most important ones. Other things that affect e-mail rates are the time and day that people receive them, language barriers, the quality of writing, and the demographics of the people that received them. Luckily, there is a way to test your e-mails.

Testing

One of the best ways to see if your e-mails are effective is to set up what's called A/B testing. This is when you write two e-mails with the same overall message but use a different sense of urgency, different title, focus on a different problem, or use a different ask. By separating your lists into two or more distinct groups of random e-mail addresses and sending similar e-mails, you can learn what is most effective when you see the open rates in your e-mail platform. It is extremely important when you set up A/B testing that you only change one thing between the e-mails, so that you can easily identify what was different. Often, simply changing the title of the e-mail is the most effective change you can make. For example, instead of "Recent Events at the Library," you could also test "Whoa! I Can't Believe That Happened at the Library!" You can also change the day and time that e-mails are sent and see if that makes any difference. Or change the picture or tagline of the e-mail. You have to learn what will make the biggest difference for your supporters. Take the time, especially early in the campaign, to test what is more effective for engaging your supporters.

In the end, it's all about being strategic with your e-mails. Take the time to work with your e-mail team to train them and keep them on task, and make sure that they are sending the highest-quality e-mails to the highest-quality lists. Your e-mails may be one of the only ways that the voters will hear from your campaign, so they are one of the most important assets to your campaign. You need to take care of them.

If the library plans on running another measure soon or has to rerun its measure because of a loss, the committee leadership should plan a schedule of "check-in" e-mails in between campaign seasons with the list. These check-ins can include progress reports about the library, invitations to participate in the next planning stage for the library, recent news affecting libraries nationally or locally, updates on the local political climate or other elections like the library's, or invitations to participate in the work of the campaign next time. In every e-mail, remember to identify a problem for the recipient to solve and include a call to action that they can do to solve it. It is important to keep fund-raising for the next campaign in between elections. However, it would be better to mothball an e-mail list in between elections than to send out boring and irrelevant messages just for the sake of e-mailing.

After a ballot measure campaign is over, the e-mail lists continue to be an asset for your library. The ballot committee should plan on donating or transferring those e-mail lists to a library support organization like the Friends or the foundation. Everyone on the list has a history of supporting, donating, or volunteering for the library's campaign—some for the very first time. They have already opted in to receive messages. They are ready and willing to continue their relationship with the library and are invested in its future success. You need to help them do it.

CHAPTER TWENTY-TWO

Facebook

THE USE OF FACEBOOK IN POLITICAL CAMPAIGNS HAS become standard practice. For many campaigns, Facebook is the primary tool that is used to communicate the need for a new library, tell the library's stories of impact, text messaging, and, most importantly, collect data about supporters. Essentially, through Facebook the campaign is attempting to identify potential yes voters and persuade the persuadable. According to a November 2016 Pew study, 79 percent of online Americans use Facebook, an increase of 7 percent from 2015.[1] If you have any hesitation about using this communications channel for a library campaign, we encourage you to get past that feeling quickly. Neither Instagram (now owned by Facebook), LinkedIn, Pinterest, nor Twitter break above 35 percent of market use. For the foreseeable future, the single most effective way to communicate with adults on a social network quickly and cheaply is through Facebook.

It is important to note that in most cases there will be two Facebook pages active throughout the campaign. One is the "yes" campaign's Facebook page. It is generally named something like "Vote yes for the XYZ Library." The other page is the library's own Facebook page. Both should be used throughout the campaign in a way that makes the most of the campaign's resources. While the library's page cannot and should not discuss voting yes for the ballot measure, the library should talk about its past successes and its current needs, as well as help the public get a vision of the future and promote the value of libraries. The campaign's Facebook page will be the place to ask people to vote yes or to take action on behalf of the campaign itself.

It's important to remember that once the campaign starts, the library should not suddenly change its behavior about the topics it posts on or the amount of money it spends to boost posts. A campaign season shift in the frequency or content of Facebook posts, or a change in how much the library spends on them could appear to be "advocacy campaigning" even if the words "vote" and "yes" never appear next to each other. Using public money and resources for specific advocacy campaigns by the library is illegal. In some communities, the mere appearance that the library is itself advocating for a specific outcome is enough to make it seem inappropriate even if it isn't technically illegal. One way to guard against this accusation is to change the library's behavior about spending money on ads and posting about election-related information in the 12–24 months before your campaign. If the library was previously spending money on Facebook ads, then it can reasonably continue that habit throughout the campaign. It's also the best vehicle for reaching the public about the library's programs and services, which doesn't hurt the library's overall storytelling. We always recommend that our libraries start spending money on Facebook ads before the campaign begins.

FACEBOOK FOR CAMPAIGNS: OVERVIEW

The power of Facebook lies in its ability to cheaply and quickly reach large numbers of highly targeted demographic populations. Facebook market saturation rates across the country stand at approximately 79 percent. E-mail is only a little higher, at about 85 percent. Most other social media tools have much smaller market shares. More importantly, they do not allow highly targeted ads based on consumer habits, self-identified interests, and demographics like age, gender, and language. We rarely recommend spending campaign time or money on other social media platforms. Facebook's advertising-targeting features are available to every page manager and are easy to use and design. That, coupled with its high saturation rate among demographic groups who are typically higher-propensity voters or are highly engaged, civic-minded members of the population, are what make Facebook an extremely effective tool in a campaign for voter ID and persuasion. The cost per each ad impression is lower than other social networks, and each impression is thousands of times cheaper and more easily customized than traditional campaign tools like direct mail. This means that a "yes" campaign can spend less money to ensure that individuals will see multiple message impressions multiple times throughout the campaign.

ADS OVERVIEW

Over the years, Facebook has changed its algorithm for "organic reach" (i.e., the number of people who are shown your page's posts for free) for pages of all types. Facebook is, as a publicly traded company, in the business of making money, after all. The decline in "organic reach" means that there is now a pay-for-play model for pages attempting to reach high numbers of individuals in the public. However, ads remain relatively cheap and can be highly targeted. While it takes money to run Facebook ads, it is by far the least expensive (in both money and time) way to reach tens of thousands of individuals in the public. Your fund-raising goals need to include a budget for Facebook ads from day one of the campaign.

For each $100 spent, you can expect a single Facebook ad or sponsored post to reach around 10,000 people one time. We typically use this number when budgeting our Facebook ad spends because this number can also take into account any organic engagements with a post. Think of the number of people reached organically as the "floor" for any post. If there is more engagement on a Facebook post that occurs organically, Facebook will not reshow the post to those people but instead increase the reach of the ad without increasing your cost. A strong, engaging, and interesting Facebook post can reach as many as 30,000–50,000 impressions in an average-sized community with the same $100. However, it is important to remember that "going viral" is not important in "yes" campaigns because, generally speaking, if a post goes viral it has left your local population of voters. It's nice that it is circulating across the country, but you don't need to spend money on people who can't vote for your library.

Demographics

When boosting a post or using the Facebook Ads Manager, setting ad demographics is exceptionally easy. Demographics can be set for each ad individually and can be saved as audiences to use in future ads. Creating these "audiences" saves time and allows you to be consistent when creating and fielding ads or boosts. Demographics can be set according to what individuals have personally "liked" such as books, reading, literacy, education, and so on. Ads can be set to target community members who have liked specific pages such as the library's Facebook page. There is also the ability to target groups who primarily speak a specific language, identify as a specific gender, are parents, seniors, retirees, business owners, and so on.

Most importantly, you can set ads to show only to registered voters so that your ad spends aren't wasted on nonvoters. These self-identified interests and data about our community of Facebook users are what allows us to run strong ads targeting them through specific messages to take actions.

For a library political campaign, it's important to begin months in advance and test a number of messages with various demographics to find the most effective messages. This is called A/B testing, as discussed in the preceding chapter on e-mail. However, if your election day is only a few weeks away, you will have to use polling data, and your "gut instinct," to determine the demographics for messaging.

Business Manager

Every page manager has access to the basic advertising tools in Facebook. We recommend that our campaigns go one step further and set up the Facebook Business Manager tools to manage your ads and boosts. By setting up a Facebook Business Manager account to manage your campaign's Facebook page, you will get access to even better targeting tools through third-party data providers like Acxiom. Acxiom is a "big data" company that specializes in connecting people in the physical world to their digital profiles while pulling in big data for comprehensive profiles that allow you to target specific groups of consumers. They even have a "data-guru" who will upload custom audiences of people into your Facebook account that aren't available with the Facebook Audience Insights Platform, such as likely voters. You can make requests for audiences at www.acxiom.com/data-guru/. By creating a "likely voters" custom audience for your precincts, you can ensure that you don't waste money by putting ads in front of nonvoters. With Business Manager, your campaign can also set narrower demographics within the voter audience such as parental status, political affiliation, interests in various causes, geographic focus, and so on. This allows you to use Facebook as an extremely powerful persuasion tool. You can put the most relevant messages about your library ballot measure in front of a group of voters who would care the most about it.

While we would love to give more specifics here about how to set up a Business Manager account and the features that are available, these are changing too rapidly. However, the Business Manager information is available at business.facebook .com/ and we will keep up-to-date guides on our website at action.everylibrary.org/ trainingguides.

Organic Reach

Organic reach is the number of people who are shown your page's post for free, either because they "like" and follow your page, or because it is shared to them by someone else. It is important to work on increasing the organic reach for your campaign page because a better organic reach will allow your paid ads to reach a higher number of individuals in your target market. Organic reach can be increased easily and quickly by using engaging photos that tie the beliefs of the individuals to the cause. Facebook will more organically show content from a page to individuals who have interacted with the page most frequently. By using unpaid posts with meme images about books, libraries, literacy, or other key subject areas most common to library supporters, you will not only see more clicks and likes and shares from those posts, but you will also see an increase in organic reach from your other paid posts. For example, some campaigns have uploaded and scheduled a few dozen memes about libraries that are easily shared throughout the community. This increase in likes will influence the Facebook algorithm and cause the cost per impression for ads to decrease and therefore increase the number of imprints of your campaign's paid ads.

If you don't have someone on your campaign team who can make inspirational, clickable images, there are websites such as Fiverr.com where you can commission library or campaign-specific images for as little as five dollars from professional designers. Your campaign provides the text for the images as well as the logo/website of the campaign to be included in the images. The text can simply be good quotes from famous people about libraries. A good design can be clicked on, or liked, hundreds of times in a day and anyone who clicks on an image or likes or comments on it is more likely to organically see other posts from the campaign. EveryLibrary provides a lot of editable image files that we have tested and shown to be highly effective at increasing organic reach across social media platforms. You can find these at action.everylibrary.org/campaignresources.

TELLING THE STORY

One of the most important things that a campaign can do is move people "up the ladder of engagement." As we discussed in chapter 1, this means moving people from unaware to evangelized. People who are "lower" on the ladder are less likely to engage in the campaign and the least likely to take action for the campaign.

Ultimately, the lower an individual sits on the ladder the less likely they are to vote for the library, largely due to their low awareness. Through inexpensive Facebook ads, the "yes" campaign has the opportunity to move community members up the ladder and change their awareness. By telling stories of impact, by communicating the importance of the library, and discussing issues in the community that a vote for the library can solve, you can prepare for a final successful GOTV effort the week before Election Day or during mail-in ballot periods.

The stories can be told through a wide range of techniques. If the campaign finds interesting content and examples of stories of impact from news sites or blog posts, these can be posted and boosted. If there are events that the campaign is creating to rally people to support the library, the "events" feature in Facebook is extremely effective. However, the most effective content is original content developed by the campaign that tells the library "yes" campaign story. Whether you publish that content on a "yes" campaign website and link it to blogs or articles from the campaign, or post it directly to Facebook, tell your local library story first.

ASKS

For those who are higher on the ladder of engagement, Facebook posts should be used primarily to make asks for the campaign. Those who are higher on the ladder are typically the individuals (and their friends) who have liked your page. These are the individuals who are most likely to respond to campaign asks and take action for the campaign.

These asks can include a wide range of actions. For example, the campaign can ask for donations, pledges of support, volunteers, spreading the word of the campaign, signing petitions, attending an event or a rally, or contacting local legislatures. There should rarely be a paid post on Facebook that does not include an ask. This is extremely important because without an ask, the campaign will get little to no return on its investment from Facebook ads besides making people aware of the campaign. While raising awareness is important, awareness can be raised while also increasing the resources of the campaign and the number of committed voters, which is the ultimate goal. Often the campaign can recoup expenses for an ad or even raise more than the ad costs by asking for donations within the ad or within the blog or article that the ad points to. We often see a significant amount of the cost for ads recouped with an ask for contributions to the campaign at the end of a strong, engaging, and informative blog post that educated the public about the need.

RECOMMENDED BUDGET

It may seem counterintuitive, but lower spends on ads early in the campaign ultimately keep the overall costs lower. If you have focused on engagement and there is a larger number of individuals higher on the ladder of engagement, your cost per engagement is smaller. For an average-sized campaign with a population of about 10,000, we would typically make the recommendation that $10–20 a week should be spent during the year's run-up to the campaign. This spend should be increased about $10 a week for every 15,000 people in the community. In the month before a campaign a much larger spend is necessary each week of typically not less than $100 to raise awareness, persuade, and identify voters through calls to pledge to vote yes on your campaign website. If there are more than 25,000 voters in your community, you should spend about $100–$250 per week for every 25,000 voters. Then you should make a large spend of about $250–$500 per 25,000 voters during the last week, primarily to those who like your page and their friends to remind them to go vote. However, if the campaign has begun Facebook ad spends later in the campaign and therefore has lower numbers of community members who have liked the page and are ultimately lower on the ladder, then that campaign needs to pay higher amounts to engage and educate the public during the last few months.

Again, these spends should be split between 3–4 ads running each week, with specific messages targeted to each demographic that complement the messaging being used in the fieldwork of the campaign for those demographics.

FACEBOOK AND E-MAIL TIME LINE

It's important to create a social media calendar for your Facebook ads as much as it is for your earned media calendar. While the time line that your campaign uses will vary based on how much time you have, here is an example time line.

One Year Out

Beginning one year from Election Day, the campaign (and the library) starts telling the story of the library with paid ads. Whether these ads are from the campaign or the library's Facebook page, the ads should be directed primarily at an audience of voters. Included in these stories should be articles about better-funded libraries and what they can provide to the community; articles that address common oppositional statements like "Why do we need libraries when we have Google?"; and 3–5 unboosted posts per week that play to a sense of fun and positivity like meme images about reading, books, or libraries that are easily liked and shared.

Three Months Out

Three months from Election Day, the campaign's Facebook page should shift to talking to voters about the upcoming election. The campaign's Facebook page should be directly addressing the need for a new library or new funding and informing the public about what they will get if the election succeeds, as well as making asks on behalf of the campaign such as calls for volunteers, or soliciting for donations, or asking people to pledge to vote yes in the upcoming election. This is the heaviest time period for the persuasion posts of the campaign, and the campaign should address as many of the "why" questions as possible.

Note: The library's Facebook page should remain consistent with what it was previously posting, and the amount that it is paying for Facebook ads should not change until after the entirety of the campaign is over.

One Month Out

One month before Election Day, the campaign should start posting endorsements and messages of success. They should begin to speak as if they won the campaign and as if everyone is with them. You can see this same behavior in a presidential campaign when the candidates begin addressing themselves more assuredly as the winner. The campaign should also focus more paid ads at asking people to pledge to vote yes and other methods of voter ID.

One Week Out

The last week before the election, the campaign will begin to specifically address those who have liked their page and their friends to ask them to show up to vote for the library on Election Day. Almost all of the voter ID work will end and most certainly the campaign should not be spending money on persuasion during the last week. It should be focusing on getting the supporters to actually go out and vote for the library.

NOTE

1. Pew Research Center, "Social Media Update 2016," www.pewinternet.org/2016/11/11/social-media-update-2016/.

CONCLUSION

VOTERS ARE INHERENTLY CONSUMERS. THEIR ATTITUDES ARE shaped by marketing messages and their perceptions are tied to brand loyalty. With the 2016 election, we saw that brand matters in politics more than anything else, because to self-identify as a Republican or Democrat is to predispose the voter to a whole set of Election Day decisions that are not based on individual candidates but on their brand loyalty. That party brand is a head start of loyal voters on Election Day that leapfrogs a major party candidate over third parties and independent ideas. Bernie Sanders ran as a Democrat because he wanted to be automatically viable within the establishment and not have to attempt to recruit voters to leave the Democratic Party to vote for an independent. It is also the same reason that Donald Trump went into the Republican primary process instead of becoming Ross Perot 2.0. Trump's base block of voters in the general election consisted of people who backed their party first and only eventually got to know the nominee. Regardless of what you thought about any national third-party candidates in 2016, they were never viable because the Green and Libertarian parties do not have the sheer numbers of automatically brand-loyal voters that the Democrats and Republicans have.

There is still a base of brand-loyal voters for libraries in this country. We hope we helped you identify some messages that activate them and some techniques for reaching them. There are also plenty of swing voters about taxes for libraries. We hope that the disciplines we shared about planning and running an effective, engaged campaign will help you persuade those voters to be a "yes" on Election Day. Trends in politics and trends in consumer behavior wash back and forth across the psyche of our country's voters. At this writing, we have just come through a national election where a particular segment of voters were activated who are not part of any traditional party base, and their particular brand loyalties are unknown or suspect. In this book, we are interested in providing you with practical advice on how to run a library ballot measure campaign. We are also deeply invested in trying to share some political theory and insights into what makes voters—and not just library users—tick.

Going into the 2016 campaign season, we highlighted that the tone and tenor of the electorate could be a problem for library campaigns.[1] As we move farther away from the 2016 election and deeper into a time when the federal policy agenda looks to be focused on deregulation, less progressive tax policies, smaller government programs, and less protection for groups and rights, how do libraries continue to serve all without fear or favor? Libraries are in the habit of serving the poor, the homeless, folks at the margins, and people in need. We work with children of all abilities and adults of any means. We are there with people at their most vulnerable: when they are truly looking for an answer. This service orientation is our biggest virtue as an industry and is our proof about being transformative in our work. It is something that we at EveryLibrary champion as the biggest value-proposition we have to users and nonusers alike.

We are particularly concerned going forward that the library community will be forced to defend the basics of its mission and purpose. We know that the library community will try to provide legitimate answers to specific questions during campaigns. But we are concerned that a certain crassness among voters will also invade the civic discourse to not only dismiss the answers but to invalidate the questioners.

> "They are building a Taj Mahal for the homeless."
> "Those people use the Internet at the library to apply for welfare."
> "The kids at the library are disruptive and their parents don't care."
> "Only poor people still use the library."
> "Why do we need the library? Everything is on the Internet."

The biggest problems that library campaigns face come from a combination of voter discomfort, voter apathy, and direct opposition to taxes. How do you inoculate yourself against potential charges coming from the opposition? How do you hold the line against disinformation and distrust of government that threatens to defund or tear down core institutions in our American society? How do you continue to support people locally when our national infrastructure is being dismantled from within?

We talk in chapter 5 about how to power map your community and segment your stories based on what topics or issues are of interest to the person or organization you are talking to. In a similar way, you need to evaluate what the impacts and outcomes are for any new services, programs, staffing, collections, or space/facilities upgrades you anticipate funding with a ballot measure. Impacts and outcomes are not abstract. They are experienced by certain groups or populations. You should name those populations or groups without fear that you are going to attract negative attention. Anyone who doesn't like the poor, the homeless, early learners, and community innovators—the folks whom libraries serve every day—is a likely "no" voter. You won't lose them during your campaign because they were already lost to you well before the campaign started anyway.

Voters are consumers. Across America, libraries have to come together to build up our brand equity and position our institutions and the people who work there as relevant in many different ways to many different communities. We have to support the image of libraries in your local market and in 9,500 other local markets around the country. Before you begin your ballot campaign, please look at how you brand and position your services, programs, and collection development approach. Voters truly want to see what the impacts are from the library. Most voters are still open to funding good outcomes with their taxes. Two weeks after the 2016 election, nearly 60 percent of Hillary Clinton voters wanted to "give Donald Trump a chance."[2] Even in the face of anger and disappointment that propels a call for change, there is still a lot of hope in this country that we can get it right. Position your library in the eyes of the electorate to help realize that hope.

Libraries won in red states and blue states in 2016—as they have for years. But libraries are not well equipped to do it in either kind of state in the face of direct opposition. With the rise of the Tea Party and the willingness of organized and well-funded agenda-driven organizations like Americans for Prosperity to campaign against library funding measures, the political landscape in the latter part of this decade has changed. If you want to win new funding for your library on Election Day after 2016, you and your team will have to work hard and work smart to reach, activate, and turn out your voters. The time when a library could simply place the measure on the ballot, run a "stealth campaign," and win is over. You have to be ready to start working now, today, to build and sustain new voter coalitions that can survive direct attacks on the core reasons that libraries exist and on the basic way that we have chosen to fund libraries historically in this country.

A winning campaign is almost never a defensive one. For your library to win you have to own your own narrative and advance your own brand. We hope we have helped you to set smart goals for your campaign, evaluate what campaign strategies are right for your community, and prepare to get started on the tactics that activate voters for your library ballot measure.

NOTES

1. John Chrastka and Rachel Korman, "Constant Campaign | Budgets & Funding," *Library Journal*, February 10, 2016, http://lj.libraryjournal.com/2016/02/budgets-funding/constant-campaign-budgets-funding/.

2. Hannah Fingerhut, "Presidential Election Reactions and Expectations," Pew Research Center for the People and the Press, November 21, 2016, www.people-press.org/2016/11/21/presidential-election-reactions-and-expectations/.

ABOUT THE AUTHORS

JOHN CHRASTKA is EveryLibrary's founder and is a longtime library trustee, supporter, and advocate. Chrastka is a former partner in AssociaDirect, a Chicago-based consultancy focused on supporting associations in membership recruitment, conference, and governance activities. He is a former president and member of the Board of Trustees for the Berwyn (Illinois) Public Library (2006–2015) and is a former president of the Reaching Across Illinois Libraries System (RAILS) multi-type library system. Prior to his work at AssociaDirect, he was director for membership development at the American Library Association. He is a member of the ALA as well as the Illinois Library Association and the American Political Sciences Association. He was named a 2014 Mover & Shaker by *Library Journal* and tweets @mrchrastka.

PATRICK "PC" SWEENEY is a tireless and innovative advocate for libraries and the current political director for EveryLibrary. A 2007 graduate of the San Jose School of Library and Information Sciences, Sweeney is a former administrative librarian of the Sunnyvale (California) Public Library and was executive director of EveryLibrary California, a statewide ballot committee to support library ballot propositions. He is active in the California Library Association and across library social media as a cofounder of the ALA Think Tank. His library blog is well respected, and he is a sought-after speaker and presenter. A recent project, the Story Sailboat, worked to provide library services and materials—by boat—in the San Francisco Bay area. He was named a 2015 Mover & Shaker by *Library Journal* and tweets at @pcsweeney.

INDEX

T

tactics
    for voter contact, 98–99
    vs. goals and strategies, 41–42
tax filings, 75–76, 78
taxes, opposition to
    case studies of, 50, 87–91, 154–158, 172–173
    counter-messages for, 140, 142, 148–151
    data on, 4, 199
    preparing for, xiv, 47, 62, 145–148, 153–154, 159–162
Tea Party, opposition from, 87, 142, 153–158, 160, 189, 191
television, 169–170, 181
testing of e-mails, 248–249, 254
themes *vs.* messages, 133–135
time, as resource, 42–43
time lines, 10–15, 257–259
titles of ballots, 90–92
Tools for Radical Democracy (Minieri and Getsos), 25–26
Toups, Lindel, 90–91
training of volunteers, 70, 123–126
transparency, need for, 71, 142, 157–158
treasurers, 78–79
Troy Public Library, 172–173
Trump, Donald, xiii, 26, 74, 133–134, 163, 171, 209, 261
turfs, 206, 214–217
Twitter, 109, 164, 172, 180–181, 251

U

unions, 60–61, 111
Urban Librarians Unite, 231
URLs, purchase of, 74

V

venues, 234, 240
verbatim polling, 197
virtual call centers, 217
volunteer chairs, 78, 80
VolunteerMatch, 69, 120
volunteers
    allocating, 127–128
    belief that libraries can be run by, 147–151
    recruiting, 69, 117–122, 217–218, 223–224
    retaining, 126–127
    roles for, 128–130
    staff members as, 7
    training of, 70, 123–126
    website page on, 204–205

vote goal, formula for, 49
"vote yes" committees. *See* committees
voter education period, 12, 258
voter guides, 92
voter identification (ID), 6, 11–12, 100, 217–221
voter universes, defined, 214
voters
    data on, 3–5, 46, 187–194, 196, 202, 215–218, 237–238
    early voters, 193, 221–222
    "no" voters, 4–6, 11, 213–214, 219
    number of, 49, 97–98
    undecided and swing voters, xiii–xv, 5–6, 11, 219–223, 261
    "yes" voters, 4–6, 11–12, 219, 221–222
voter-to-voter contact. *See* canvassing

W

walk lists, 216
wants *vs.* needs, 99–100
websites
    for campaigns, 201–207
    for EveryLibrary resources, 15, 62, 75, 84, 96, 238, 241, 254–255
    for opposition research, 160
    for political data on districts, 46
    for Public Library Vote Toolbox, vii
    for volunteer recruitment, 120
Wellstone Center, 217–218
Werner, Lance, 154–158
"will" *vs.* "can," 114–115
win numbers, 49, 97–98
worksheets, for power mapping, 62–63

Y

Yes, Helen! campaign, 230
"yes" committees. *See* committees
"yes" voters, 4–6, 11–12, 219, 221–222